D0492754

ELECTRONIC BYWAYS

The Aspen | Institute

A report prepared for
The Ford Foundation and the
Rural Economic Policy Program
of The Aspen Institute

ABOUT THE RURAL ECONOMIC POLICY PROGRAM OF THE ASPEN INSTITUTE

The Rural Economic Policy Program (REPP) was created in 1985 as a collaborative program of The Aspen Institute, The Ford Foundation, and the Wye Institute. Working closely with The Ford Foundation's Rural Poverty and Resources Program, the REPP encourages greater attention to rural policy issues through a program of research grants, seminars, and public education. The Program is focused on rural concerns, including community economic development, resource management, agricultural policy, and enhanced livelihoods for the rural poor. REPP is funded by a grant from The Ford Foundation.

The Rural Economic Policy Program is housed at The Aspen Institute in Washington, D.C. The Aspen Institute is an international nonprofit organization whose broad purpose is to seek consideration of human values in areas of leadership development and public policy formulation. Since its founding in 1949, the Institute has operated a program of Executive Seminars in which leaders of business, government, the arts, education, law and the media convene with distinguished scholars to reinforce the application of traditional humanistic values in their personal and professional deliberations. The Aspen Institute's Policy Programs seek to advance the formulation of public policy.

ELECTRONIC BYWAYS

State Policies for Rural Development Through Telecommunications

Edwin B. Parker and
Heather E. Hudson

with Don A. Dillman, Sharon Strover,
and Frederick Williams

Westview Press

BOULDER • SAN FRANCISCO • OXFORD

The Aspen Institute

Copyright © 1992 by Westview Press, Inc.

Published in 1992 in the United States of America by Westview Press, Inc., 5500 Central Avenue, Boulder, Colorado 80301-2847, and in the United Kingdom by Westview Press, 36 Lonsdale Road, Summertown, Oxford OX2 7EW

Library of Congress Cataloging-in-Publication Data
Parker, Edwin B.
  Electronic byways : state policies for rural development through telecommunications / by Edwin B. Parker and Heather E. Hudson, with Don A. Dillman, Sharon Strover, and Frederick Williams.
    p. cm.
  Includes bibliographical references and index.
  ISBN 0-8133-1592-1 — ISBN 0-8133-1593-X (pbk.)
    1. Rural development—United States. 2. Rural development—Government policy—United States. 3. Rural telecommunication—United States. I. Hudson, Heather E. II. Title.
  HN90.C6P36 1992
  307.1′412′0973—dc20   92-9247
                                                                    CIP

Printed and bound in the United States of America

The paper used in this publication meets the requirements of the American National Standard for Permanence of Paper for Printed Library Materials Z39.48-1984.

10   9   8   7   6   5   4   3   2   1

CONTENTS

v

FIGURES, MAPS, AND TABLES

FIGURES

MAPS

TABLES

ACKNOWLEDGMENTS

This book was prepared for the Rural Economic Policy Program of The Aspen Institute, under a grant from The Ford Foundation to the University of San Francisco. The Principal Investigator was Heather E. Hudson. Edwin B. Parker and Heather E. Hudson coordinated the preparation.

The authors of the book and their affiliations are:

Edwin B. Parker

President, Parker Telecommunications, Gleneden Beach, Oregon (former President of Equatorial Communications Company and Professor of Communication at Stanford University);

Heather E. Hudson

Professor and Director of the Telecommunications Management and Policy Program, McLaren School of Business, University of San Francisco;

Don A. Dillman

Professor and Director, Social and Economic Sciences Research Center, Washington State University;

Sharon Strover

Associate Professor, Department of Radio-TV-Film, University of Texas at Austin;

Frederick Williams

Professor and Director of the Center for Research on Communication Technology and Society, University of Texas at Austin.

Edwin Parker had primary responsibility for chapters 1, 6 and 7. Heather Hudson had primary responsibility for chapters 2 and 3. Don Dillman had primary responsibility for chapter 5. Sharon Strover and Frederick Williams had primary responsibility for chapter 4. David Bollier edited the text.

The authors would like to acknowledge the support of E. Walter Coward, Director of the Ford Foundation's Rural Poverty and Resources Program, and Susan Sechler, Director of The Aspen Institute's Program on Rural Economic Policy. Maureen Kennedy managed the project for The Aspen Institute and moderated a workshop on rural telecommunications in September 1990 that provided valuable guidance to the authors.

Many people contributed to the preparation of this book. At the University of San Francisco, research assistants included Jane Carmina, Anita Del Bello, Susan Ho, Mark Milatovich, Joseph Ngallo, Michael Paetsch, and Joaquin Vicente-Ausina. Kattie Miles provided administrative and secretarial support.

Kenneth L. Deavers, Director, Agriculture and Rural Economy Division, Economics Research Service, U.S. Department of Agriculture, was particularly helpful in providing background information on the U.S. rural economy and in reviewing an earlier draft of chapter 1.

Many people in Demopolis, Eagle Pass, Glendive and Kearney gave their time and thoughts to help us understand the characteristics and unique dynamics that made each what it is today. Research assistants on the project that resulted in chapter 4, Richard Cutler and Liching Sung, made major contributions; Joan Stuller and James McCain also helped with the field work and economic base analyses. Dr. Amy Glasmeier at the University of Texas provided interpretive help, and Drs. Jurgen Schmandt and Robert Wilson from the LBJ School of Public Affairs at the University of Texas influenced the earlier research that led to the community study. Connie Crytzer patiently typed early drafts and helped with field work arrangements.

Chapter 5 was prepared with additional support from the Social and Economic Sciences Research Center and the Department of Rural Sociology at Washington State University. Helpful comments on an earlier draft of chapter 5 were provided by Susan McAdams, John Niles, Tom Kneeshaw, Lucy Burton, Steve McLellan, David Gray Remington and Don Hanna.

Andrew D. Roscoe and Robert G. Wysor, both of Economic Management Consultants International (EMCI) of Washington, DC, provided the data for Appendix A and played a major role in collecting the data for chapter 6. Ed Morrison of the Oregon Public Utility Commission provided invaluable assistance in collecting the Oregon telecommunications data. Doug Scott of Washington State University performed most of the data analyses for chapter 6, under the direction of Edwin Parker and Don Dillman. Marie Howland contributed helpful comments on an earlier draft of chapter 6.

The authors are also grateful to various individuals in state governments and the telecommunications industry who provided numerous helpful comments on earlier drafts of chapter 7.

FOREWORD

Nearly five years ago, the Rural Economic Policy Program (REPP) and the Communications and Society Program of The Aspen Institute organized a meeting in Aspen, Colorado, in which the participants considered three basic questions: How is rural America likely to fare as the national economy becomes more dependent on information technologies? Is the telecommunications infrastructure gap between rural and urban parts of the country expanding, and at what long-term cost to rural America? How can policymakers formulate new policies that would help to harness telecommunications in support of good jobs and a high quality of life in rural places?

At the time, there was little evidence upon which to base a discussion. Many of the hard numbers presented in this book and in its predecessor, *Rural America in the Information Age*, were yet to be developed. But there were anecdotes: of rural hospital suppliers blocked from metropolitan inventory resupply networks because they could not access on-line databases, and of remote businesses forced to move to urban communities whose telecommunications utilities could support simple fax communication.

Those who met in Aspen that summer hypothesized that telecommunications technology was the tool rural communities could use to overcome the rural "distance penalty" and bring about economic vitality. In an increasingly services-dependent global economy, rural firms could provide services to businesses anywhere in the world provided good-quality telecom infrastructure was built. Workers could "telecommute" from rural places, forming the basis for a rural economic and social renaissance.

It was heady stuff.

After several years of further research, evaluation and hard thinking, we have come to more realistic conclusions. The REPP staff organized a series of conferences and workshops, first to identify the research agenda, and then to compare notes and move toward consensus on findings. In 1988, *Rural America in the Information Age* identified policy options available to federal policymakers hoping to foster rural development through telecommunications. Later that year, the authors of this book turned their attention to state and local policy.

xiii

As they argue here, rural America will undoubtedly fall further behind the national economy if its telecommunications infrastructure is not upgraded in short order. But simply installing fiber optic cable across the country will not resolve rural America's economic problems. Leaders representing rural areas must understand their comparative advantages—and there are many—and create an economic future that meshes with the sophisticated needs of the global economy. Both telecommunications experts and state and local leaders have much to learn from this volume and from each other in progressing toward this vision.

The Rural Economic Policy Program and the Rural Poverty and Resources Program of The Ford Foundation have worked with researchers and practitioners for nearly a decade to come to a better understanding of the obstacles and opportunities facing rural communities, and the policy options available to their leaders. Foundation grantees examining other topics have informed our work on telecommunications and development, and over 100 individuals, including rural mayors, economic development officials, state regulators, utility executives and business owners have participated in project meetings. We thank each for his or her involvement. We particularly thank Ed Parker, Heather Hudson, Don Dillman and David Bollier, whose work forms the core of this five-year effort.

Maureen Kennedy
Associate Director
Rural Economic Policy Program
The Aspen Institute
December 1991

EXECUTIVE SUMMARY

INTRODUCTION

After a bruising series of economic reversals in the 1980s, rural America stands at the threshold of a new economic era. Rural economies are not simply suffering through yet another cyclical decline which will eventually, at some point, generate prosperity. Quite the contrary: they are in the midst of a major structural decline for which there is no obvious or easy remedy. How, then, can concerned rural communities and state governments begin to construct a new economic and community vision for themselves?

Given the dynamics of today's global and national economies, we believe that a modern telecommunications infrastructure holds one promising answer for rural economic development. It is not a magic solution, certainly. But advanced telecommunications is a versatile enabling tool that, in combination with strategic community development planning, can open up a wealth of new opportunities—to "grow" businesses, improve government and social services, enhance public education, and build new bonds of local and regional community. This book explains how these goals can be achieved through state government policies designed to exploit telecommunications potentials for rural development.

An earlier book by some of the same authors, *Rural America in the Information Age*, provided a general overview of the role of telecommunications in rural development. That book made recommendations directed to the U.S. Congress, the Federal Communications Commission, other federal agencies and state governments. This book is a companion volume, providing more detailed analysis and recommendations for state and local policies.

CHAPTER 1
RURAL AMERICA IN THE GLOBAL ECONOMY

The 1980s were hard on rural America. While urban America expanded, rural America resumed the decades-long decline of its historic

1

rural industries, agriculture and natural resources, without compensating growth in other industries. Rural Americans fell further behind urban Americans in terms of new job creation, unemployment rates, poverty rates, wages and total income.

The root causes of these disturbing trends can be traced to massive changes in the global economy that are restructuring the very foundations of the rural economy. In an earlier time, rural Americans were more sheltered from the competitive global economy. Rural life had two main economic penalties—higher travel and transportation costs, and the inability to achieve economies of scale due to lower population density. Yet rural areas also benefited from their isolation; local businesses were more protected from outside competition. As transportation and communications improved, however, rural communities became more closely connected with the rest of the world—introducing new forms of competition to local economies.

At the same time, rural businesses, like urban businesses, need timely access to reliable information. Goods and services today have a greater percentage of "information content"—that is, knowledge that improves quality, reduces costs, aids distribution and marketing, and in other ways enhances competitiveness. The competitive survivors of today's economy have discovered that they must not only work harder, they must work "smarter." Their manufacturing or services must be more efficient, responsive and flexible. If rural America is going to compete in this new global economy, it needs a telecommunications infrastructure that will allow it to exchange information with the rest of the economy—by voice, facsimile and data interchange.

Rural development strategies also must keep pace with the changes in the global economy. In the 1980s, rural communities updated the rural development strategy of "smokestack chasing" to lure telemarketing and other "back office" industries. A more effective long-term strategy, however, may be "capacity building" in one's own community rather than recruitment of outside industries. To help this process, state governments should concentrate on acting as a catalyst, leveraging development investments from the private sector, stimulating competition, and providing incentives and information to help communities and businesses help themselves.

The key is to mobilize whatever human and physical resources are available, often in collaboration with nearby communities. Tempting as it may be for a community to focus on the short-term goal of jobs creation, sustained development is more likely to occur if a community deals with three interrelated concerns: investment in human capital; investment in basic physical infrastructure; and social infrastructure development. Leadership, cooperation and risk-taking are the three key characteristics of the social relations in communities that develop successfully.

Telecommunications is a key part of the physical infrastructure needed for development. At a minimum, rural communities need single-party touchtone calling and line quality that can reliably transmit voice, data and facsimile messages. Many other services are highly desirable. Call waiting, call forwarding and three-way calling have become useful small business productivity tools. Other policy changes and enhanced services such as expanded local calling areas, lower long-distance toll charges for intrastate calls, and 800 numbers also can affect the competitiveness of rural businesses.

However necessary these telecommunications services, it may be difficult for rural areas to obtain them. The telecommunications industry is currently navigating through a regulatory transition, a period during which old pricing subsidies are giving way to market forces that are driving prices closer to the actual costs of each specific telephone service. This transition poses daunting challenges for rural communities. As telephone carriers struggle to cut costs, service quality may deteriorate and rates of investment in modern equipment may slow, especially in rural areas.

In this difficult transition, rural America faces great risks to its economic well-being if it leaves policy decisions entirely in the hands of the telephone carriers and their regulators, who often are more concerned with the more lucrative and competitive urban markets. Rural leaders must mobilize to prevent rural areas from being hurt in the transition. This period of transition is also a time of genuine opportunity. If rural communities can forge cooperative development plans with development agencies, state government telecommunications network managers, regulatory agencies, and the telecommunications industry, all parties have a unique opportunity to achieve significant benefits.

Three key issues must be addressed:

1. The transition from telecommunications monopoly to telecommunications competition;

2. Spurring investment in rural telecommunications infrastructure as a means for economic growth; and

3. Exploiting the existing and future telecommunications network to achieve development goals.

CHAPTER 2
STATE TELECOMMUNICATIONS PLAYERS
AND POLICIES

Understanding why policies have not kept pace with the times requires, first, an understanding of the major policy players in state telecommunications and development. Often there are identifiable reasons why state governments, telecommunications carriers, and businesses have failed to exploit telecommunications as a development tool. One of the most important reasons, we believe, is that the two cultures of telecommunications and development—their respective policy makers, industry representatives, research analysts, academic experts, and public constituencies—do not really understand each other.

Chapter 2 provides an overview of the chief players in telecommunications and development policies. Based on a survey of state regulatory commissions, legislative committees, and telephone associations, we describe how states legislate, manage and regulate their rural telecommunications infrastructure—and how this work is and is not coordinated with development agencies. It is our hope that, by de-mystifying the basic policy apparatus that animates telecommunications and development, respectively, a new and fruitful conversation between the two cultures can begin.

Three different parts of state government all influence state telecommunications policy—the legislature, the executive branch headed by the governor, and the state regulatory agency. Telephone carriers are also important because they make the actual investments in rural telecommunications infrastructure and provide telecommunications services to rural areas.

Typically, state legislatures have little telecommunications expertise. With limited staff, legislatures must rely on other sources of expertise, usually the state regulatory commission. The second most important source of expertise is not a state agency, but the telephone companies themselves.

The governor's most direct influence on telecommunications policy in many states is through appointments of regulatory commissioners. Governors also can play a critical role in other areas of the executive branch: through state telecommunications agencies, the state government procurement process, and through special task forces and studies designed to forge a consensus on new telecommunications policy.

In many state governments, a separate office manages the state's internal telecommunications facilities. An often-overlooked instrument for improving rural telecommunications is the state government's own telecommunications network. State governments can provide leadership in two key areas: the creative use of the state network to reach dispersed rural users, and the innovative use of the procurement process to leverage new telecommunications infrastructure and services into existence.

State regulatory commissions have more influence on rural telecommunications than any other state agency. Most state commissions see their role as both regulatory and policy making. However, the amount of telecommunications expertise differs greatly from state to state. Thirty-two states have ten or fewer staff working exclusively on telecommunications; five states have no staff assigned exclusively to telecommunications.

Although they often set policies affecting rural services, the regulatory commissions generally do not consider rural development goals in their regulatory decisions. Most commissions do not have explicit legislative authority to consider economic development, although their authorizing legislation usually provides a broad "public interest" standard that could be used to justify development goals.

Changes in telecommunications technology and competitive pressures are forcing regulatory commissions to revise traditional rate of return regulation. The most common alternative to rate of return regulation is incentive regulation designed to give carriers a profit incentive to reduce costs and offer new or improved services. Such plans give telephone companies flexibility in setting rates and opportunities to keep more profits if the companies improve their productivity.

Critics charge that large companies will be tempted to cut corners on service and quality in the less profitable regions. Even when the regulatory commission stipulates statewide benchmarks for service quality, poorer rural areas may suffer worse service because the declines might not show up in statewide averages. An alternative would be for states to achieve state policy goals through "management by objectives." Under such a regulatory scheme carriers that achieved state goals would be permitted a higher profit potential and greater flexibility in their investments, technology choices, and management. The advantage is that instead of tempting carriers to reduce the quality of rural service to reap higher profits, such regulation would reward carriers for improving rural service.

Three regulatory issues are of particular concern to rural users of telephone services:

Service availability: In many states telephone carriers are introducing new services to urban areas. Meanwhile, many rural users still do not have services that have long been available to urban users, such as single-party touchtone service. Rural development advocates should pay particular attention to how quickly carriers offer new services to rural users.

Service quality: It will be important to monitor the quality of telecommunications services in rural areas under the new incentive regulation plans, because carriers may pay more attention to their urban and interurban networks than to rural facilities.

Rural rates: In major cities most telephone calls are local. In rural areas, however, a much higher percentage of calls for the identical purposes are long distance. The appropriate, financially feasible response is "extended area service" (EAS), a tariff that lets rural residents make calls within an extended area for a flat rate. This policy helps reduce the disparities between rural and urban subscribers.

Another approach to expanding services available in rural areas is aggregating demand. Rural areas often lack economies of scale that would make it attractive to provide new services such as equal access to alternate long distance carriers. Iowa Network Services pioneered rural demand aggregation through cooperation of rural telephone carriers. Similar cooperation is being planned for Minnesota, Kansas and South Dakota.

For states to harness the new telecommunications for development purposes, they should begin with a broader perspective. State regulators and other policy makers should appreciate the larger economic and social context in which modern telecommunications operates, and explore new regulatory approaches that can unleash new infrastructure, applications and benefits that will contribute to economic development.

CHAPTER 3
RURAL DEVELOPMENT PLAYERS:
STATE AND LOCAL INITIATIVES

Chapter 3 examines the rural development players at the state and local level, and reviews telecommunications projects that support rural social and economic development goals.

State rural development responsibilities are spread across many departments and agencies, several of which may have some connection with telecommunications. They include agencies directly involved in rural development such as agricultural extension, forestry and fisheries, and parks and wildlife. They also include state and county commerce or economic development agencies, and social service agencies providing emergency services, health care, welfare and other community services. Educational institutions for preschool through adult learners are particularly important for rural development.

Through our survey, we identified two major reasons why development agencies at both state and local levels are not involved in telecommunications planning and policy. First, they typically do not have a formal mandate for telecommunications planning or policy, even if they are involved in telecommunications projects. Second, the regulatory commissions usually do not perceive any ongoing role for development agencies in state telecommunications policy. At the local level, many communities are unaware of what services could be available or how to make their needs known to regulators and carriers. Even when services are available, they may be unaware of how they can use them to achieve local development goals.

Many state and county economic development agencies are trying to diversify their economies by attracting businesses that are information-intensive such as telemarketing, customer support, mail order fulfillment and data entry. By upgrading the local telecommunications infrastructure, these agencies can make attractive overtures to businesses that require sophisticated services such as alternate routing of 800 number calls and improved data transmission services.

This chapter includes several examples showing how telephone carriers can stimulate economic development in the communities they serve, and thereby increase their revenues. Beyond installing and marketing advanced telecommunications services, carriers can improve their expertise on development issues, actively participate in local economic development councils, and help finance some development projects.

As a means to reduce costs and improve quality, one of the most promising applications of telecommunications and information technologies is rural health care services. Many hospitals already use Electronic Data Interchange (EDI) to communicate with their suppliers. Using data networks and video conferencing, rural general practitioners can consult with specialists in major urban hospitals. Physicians and other health care professionals can use the network for remote diagnostics, video consultations, in-service training and continuing education.

Another innovative rural use of telecommunications is known as "distance learning." Rural educators have demonstrated valuable new applications of rural telecommunications and explored key issues that must be addressed to put these technologies to effective use. Rural schools have embraced telecommunications as a response to two major challenges that have arisen in recent years. First, as the rural economy has declined and residents have moved away, rural taxpayers have faced unbearably high costs to operate their schools. Second, many states have revised their curricula and introduced tougher new standards for high school graduation, including requirements in foreign languages, mathematics and sciences. Many rural school districts do not have the necessary expertise on their faculty, and are unable to attract or afford the specialized teachers.

We identified 50 current rural education projects that use telecommunications and gathered information about each of them. Most of the projects deliver instructional materials exclusively to rural schools, while some serve colleges and adult education programs. Local school districts and universities together initiated 70 percent of the projects. State governments, through departments of education or administration, originated many other projects. State governments have been the major sources of funding.

One lesson learned from successful projects is that new bridges must be built—between rural communities and state government, between development experts and telecommunications experts, between those who use technical jargon and the lay public whose future is being decided. Ultimately, rural development is a community process. There is an old saying, "You can lead a horse to water, but you can't make it drink." State development agencies cannot make rural development happen. Development depends on local leadership, local initiative and local cooperation.

Development agencies should work with the state regulatory commission to ensure that telephone carriers have appropriate incentives to put a basic "equal opportunity" telecommunications infrastructure in place for all rural communities. In addition, state development agencies should look for "thirsty" communities that do have the leadership, initiative and cooperation to attempt development projects making use of telecommunications.

CHAPTER 4
LOCAL PERSPECTIVES ON TELECOMMUNICATIONS AND DEVELOPMENT: FOUR COMMUNITY STUDIES

Chapter 4 explores how four different rural communities and their nearby regions promote community development. The four sites— Glendive, Montana; Kearney, Nebraska; Demopolis, Alabama; and Eagle Pass, Texas—were selected because of their varying geographic, economic and population characteristics and their varying uses of information technologies, especially telecommunications.

The four communities offer a range of perspectives on how telecommunications can foster rural development. Despite their differences, the experience of the four communities provided two related principles: development strategies must be based on vigorous local involvement; and state policies and programs should provide incentives carefully structured to stimulate community participation.

We conclude that economic development must be nurtured among all segments of the community, from citizen groups to business leaders, from elected officials to the schools. New partnerships for using telecommunications—among several rural communities or among segments of a single rural community—have a large, untapped potential. Partnerships help achieve economies of scale that are otherwise unattainable, creating new "win-win" situations for everyone. Towns can be allied with each other and reap the benefits enjoyed by much larger towns and cities—lower costs, access to diverse information sources, a greater differentiation of products and services. The participants all gain new telecommunications capacities, and the process itself helps build the civic culture of rural regions.

State development policies and programs usually do not take much account of local resources and needs. Nor do they generally consider how telecommunications could help a community exploit new opportunities. Another shortcoming of existing state development is its oversight of needy towns that do not have the leadership or expertise to seek state aid. If state development programs are truly going to reach the most needy and less developed regions, they must undertake a more aggressive outreach program to inform communities about state aid programs and help them develop local leadership. Local and state authorities should explore the development potential of telecommunications alliances, and help test their effectiveness in different marketplaces.

One of the most important development players in rural America is the local telephone carrier. The smaller rural telephone carriers tend to have better facilities and to provide more development support for rural communities than the larger carriers that lack management presence in rural communities. By contrast, carriers with large urban markets and monopoly franchises protecting them from competition in their rural service areas do not have much financial incentive to improve rural service. To deal with this problem, state policy makers should devise incentives for rural telephone companies both to upgrade their facilities and to ensure their creative use in community development.

Based on our investigations of the four communities, we believe state policy must:

- Create incentives for telephone companies to be more responsive to users in providing both existing and new services;

- Develop strategies for aggregating telecommunications demand so that economies of scale can be realized by providers and users;

- Foster a long-term, community-based approach to economic development by promoting the active participation of diverse constituencies;

- Identify the areas where the telecommunications marketplace works adequately and where it does not, and then forge new policies to spur competition or compensate for its absence; and

- Set priorities for the most important social services in rural areas, such as education and health care delivery, and identify how telecommunications might aid them.

CHAPTER 5
RURAL TELECOMMUNICATIONS AND ECONOMIC DEVELOPMENT IN WASHINGTON STATE: A CASE STUDY

There is no single process by which a state comes to see how telecommunications can enhance rural development. So much depends upon a state's political culture, economic base, existing telecommunications infrastructure, and many other factors. That said, it is instructive to look at how one state developed its rural telecommunications services in the 1980s to stimulate economic development. Chapter 5 describes the process of change in Washington State.

Between 1983 and 1990, the rural residents of Washington State received significantly improved telephone services after many people—university professors, rural advocates, entrepreneurs, telecommunications experts, legislators and regulators—began to focus on the problems of rural telecommunications. As initial interest in the issue grew, a critical mass of researchers and advocates propelled changes in people's expectations and in state policy. A new body of literature and a new network of experts emerged; regulators started new policies and programs; carriers made significant new investments in telecommunications; and new varieties of rural development ensued.

In 1989, the Washington Utilities and Transportation Commission (WUTC) completed an inventory of the state's telecommunications infrastructure and proposed a new, minimally acceptable level of basic telephone service: single-party touchtone service at affordable rates, without suburban mileage charges. The WUTC has established that policy, and expects to achieve the new goal by 1995 for all locations, with most locations upgraded to single-party touchtone service by the end of 1992.

Another WUTC project bore fruit in December 1990, when the commission issued new rules for enlarging the boundaries for extended service areas. The chief goal was to allow toll-free calling to those areas where phone calling is consistently heavy. To this end, the WUTC ordered telephone companies to identify exchanges where an average subscriber paid long-distance toll charges for more than 20 percent of the minutes of phone calls within the Local Access and Transport Area (LATA). The commission ordered the carriers to prepare new extended area rate plans that would include 80 percent of intraLATA call minutes in flat rate EAS services. Any increased costs for the new extended local calling will be recovered primarily from customers who directly benefit.

The Palouse Area Economic Development Council and the Center for the New West collaborated on a proposal for an experimental office that would use telecommunications and computer linkages to help farmers and businesses in the Palouse region learn about international marketing opportunities. With a $95,000 state grant, the new office, called AgriTechnics International, began to identify export opportunities for businesses in four adjacent counties and to provide information on export and international shipping documentation, letters of credit and the mechanics of doing business internationally. By 1990, eleven counties in eastern Washington were participating in the program. An indispensable factor in AgriTechnics' success has been access to modern telecommunications networks and services, such as international facsimile transmission and remote access to electronic databases.

An important lesson of the Washington experience is that change in the quality and use of rural telecommunications can be achieved through the cooperation of many individuals and organizations who together reach a consensus concerning what should be done. Mobilizing the potential power of this array of players requires some means to bring them together in constructive ways. A process must emerge through which these individuals can forge personal relationships, discuss and debate new research, identify common concerns, develop political alliances, and learn leadership skills.

A vital instrument throughout the process of change in Washington State was rigorous research. Research on a state's telecommunications needs is often quite limited. With the introduction of thorough research and analysis a persuasive case was made for specific policy reforms. Uncertainties were resolved and minds were changed, opening the door for action.

Important as research is, its vital partner is the real-life experiences of rural residents. Much of the emotional and political power fueling telecommunications improvements in Washington State came from the concrete anecdotes and personal testimony of ordinary people. Their testimony, when combined with more generalized, systematic survey research, spurred the legislature and the WUTC more than either could have achieved alone.

CHAPTER 6
TELECOMMUNICATIONS AND RURAL DEVELOPMENT:
QUANTITATIVE ANALYSES

Chapter 6 provides quantitative statistical evidence that strengthens the argument that telecommunications can help rural economic development. There were two major gaps in the prior research. First, there was little evidence showing how improvements in telephone service beyond the provision of basic voice communication helped rural economic development. Second, there was an absence of reliable quantitative data comparing rural and urban locations in the United States.

Two recent quantitative studies go a long way toward filling these two gaps in the telecommunications research literature. The first is a national time series analysis providing definitive statistical evidence that investment in U.S. telecommunications infrastructure in earlier time periods generally "causes" increases in the U.S. Gross National Product in later time periods. These results show that, more often than not, when telecommunications investments are made, the resulting networks are used in ways that lead to economic growth. The second study analyzes recent data from both rural and urban counties in two Pacific Northwest states, Oregon and Washington. It concludes that counties with better telephone networks perform better economically.

The first study confirmed a "cyclical, positive feedback process": telecommunications investment stimulates economic growth, and economic growth in turn stimulates further demand for telecommunications investment (Cronin and others, 1991). A related study (DRI/McGraw-Hill, 1990) also measured the amount of savings for the U.S. economy resulting from telecommunications infrastructure production and utilization in the period from 1963 to 1982. The savings came in two forms. First, after adjusting for inflation, prices for comparable communications services were lower in 1982 than in 1963. Capital investment in more advanced technology was a major factor in achieving those lower costs. Second, the use of telecommunications increased as telecommunications substituted for more expensive alternatives, such as travel, or made the production processes of other industries more efficient. Partly offsetting this second form of savings is the cost of the additional telecommunications services themselves.

Most of the telecommunications-related savings in other industries benefited those industries and their customers. Significantly, these benefits were largely "external" to the telecommunications industry. It is the confirmation of these external benefits that justifies policy intervention to ensure that regulated telecommunications carriers, especially local monopolies, provide the infrastructure that is necessary for growth in the rest of the economy.

The benefits of improved telecommunications were spread widely over almost all industries, with the most information-intensive industry—finance and insurance—increasing telecommunications usage by more than 800 percent. The service sector of the economy, which is now the largest and fastest growing sector, accounted for nearly three-quarters of the total increase in telecommunications utilization.

These national statistics provide convincing evidence that the economy as a whole benefits from increased investment in telecommunications infrastructure. The causal connection observed in the time series analysis is indirect, however; telecommunications was not the direct "cause" of economic growth but rather, a vital catalyst. The economic growth stemmed from the ways that other industries used telecommunications to make their production processes more efficient.

To provide more evidence concerning the relationship between telecommunications infrastructure and rural development, we gathered data on the telecommunications infrastructure in two Pacific Northwest states, Oregon and Washington. The key question to be answered was whether the benefits from improved rural telecommunications were sufficiently large that they would result in higher income levels or lower unemployment rates.

The county data from two states provide a more detailed picture of the interrelationship of population density, telecommunications infrastructure and rural economic performance. This more detailed picture confirms that counties that have upgraded rural multiparty phone service to single-party service and replaced electromechanical telephone switches with modern digital switching capability, perform better economically than counties that have not done so. This result remains true after controlling for the effect of population density on economic performance.

The process of achieving the economic benefits is complex. Upgrading the telephone technology improves the quality and variety of telecommunications services available. It is the use of those services by rural residents, businesses, government and other institutions that causes the resulting economic gains. Those gains may result from a better informed workforce, productivity gains in local businesses, or from better information about markets and business opportunities. Modern telecommunications infrastructure is the enabler that makes such gains possible.

CHAPTER 7
BUILDING ELECTRONIC BYWAYS:
GOALS AND RECOMMENDATIONS

How can we ensure that the electronic byways are built, and that their full developmental benefits for rural America are realized? Chapter 7 discusses detailed sets of policy goals and recommendations for four different audiences: governors and legislators, state and local development agencies, state regulatory commissions, and the telecommunications industry. These goals and recommendations are listed below.

The infrastructure recommendations are cast in terms of services that should be available to users, not particular technologies. It is not necessary for regulators to micro-manage the carriers' technology choices to achieve service and quality goals. Rather, it is preferable to give carriers economic incentives to provide the needed variety and quality of services in the most efficient manner.

Many experts have compared the telecommunications infrastructure to an "electronic highway," an analogy that may lead some people to conclude that it will be too costly to provide access to modern electronic superhighways from every community. This assumption is incorrect. It *is* economically feasible to provide broadband service connecting every telephone exchange in the county, including those in small rural communities, and high quality narrowband access (for voice and data) for every household in the country. Broadband links for video and high-speed data can be provided wherever the business, educational or other applications require them.

Universal access to high quality telecommunications networks is not only affordable; it can be provided without tax dollars. Although large investments will be required, the anticipated profits should be sufficient to raise the necessary capital. Telephone subscribers, on the average, are unlikely to have higher telephone bills, except for increased usage. As the new investments lead to lower costs and increased usage, subscriber revenues will repay, over time, the costs of the new investments.

In order to harvest the many benefits of telecommunications technologies, the challenge is to craft incentives that will extend electronic highways and byways throughout rural America. Telecommunications providers and rural development advocates should both remember, however, that telecommunications alone is not enough. Putting a modern infrastructure in place is a necessary starting point. The continuing challenge is to develop the uses and applications of modern electronic byways that will contribute to economic development and improved quality of life for all rural Americans.

≡ GOALS and RECOMMENDATIONS

RECOMMENDATIONS FOR STATE GOVERNORS AND LEGISLATORS

1. State governors and legislatures should develop a comprehensive telecommunications plan with specific goals appropriate to the conditions of their states.

2. Each state should establish a full set of performance measures to monitor progress toward meeting state goals for its telecommunications infrastructure.

3. State legislatures should authorize their regulatory commissions to consider economic development potential as they regulate telecommunications.

4. State legislatures should authorize their regulatory commissions to use incentive regulation as an alternative to traditional rate-of-return regulation.

5. State economic development agencies should be authorized to become advocates for telecommunications policies that serve economic development goals.

6. State governments should establish a high level, centralized telecommunications authority within the state government. This body would coordinate, evaluate and set priorities for the state's own telecommunications and information technology efforts, including voice, data and image processing and transmission.

7. Planners of state government telecommunications services should design them to increase citizens' access to public information and services without regard to geographic location or income.

8. The state government process for procurement of telecommunications should be used to help develop a modernized public switched network throughout the state.

9. State governments should support pilot projects involving telecommunications applications that could benefit rural development.

GOALS AND RECOMMENDATIONS
FOR DEVELOPMENT AGENCIES

1. *Increased Statewide Awareness of the Linkages Between Telecommunications and Development*

   1.1 Development agencies should sponsor regional workshops to share information about innovative uses of telecommunications and identify rural telecommunications needs.

   1.2 Development agencies should convene task forces to set goals for modernization of the state's telecommunications infrastructure and plans for its use to stimulate development.

2. *More Sophisticated Advocacy for Telecommunications Policies that Serve Development Goals*

   2.1 State development agencies should become credible advocates for rural development interests at the state regulatory commission.

3. *Better Understanding among Small Businesses and Rural Communities of the Many Valuable Uses of Telecommunications Services*

   3.1 State development agencies should build a telecommunications component into small business assistance and rural community development programs.

   3.2 Development agencies should sponsor training courses on telecommunications for community and economic development professionals.

4. *A Rural Workforce Trained to Meet the Telecommunications Needs of Rural Business*

   4.1 Development agencies should work with community colleges to establish telecommunications training courses.

4.2 State development agencies should encourage the establishment and expansion of distance learning programs for both student and adult education.

5. *Aggregation of Rural and Small Business Demand for Modern Telecommunications Services*

5.1 Development agencies should work with rural communities and small businesses to help them to obtain collectively the telecommunications services they might not be able to obtain individually.

GOALS AND RECOMMENDATIONS
FOR STATE REGULATORY COMMISSIONS

1. *Universal Single-party Touchtone Service*

1.1 All state regulatory commissions should participate to the maximum extent allowed in the FCC's "lifeline" program, which reduces the monthly basic telephone service fee for eligible households by as much as $7.00 below the normal charges.

1.2 All state regulatory commissions should participate in the FCC's "Link-up America" program, which reduces the installation and deposit charges for telephone service for eligible poor households by $30.00.

1.3 State regulatory commissions should encourage "local service only" options for subscribers who would otherwise be denied access to both local and long-distance service.

1.4 All state regulatory commissions should establish "relay services" that enable persons using teletype or other terminals for the speech- or hearing-impaired (or those with other disabilities) to communicate through the telephone network with people using ordinary telephones.

1.5 State regulatory commissions should encourage competition for service to all locations where telephone carriers charge extraordinary installation fees.

1.6 State regulatory commissions should solicit competitive bids for telephone service to locations outside telephone franchise boundaries. The commissions should then grant franchise authority (and corresponding service obligations) to qualified low bidders.

1.7 All state regulatory commissions should eliminate "suburban mileage charges" from basic single-party telephone service rates.

1.8 State regulatory commissions should redefine basic telephone service to include touchtone service.

1.9 State regulatory commissions adopting incentive regulation plans should include an incentive to encourage universal access to single-party touchtone service.

2. *Service Quality Sufficient for Voice, Fax and Data*

2.1 State regulatory commissions should establish mandatory, audited telephone service quality standards and should include a service quality component in any incentive regulation program they adopt.

2.2 State regulatory commissions should change regulatory policies that inhibit network modernization, including depreciation schedules and rules for amortization of costs of older equipment taken out of service.

3. *Extended Area Service (EAS) and Reduced Intrastate Long-distance Rates*

3.1 State regulatory commissions should establish Extended Area Service policies that enable residents to reach their major communities of interest with "local" calls.

3.2 State regulatory commissions should maintain geographic rate averaging for intrastate long-distance calls.

3.3 State regulatory commissions should allow intrastate long-distance competition within each LATA established by the Modified Final Judgment of the AT&T Consent Decree.

3.4 State regulatory commissions should encourage lower intrastate long distance rates.

4. *Universal Enhanced 911 (E911) Service*

4.1 State regulatory commissions should work with local government agencies to make E911 services available from all telephones throughout the state.

5.   *Widespread Access to Optional Information Services*

> 5.1 State regulatory commissions should encourage statewide local access to information services that are generally available in urban areas.

6.   *Public Network Utilization for Distance Education*

> 6.1 State regulatory commissions should encourage flexible tariff structures for distance learning networks.

RECOMMENDATIONS
FOR TELECOMMUNICATIONS PROVIDERS

1.   Telephone carriers should upgrade their facilities to provide universal single-party touchtone service with quality levels suitable for reliable data and facsimile transmission. They also should upgrade facilities to meet demands for access to distance learning, other video and data applications, and a variety of enhanced services as they become available.

2.   Telecommunications equipment and service providers should design and promote equipment and services to meet the needs of rural users.

3.   Telecommunications providers should market their products and services effectively.

4.   The telecommunications industry should offer telecommunications training for the present and future workforce.

5.   Telephone carriers should provide local leadership for economic development programs in the communities they serve.

6.   Telephone carriers should contribute trained staff to economic development programs in their service areas.

7.   Telephone carriers should help local entrepreneurs and economic development projects obtain financing.

8.   Telephone carriers should make direct investments in rural economic development.

INTRODUCTION

After a bruising series of economic reversals in the 1980s, rural America stands at the threshold of a new economic era. Rural economies are not simply suffering through yet another cyclical decline that will eventually, at some point, generate prosperity. Quite the contrary: they are in the midst of a major structural decline for which there is no obvious or easy remedy. How, then, can concerned rural communities and state governments construct a new economic and community vision for themselves?

Given the dynamics of today's global and national economies, we believe that a modern rural telecommunications infrastructure holds one promising answer for rural economic development. It is not a magic solution, certainly. But advanced telecommunications is a versatile enabling tool that, in combination with strategic community development planning, can open a wealth of new opportunities—to "grow" businesses, improve government and social services, enhance public education, and build new bonds of local and regional community. To achieve these results, rural communities must have electronic byways that will serve as their feeder roads and on-ramps to the modern interurban electronic superhighways.

This book explains how these goals can be achieved through state government policies designed to exploit telecommunications potentials for rural development. An earlier book by some of the same authors, *Rural America in the Information Age* (Parker, Hudson, Dillman and Roscoe, 1989), provided a general overview of the role of telecommunications in rural development. It made recommendations directed to the U.S. Congress, the Federal Communications Commission, other federal agencies and state governments. This book narrows the focus to state issues and provides more detailed analyses and recommendations for state and local policies.

One reason that the importance of telecommunications for rural development has not been well-recognized until recently, is the gap between two "cultures"—the telephone industry and its regulators on the one hand and the culture of economic development advocates and agencies on the other. Both cultures are in the midst of difficult transitions and inhabit worlds marked by distinct technical jargons and complex policies. As a result, members of the two cultures have rarely had occasion to speak to each other.

21

As changing technological and economic realities made obsolete the old policies in both telecommunications and rural development, a new terrain of common ground appeared. As each culture adjusts to its newly changed environment, there are now significant opportunities for the two of them to cooperate for mutual benefit. A major goal of this book is to help bring the cultures of telecommunications and rural development together.

Necessarily, the argument of this book requires a brief primer on the current challenges facing both telecommunications policy and rural economic development. We therefore begin in chapter 1 with an exposition of the structural shift in the rural economy over the past decade, prompted in large part by intense global competition and the growing importance of information in nearly all business activities. Chapter 1 also explains the changes that are sweeping through the world of rural telecommunications, and how they both threaten and open new opportunities for rural economic development.

Planning telecommunications-based development requires an understanding of how state governments legislate, regulate and manage their rural telecommunications infrastructure. That is the topic of chapter 2, which also examines how state policies affect telecommunications investments and economic development opportunities.

If there is one lesson to be learned in rural development, it is that there is no simple prototype that can be easily replicated in rural communities; each locality has its own distinctive identity, economic resources and social needs. In recognition of this diversity, chapter 3 explores specific rural development projects that use telecommunications. It gives special attention to the fastest-growing rural development use of modern telecommunications networks, "distance learning"—that is, the use of satellite, fiber optic and other distance-spanning technologies to share teachers in rural regions or to bring to rural locations special instruction in subjects not otherwise locally available.

Rural communities that aspire to exploit telecommunications need to know more than the development potential of different telecommunications networks and services. They also need to understand that the *community context* of telecommunications networks is vital to their successful use in spurring economic development. Toward this end, chapter 4 reports how four rural communities are using telecommunications as a tool for long-term regional development.

Although much of the impetus for change necessarily resides in individual rural communities, little can be done without statewide policy changes. Chapter 5 illustrates the complex dynamics of state and local interaction on telecommunications and development policy, as experienced in Washington State between 1983 and 1990. This case study shows how a diverse state network of telecommunications and development experts acted as catalysts for significant reform.

While much of the enthusiasm for improved rural telecommunications comes from compelling anecdotal accounts, legislators and other policy makers understandably want to review hard evidence showing quantitatively the relationship between telecommunications and economic development. Chapter 6 marshalls the latest statistical evidence showing how a modern telecommunications infrastructure contributes to a community's economic success.

Finally, chapter 7 presents a series of policy goals and recommendations for each major constituency with a stake in telecommunications and development policy issues: governors and legislators, state and local development agencies, state regulatory commissions, and the telecommunications industry. It is our hope that these recommendations will stimulate careful consideration of these issues and point the way toward an economic revitalization of rural America.

CHAPTER 1

Rural America
in the Global Economy

1. THE U.S. RURAL ECONOMY IN THE 1990s

Structural Shifts in the Past Decade

The 1980s were hard on rural America. The 1970s, in retrospect, had been a time of relative prosperity, as rural manufacturing flourished and the rural population grew. Then came the recessions of 1980 and 1982, which hurt both urban and rural Americans. Urban economies soon recovered, despite a variety of regional problems, while rural Americans found themselves left behind in the economic expansion that stretched from 1982 to late 1990. While urban America expanded, rural America resumed the decades long decline of its traditional industries, agriculture and natural resources, without compensating growth in other industries.*

As the 1980s wore on, rural Americans began to realize that they were not just suffering through another cyclical recession in the familiar series of rural booms-and-busts. They came to realize that the very structure of the rural economy was changing—permanently. Rural Americans fell further behind urban Americans in terms of new job creation, unemployment rates, poverty rates, wages and total income.

In the 1970s, employment growth in rural America had been strong. Agricultural employment had been stable, the number of mining jobs had grown, and manufacturing jobs had increased by an impressive 20 percent. Rural unemployment was under 6 percent at the end of the decade. In the 1980s, however, rural employment began a new, more ominous decline. Until the 1980–81 recession, the rural unemployment rate had stayed lower than the metro rate in good times and bad. Now, as the recession grew

---

* For purposes of statistical comparison, rural America is defined as counties outside Metropolitan Statistical Areas (MSAs), as defined by the Census Bureau.

25

deeper, the rural unemployment rate rose faster than the metro rate and peaked at a higher level. Throughout the rest of the decade, as urban areas recovered, the relative performance of rural areas worsened. Total metro area employment grew by more than 18 percent, but rural areas enjoyed only about 8 percent growth. Not until 1989 did rural unemployment rates come back down to under 6 percent. That temporary improvement in the rural unemployment rate late in the decade, which came just before the 1990–91 recession raised unemployment rates again, resulted from workers migrating to the cities to find work. Even so, the rural unemployment rate in 1989 was 110 percent of the urban unemployment rate.

Rural poverty rates similarly worsened throughout the decade. The rural poverty rate—that is, the percentage of people living below the federally established "poverty line"—was 13.8 percent in 1979. It rose rapidly during the recessions of the early 1980s, as did urban poverty rates. However, unlike previous experience and unlike the urban poverty rate, the rural rate remained stubbornly high throughout the national economic expansion of the 1980s. In 1982, the rural poverty rate was 17.8 percent. The most recently available data, for 1989, show the rural poverty rate at nearly 16 percent, almost four percentage points higher than in metro locations. The average 1989 per capita income of residents of metropolitan counties was $18,771, compared to an average per capita income of $13,557 for rural county residents (Deavers, 1989; U.S. Department of Commerce, 1990).

Given the dismal circumstances in rural employment and poverty, it is not surprising that large numbers of rural Americans moved to the cities. The 1990 census confirmed that rural populations had declined over the previous decade in more than half of rural counties. The worst hit regions were the corn belt, great plains, Mississippi delta, Appalachian coal fields and mining areas of the west. Overall, rural counties grew at one-third the rate of metropolitan counties.

Modest rural growth occurred in desirable retirement locations and on the periphery of some metropolitan areas. These regional variations in population growth and decline generally follow variations in regional economic performance: only recreational, desirable retirement locations and those rural areas near major metropolitan areas enjoyed robust growth; most other rural areas suffered (USDA, 1991).

After a decade of decline, the 1990s did not open with any greater promise. The 1990 recession hit rural America early and hard. By the third quarter of 1990, rural job growth had declined for four consecutive quarters, leaving fewer total jobs than a year earlier.

What was happening to rural American families and communities, as they attempted to cope with their local economic problems, was an acceleration of the structural transformation of the rural economy. The traditional rural economic base of farming and natural resource extraction now supported only a tiny fraction of the rural population. By the late 1980s, farming accounted for fewer than 9 percent of rural jobs and mining fewer than 2 percent. Manufacturing, which had provided 17 percent of jobs in rural counties in 1986, no longer provided rural job growth. Many manufacturing jobs moved to Third World countries with even lower wage rates. Factory automation kept jobs in the United States, but the net result was fewer jobs and jobs requiring different, more advanced skills.

As in urban areas, the primary source of new rural jobs was service businesses. The rate of growth of service jobs in rural locations was lower than in cities, and the pay was more likely to be low. Many rural people were able to find work without moving to the city. But trading a $10 an hour mill job for a $5 an hour services job did not improve their standard of living.

The Penalties of Isolation

In an earlier time, rural Americans were more sheltered from the competitive global economy. They exported to cities the food and natural resources that were uniquely available in rural areas. In exchange, they purchased goods manufactured elsewhere, either by mail order or at nearby retail stores. There were two main economic penalties of rural life. One was the higher travel and transportation costs associated with rural distances. The other was the inability to achieve economies of scale due to lower population density. With fewer customers, the local rural market could not sell as much—either in volume or variety—as successful urban stores, and therefore had to charge more per item if the proprietor was going to cover total costs and earn an adequate living. In the 1980s, Wal-Mart discount department stores, among others, overcame this historic rural disadvantage by using telecommunications in innovative ways to create new economies of scale and minimize the rural "distance penalty." Wal-Mart put satellite earth stations at rural store locations and used them for voice, data and video communication with headquarters. The data network permitted efficient inventory control, and the video network was used for employee training.

In the past, the rural barrier of distance also provided an advantage. It often served to protect local services from outside competition. The local bookkeeper did not face competition from an urban accounting firm. The local restaurant did not have a national fast food chain outlet across the street. The local storekeepers did not have to worry about national chain stores twenty miles away. And the town poolroom did not lose customers to Japanese video games. Some goods and most services consumed in each rural location were produced in the same rural location, helping the local economy to flourish.

As transportation and communications improved, rural communities became more closely connected with the rest of the world—introducing new forms of competition to local economies. The economic advantage of rural distance disappeared. Both goods and services consumed in rural communities now come from whatever part of the world can most economically produce them. Imported goods and services displace rural goods and services that are not competitive in the larger economy. Rural payroll clerks can lose their jobs to more highly automated payroll processing businesses. Rural firms serving national and international markets can prosper—as the L.L. Bean catalog retail business has shown. Businesses that effectively use new technology to achieve productivity gains—that is, greater or higher quality output with the same or lower costs—have usually survived. Many businesses that resisted such changes to protect local jobs have gone out of business altogether.

Successful businesses, both urban and rural, are usually well connected with national or global marketplaces and have good communication links giving them feedback about what their customers want. Successful businesses everywhere seek their sources of supply from wherever in the country or the world they can get the most economical goods and services quickly and reliably. Rural suppliers without connections to their customers and suppliers by facsimile and data networks, or 800 numbers, can lose to those who have these links. Instant national or global connectivity has become the norm for successful businesses.

Quality and Productivity

One major result of intensified global competition is a new emphasis on quality. The Japanese have been so successful in taking market share from U.S. manufacturers and in forcing innovations in U.S. motor vehicles because of their legendary commitment to quality. In other products and services, too, quality has become an important means of adding competitive value. Although it may seem counter-intuitive at first, U.S. manufacturing companies have found that improving quality also lowers manufacturing costs. Higher quality also saves maintenance and repair costs.

In the production process itself, ensuring quality is less expensive with a "do it right the first time" process than with post-production inspection and repair. Just-in-time manufacturing inventory systems help improve quality while also reducing inventory costs. One essential component of these new manufacturing, management and supply systems is excellent communication—which has obvious implications for rural businesses that wish to compete in the national or global economy.

To succeed in today's competitive environment, businesses have to improve their productivity at least as rapidly as their competitors. There are two ways to achieve productivity gains. The first is to lower costs, usually by introducing technology or process improvements that reduce labor costs. This is the classic form of productivity gain. Businesses use less labor per unit of production, making it possible to both lower prices and raise the standard of living for the remaining workers, who are likely to need more advanced skills and to get higher pay. If the lower prices create a larger market, as often happens, then even more workers may be hired to meet the demand.

The second method of achieving productivity gains is to add value. Finished lumber commands higher prices than uncut logs. Fine furniture commands higher prices than basic lumber. Packaged fancy foods command higher prices than commodity produce. It is often cheaper to add value to basic products locally because packing and shipping costs can be reduced.

This search for productivity gains is not a one-time event. Staying competitive in today's regional, national and global markets is an ongoing *process* of seeking out opportunities for further gains. Small businesses have found major productivity gains through the increased use of answering machines, 800 telephone numbers to provide free calling for customers, computer network access to suppliers, and other improved telecommunications. Businesses also have benefited from personal computers and myriad applications software packages for word processing, financial spread sheets, and accounting, among other functions. For offices and service businesses, as well as manufacturing and materials processing, a variety of new technologies in computing, communication and electronics is helping to improve quality and enhance productivity—a trend that will continue as equipment costs decline. Business partners are increasingly using data networks to gain remote access to computer applications and to conduct two-way computer communications. Retailers and their wholesalers are gaining new efficiencies in inventory control and stocking practices through jointly accessible computerized retail inventory systems.

What makes these new telecommunications services so significant is not just their potential for improving quality and reducing costs, but their great accessibility. Rural businesses can use these services just as easily as those in urban locations—and in the process, take advantage of new opportunities to rebuild the rural economy.

The Growing Need for Information

For most businesses today, success in the marketplace requires access to timely, reliable information. To be competitive in today's economy, rural America needs a telecommunications infrastructure that allows it to exchange information with the rest of the economy—by voice, facsimile, and data interchange. This is particularly true as more information-intensive service businesses supplant the traditional sources of jobs in rural America—manufacturing, agriculture and natural resource extraction—both in the absolute number and percentage of jobs created.

As the competitive survivors of today's economy learn to work smarter instead of just harder, all goods and services have more "information content"—that is, knowledge that improves quality, reduces costs, aids distribution and marketing, and in other ways enhances competitiveness. More intelligence now goes into the automation of manufacturing processes. More knowledge of customer needs goes into product design. More electronic communications link suppliers with each other and with their customers, for ordering, billing and shipping instructions. More small businesses find it necessary to have a personal computer and facsimile machine, and to add an answering machine to their telephone.

The shift to "just-in-time" inventory systems and on-demand manufacturing systems requires rapid transfer of information. Customers may order items from a mail order catalog through a free 800 telephone number, expecting quick delivery. Rather than keep a large inventory, the catalog vendor may get the supplier to deliver the item after receiving the customer order. The supplier may ship directly to the customer, using the catalog vendor's shipping labels. All of the information for production, billing and shipping can be transferred via computerized "electronic data interchange" or specialized electronic mail services. To compete in this new electronic marketplace, rural businesses must be connected by telephone, facsimile and data networks to their customers and suppliers.

Downsizing and Outsourcing

In the national economy, the increased importance of information has led to phenomenal growth of professional information services jobs. Consultants and expert advisors of all kinds are in demand to help businesses cope with a changing variety of technical and economic concerns. One reason for this robust growth in information services is that large businesses buy specialized services as needed, rather than rely only on their own full-time employees. It is now common, for example, for companies to purchase payroll and accounting services from specialized firms ("outsourcing") rather than try to keep up with the vast array of government reporting requirements and confusing advances in data processing techniques. Instead of trying to do everything within their own organizations, more managers are buying the goods and services they need from smaller or more specialized firms. Outsourcing gives companies more efficiency and flexibility in responding to a changing marketplace.

A 1980s business trend likely to continue through the next decade is the relative decline of large businesses. As more companies introduced labor-saving productivity improvements or lost market share to competition that did, they reorganized and laid off staff, including managers. This trend, often called "downsizing," is a visible symptom of the new competitive environment.

The downsizing and outsourcing trends will continue to provide opportunities for rural communities with entrepreneurial risk-takers who have both telecommunications and personal links to larger businesses in urban locations. Taken by themselves, downsizing and outsourcing do not create rural advantages, but they may reduce rural disadvantages.

2. THE PROCESS OF RURAL DEVELOPMENT

From Smokestacks to Incubators

Rural developers and the people they are trying to help have discovered, sometimes painfully, that there is no simple technique that will achieve economic development. In an earlier time, when rural primarily meant agricultural, the national network of agricultural research and extension services created impressive improvements in agriculture, through the knowledge it generated and distributed. Now, agriculture employs less than 9 percent of the rural population. No matter how well-conceived, agricultural policy cannot revitalize rural America or improve its standard of living.

A successful rural development strategy of the 1960s and early 1970s was industrial recruitment, sometimes called "smokestack chasing." Rural counties with a surplus of unemployed people willing to work hard for low wages attracted manufacturing jobs. Now, in non-metropolitan counties, there are almost twice as many manufacturing jobs as farming jobs. For the past decade, as more companies have exported low-wage manufacturing jobs abroad, rural manufacturing has declined. Weeds have overgrown many rural "industrial parks." With rare exceptions, industrial recruitment is no longer a promising rural development strategy. Development analyst Doug Ross describes this change as the rise and fall of the "first wave" of modern rural development (Ross, 1990).

In the 1980s, many rural regions came up with a creative variation on smokestack chasing: rural telemarketing and "back office" relocation. Citibank moved its credit card processing operations to South Dakota. Other large companies moved data entry and other clerical jobs to rural locations that had appropriately educated labor forces and telephone service good enough to support the necessary data networks. One motivation for such relocation was lower labor costs. The growth of 800 telephone numbers enabled customers to make free long distance calls to merchants and increased mail order business. Many urban customers buy from rural "mail order" businesses. (Typically, the mail is not used at all: telephone orders are accepted, charges are billed electronically to national credit cards, and goods are shipped via a commercial national parcel service.)

Rural telemarketing is not just the answering of incoming calls. It also involves the making of unsolicited telephone sales calls: the modern equivalent of the door-to-door salesmen of the 1930s. The main difference is that rural people can do urban selling without moving to the city. Despite some successes in bringing jobs to rural areas, strategies based upon back office or telemarketing relocation have limitations. They cannot sustain rural development on the scale needed to improve the standard of living of most rural Americans. Furthermore, there may not be enough "relocatable" jobs. Relocation implies that one community's gain is another's loss. What rural regions need is a sustainable long-term path to local development that does not necessarily succeed at someone else's expense.

A development approach favored by Ross and other commentators focuses on "capacity building" in one's community, rather than the recruitment of new industry or back offices. This "second wave" of rural development tries systematically to help rural small businesses. One rationale for this approach is that small- and medium-sized businesses create most new jobs in the United States. According to Ross (1990), the expansion of existing companies and new startup businesses now account for more than 80 percent of job creation in most states. Except for aircraft exports (a phenomenon of Boeing's success as aircraft manufacturer for the world), most growth in U.S. exports in the 1980s came from small- and medium-sized businesses. Many rural development advocates believe that strengthening indigenous small businesses holds the most promise for self-sustaining, stable growth in rural areas.

To this end, some communities have created business "incubators" that provide shared office space and services (secretarial, accounting and computer services) and sometimes, consulting assistance to help new businesses. Some states and communities have loaned funds to startup businesses, only to discover that they were no more skilled than venture capitalists and investment bankers in picking future winners. John Herbers (1990) describes a more promising variation of state assistance as "wholesaling." In this variation, funds are given to recipients through intermediary "wholesalers." One example is North Carolina's Microenterprise Loan Fund. Groups of five small businesses work together to give advice to each other and to decide collectively which two will be eligible first for loans. The others become eligible only after the first borrowers make four installments of repayments on their loans.

Although the "second wave" capacity-building approach to development represents a significant advance over "first wave" smokestack chasing, Ross and other development experts believe that the second wave may be reaching its limits. They argue that state government agencies are inherently unable to bolster a state's business capacity. Government simply does not have the resources to make a big enough difference, nor is it sufficiently responsive and market-oriented to spur effective development. Instead of relying so heavily on government agencies, Ross argues that state government should concentrate on acting as a catalyst. It should leverage development investments from the private sector, stimulate competition, and provide incentives and information to help communities and businesses help themselves. To ensure that development programs respond to actual needs, state governments should measure performance and establish a self-correcting feedback process.

Mobilizing Available Resources

The advocates for a "third wave" development approach offer excellent advice and insightful critiques of state government. Their analysis is incomplete without a discussion of the most important player in any development plan, the community itself. Successful rural development requires strong community leadership and a plan that considers the community's special circumstances. At the start, the community should prepare an inventory of local strengths, needs and opportunities. Can certain "imported" goods or services be provided locally, thereby capturing funds that would otherwise flow out of the community? Are there certain "export" market opportunities, in which local businesses can add value to goods or services that can then be sold outside the community?

The key is to mobilize whatever human and physical resources are available, often in collaboration with nearby communities. Tempting as it may be for a community to focus on the short-term goal of jobs creation, sustained development is more likely to occur if a community deals with three interrelated concerns:

1. **Investment in human capital.** The "human capital" of a community is its most important asset. Funds spent to improve the quality of education and health services, are not merely social service expenditures, they are vital development investments. Good schools and health care not only provide an educated, healthy workforce for local businesses, they can help communities attract or create new businesses whose managers and employees value good education and health care.

Yet investment in human capital, taken alone, is a "necessary but not sufficient" condition for long-term development. If a community does not nurture other factors that build the community's economy, well-educated young people may move to cities to find work.

2. **Investment in basic physical infrastructure**. For decades, rural areas have lagged behind more populated regions in obtaining the basic physical infrastructure needed for development—water and sewage systems, electrification, transportation, and telecommunications. In the 1930s, the Rural Electrification Administration (REA) began bringing electricity to isolated communities and homesteads. In the 1940s and 1950s, the REA turned its attention to basic telephone service in rural areas. In the 1960s and 1970s, federal and state governments made huge investments in the interstate highway systems that helped integrate rural regions with the rest of the country.

    In the 1990s, the economy has changed still further. Information-based jobs are increasingly replacing agriculture and traditional manufacturing in rural America. A good telecommunications infra-structure, generally available in urban areas, has become essential to rural regions also.

3. **Social infrastructure**. Equally critical to development are institutional reforms, that is changes in the way communities and businesses interact to improve the local economy. Leadership, cooperation and risk-taking are the three key characteristics of the social relations in communities that develop successfully. Much rural economic development happens only because certain individuals and groups provide leadership and take risks. To sustain momentum in any development process, there must be social support and encouragement for development ventures. The players in the process should not have exaggerated expectations that easily lead to disappointment. They should be flexible and broad-minded enough to realize that success requires experimentation, and that experimentation inevitably results in some failures. Cooperation within the community and among neighboring communities is often necessary to achieve development successes.

    Encouragement and social support by themselves are not enough, of course. Rural communities need access to support services such as banking, accounting, computer consulting and business consulting. These services need to be accessible in every rural community, although not necessarily local. It is easy to overlook these sorts of "secondary" services, which can play important roles in business development. Yet when strategically used, they can provide useful guidance and leadership to rural entrepreneurs and businesses. One example is AgriTechnics International, a consulting service in Pullman, Washington, that provides technical expertise to rural businesses seeking to find international markets (see chapter 5).

3. THE ROLE OF TELECOMMUNICATIONS

As the earlier sections make clear, telecommunications has come to play a much larger role in business success. Yet rural America faces a double whammy in grappling with this reality: it is no longer insulated from fierce global and national competition, thanks in part to telecommunications, and it is not yet fully prepared to use telecommunications to develop its own economic potential. Better integration of rural America into the larger national economy—a process that telecommunications can expedite—will help rural America develop instead of stagnate.

Telecommunications services are only one part of a multi-faceted strategy for rural development. Laying fiber optic cables across a desert will not make it green. But the absence of modern telecommunications services will block economic development at any oasis. Rural communities that still depend on multiparty telephone lines, or lines that cannot reliably transmit facsimile messages and data, will face a stunted future. The most promising development opportunities in today's economy will not be available to them.

Rural communities will face new threats to their viability if they cannot keep pace with businesses in the larger national and global economy. As more outside firms such as Wal-Mart use telecommunications to bring in new competition, indigenous rural businesses that fail to innovate in similar ways will suffer. If only to provide an equal footing, rural businesses must use modern technology to place orders with distant suppliers, access information from outside data banks, learn about distant market trends, and reach wider markets themselves.

For rural America, modern information technologies are double-edged swords. The distance barriers are falling for both rural businesses and their outside competitors. Rural businesses may be able to use telecommunications to reduce costs and enhance productivity, yet urban businesses with greater experience and technical knowledge can do the same thing—and use that capability to bring their services and products into rural backwaters.

Being compelled to compete on the same playing field with larger and more experienced competitors is, at best, a mixed blessing for rural businesses. Yet there is really little choice. Given the competitive realities, rural businesses must compete as best they can while learning how to seize new opportunities. Good telecommunications ensures a broader array of choices and opportunities.

Unfortunately, most decisions concerning when and how to modernize telecommunications networks are not made in the affected communities. They are made in urban corporate offices or state regulatory commissions. If this were not itself a formidable barrier to rural participation in the Information Age, the great complexity of telecommunications technology and policy also serves as a barrier. If rural development advocates are to make telecommunications serve rural interests, and not let them be used to bypass or victimize rural America, they must first learn more about the changing world of telecommunications. Only then will rural communities be able to shape the technologies, investment choices and policy options that will affect the rural economy for decades to come. The remainder of this chapter provides an overview of the telecommunications industry and telecommunications policies that are most important to rural Americans.

4. THE CHANGING TELECOMMUNICATIONS ENVIRONMENT

The Telecommunications Industry

In the United States, there are approximately 1,400 different local telephone companies and cooperatives, most of which are small and rural. These providers are called carriers because they carry information traffic on their networks just as transportation carriers carry people and physical goods. (Sometimes local carriers are called "local exchange carriers" (LECs) to distinguish them from long distance or "interexchange carriers" (IXCs). The local exchange carrier switches local calls from one party to another while the interexchange carrier provides the long distance connections.)

Some rural areas are served by regional Bell operating companies (RBOCs) or other large telephone carriers that have most of their business in urban locations. The Bell operating companies were spun off from AT&T in the 1984 court-ordered "divestiture" of AT&T's local telephone monopoly businesses. Map 1-1 shows the states served by each of the seven RBOCs.

There are also several major "independent" (non-Bell) telephone companies, the largest of which is GTE, sometimes known as General Telephone. Others include United Telecommunications, Centel, Alltel, Century Telephone, Pacific Telecom, and Telephone and Data Systems (TDS). The number of major independent telephone companies serving rural areas in each state ranges from none to seven. States with five or more major independent companies serving rural areas include Georgia, Illinois, Maine, Ohio, Pennsylvania, and Wisconsin.

37

Map 1-1   Regional Bell Operating Companies

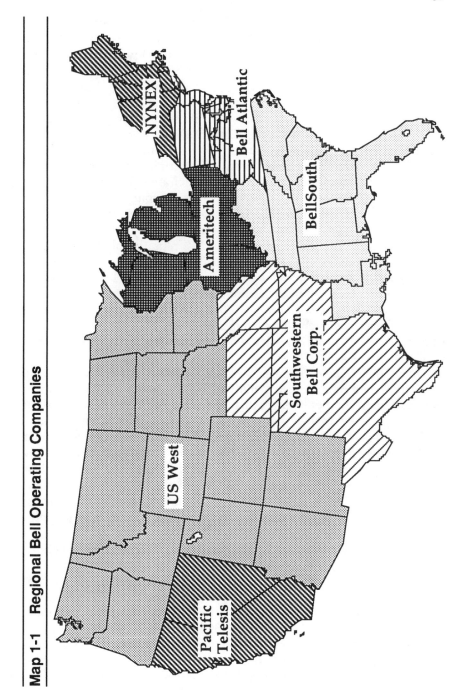

Other rural areas are served by small rural carriers. The number of small rural telephone carriers varies widely from state to state. Some states, such as Delaware and Hawaii, have none, while three—Iowa, Minnesota and Wisconsin—have more than 90. States with more than thirty small rural telephone carriers are located primarily in the west and south. See Map 1-2.

AT&T remains the largest provider of long distance telephone services, although MCI, US Sprint and others offer increasing competition. AT&T continues to provide interstate long distance service to locations not served by any other long distance carrier. Data obtained from one major interexchange competitor show that it offers originating service to more than 1,200 local exchange carriers, most of which are small, with from a few hundred to a few thousand subscriber lines. Despite these competitive advances, many rural areas still do not have equal access to more than one long distance carrier. ("Equal access" means the ability to use an alternate long distance carrier simply by dialing "1" plus the phone number—without having to resort to long numerical codes.)

Besides its leadership in long distance service, AT&T is also a major manufacturer of competitive telecommunications equipment. That market includes such products as central office switching equipment for local exchange carriers, switches on customer premises (better known as private branch exchanges or PBXs), telephone sets, answering machines and facsimile machines.

Many telephone companies, whether they like it or not, are moving away from their monopolistic "utility mentality" and are becoming more innovative and competitive. Yet this change may or may not benefit rural America. In sizing up their new investment opportunities, large telephone companies may choose to invest in foreign cable television ventures rather than in modern digital telephone switches for their rural service areas. They have a duty to their shareholders to provide the best return on their investment. State regulatory commissions greatly influence those investment decisions. For example, some state regulatory agencies have authorized higher total profits for telephone companies, but only if they modernize their rural facilities (see chapter 2).

As we will see in chapters 3 and 4, small, locally owned rural telephone companies and cooperatives tend to be more responsive to rural communities and their development needs. These companies are particularly dependent on federal and state government policies. Rural independent companies and cooperatives often rely upon the federal REA for their capital equipment financing. They also benefit from Federal Communications Commission (FCC) regulations that set nationwide rates for long distance telephone calls based on distance, not on the specific location called or calling. The "averaging" of long distance rates under FCC regulations

Map 1-2 Small Telephone Companies Serving Rural Areas

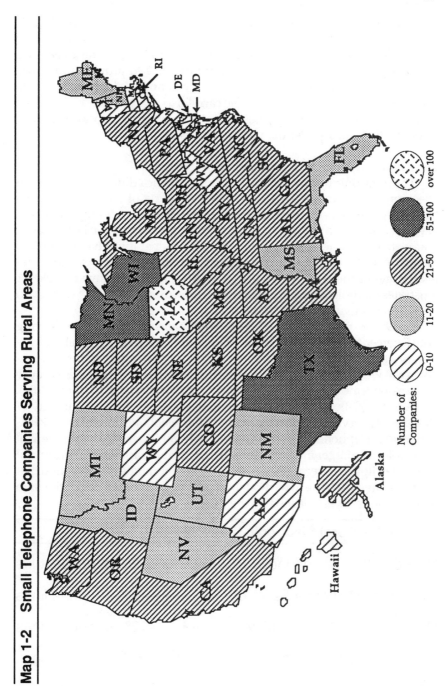

Number of Companies:

0-10   11-20   21-50   51-100   over 100

allows a portion of the local telephone company's costs to be charged to long distance carriers. Most states also require averaging of intrastate long distance rates. This is an important policy for rural communities because rural telephone carriers usually incur higher costs to provide subscriber access to the national telephone network. The national "pooling" of costs and revenues permits rural telephone carriers to recover their higher costs from averaged long distance rates without charging their local customers significantly higher prices than other carriers.

The Rural Telephone Infrastructure

The electronic byways of much of rural America differ from the urban telecommunications infrastructure. In many parts of rural America the basic telephone service is as good as that in most cities, although access to newer services such as high-speed data transmission may not be available. Many small rural telephone companies and cooperatives have used low interest loans from REA to install modern facilities. Other parts of the rural telecommunications infrastructure need to be greatly improved. Table 1-1 illustrates this point by using the common "electronic highway" analogy so often applied to urban telecommunications.

By 1990, 93 percent of all U.S. households had telephone service, leaving only 7 percent unserved. In rural areas, about 12 percent of households are unserved, mostly because of poverty. About 200,000 unserved rural households can well afford telephone service but do not have telephones because they are too remote from existing service locations (Parker and others, 1989).

Another deficiency in rural telephone service is the unavailability of single-party service. In 1989, 5 percent of the telephone lines of rural REA-supported telephone carriers provided only multiparty service. The Bell companies and larger independents also have multiparty lines in their rural service territories. A recent survey of rural telephone line quality found that approximately 12 percent of rural local telephone lines fell below the high quality standards established by the REA.

Table 1-1   Rural Electronic Highways

No Road (No Telephone) --------------------- 12% of households

Dirt Road (Multiparty Service) ----------------- 5% of phone lines

Pothole Road (Poor Quality) ----------------- 12% of phone lines

Winding Road (Analog Phone Switch) ---- 59% of exchanges

Source: FCC, REA, EMCI.

The best single indicator of a rural telephone company's capacity to provide the full variety of modern telephone services is the availability of digital, rather than analog, telephone switches. Older analog switches usually are less reliable and make it more difficult, if not impossible, to offer touchtone calling, Centrex business services, equal access to long distance carriers, custom calling services (such as call waiting, call forwarding, and three way calling), and enhanced emergency services such as E911. By 1989, 59 percent of the telephone exchanges of REA-supported carriers were still using analog switches.

Many non-REA companies serving rural communities were further behind. For example, US West, which serves rural territory in thirteen western states, was still using analog switches in 62 percent of all of its local telephone exchanges (rural and urban) in 1990. For more details on the state of U.S. rural telecommunications infrastructure, see Appendix A and Parker and others (1989).

While the kind of equipment in place provides a rough standard for evaluating rural America's electronic byways, a more significant standard is the kind and quality of services provided. At a minimum, rural communities need single-party touchtone calling and line quality that can reliably transmit voice, data and facsimile messages. This basic level of service is essential to rural small businesses, like businesses anywhere else. It is also important to residential users who may wish to access information through their telephones, either for professional or personal reasons. Multiparty service is another major barrier to rural development because it does not permit answering machines or fax machines, data transmission, or even private telephone conversations.

Many other services are highly desirable. Call waiting, call forwarding and three way calling have become useful small business productivity tools. Other policy changes and enhanced services such as expanded local calling areas, lower long distance toll charges for intrastate calls, and 800 numbers also can affect the competitiveness of rural businesses.

To help states achieve a more meaningful form of "universal service," which has long been a national policy goal, chapter 7 offers a specific set of policy recommendations.

Allocating Costs and Setting Rates

Through its authority to regulate interstate communications, the FCC greatly affects rural telecommunications and, indirectly, the possibilities for rural economic development. Under current FCC regulations, interstate long distance telephone rates cover about 25 percent of the costs of the local telephone equipment and outside plant (such as wire and cable) that is used for all calls, whether local or long distance. The local telephone carriers charge the long distance carriers a "carrier access charge" to recover these costs, which are in turn passed on to consumers as part of the prices of long distance phone calls.

The FCC reduced the amount that local telephone carriers could recover from long distance rates when it ordered that subscribers pay a monthly fixed charge for access to long distance services. The fee, charged to all subscribers, now stands at $3.50 a month. This increase in "local" rates meant that local carriers had to reduce their charges to long distance carriers; in turn, the FCC required long distance carriers to pass this reduction along to consumers through lower long distance rates.

This was one of four factors contributing to substantial reductions in interstate long distance rates in recent years. The other factors: improved technology that reduced the average cost of long distance calls; higher call volumes, which allowed fixed costs of the telephone network to be spread among more calls (and thus reduce the cost per call); and competition among long distance carriers that have undercut AT&T's prices.

Interstate long distance rates are based on the distance between the calling and called telephone exchanges, independent of the specific costs at each of those exchanges. This is called nationwide rate averaging. Long distance carriers pay "carrier access charges" to local telephone carriers so that long distance calls can be connected through local telephone exchanges. Sometimes the carrier access charges are not offset by the long distance revenues paid by subscribers of those local telephone companies. However, on the average, long distance carriers charge prices that recover all of their costs, including carrier access charges, plus a profit.

The long distance carriers often use the local exchange carriers as their billing and collection agents, so that local and long distance charges can be shown on the same phone bill. FCC regulations also allocate some interstate long distance telephone revenue to a "lifeline" fund, to help subsidize the phone bills of low-income subscribers. Additional monies are allocated to a "universal service" fund to subsidize rural telephone carriers with high fixed costs, helping to keep local rates lower and telephone service more affordable.

Many state regulatory commissions require similar rate-averaging and pooling of revenues and costs for the intrastate long distance calls under their regulatory jurisdiction. To help keep local phone rates low, state regulators often allocate a higher proportion of local telephone carrier costs to long distance services than do federal regulators. One consequence of this policy is that intrastate long distance calls often cost more than transcontinental calls.

Since both the federal and state rate averaging processes involve many different telephone carriers, there is a complicated procedure called "separations and settlements." The National Exchange Carriers Association (NECA) and comparable state organizations administer the process, under regulatory supervision of the FCC and state regulatory commissions. In this process, local telephone carriers allocate their costs to federal or state regulatory jurisdictions. Carriers serving more than one state also must allocate costs to the appropriate state. These separations of costs in turn determine how revenues are allocated.

In the FCC's interstate jurisdiction, NECA establishes, subject to FCC approval, the price that participating local carriers charge the long distance carriers. NECA sets prices at a level that recovers the local exchange carriers' total access costs plus a reasonable profit. Each participating local exchange carrier charges that price to the long distance carriers for use of their local facilities to complete long distance calls. Each local carrier then pays to, or receives from, NECA the difference between what it receives from the interexchange carriers and what it is entitled to receive under the cost allocations. Bell operating companies do not receive funds from the NECA pool, but are required by the FCC to contribute their share. Most states follow similar procedures for costs allocated to states.

Changing Regulatory Policies

Regulatory commissions have traditionally used "rate-of-return" regulation to decide what prices the telephone carriers can charge their customers. In this form of regulation, telephone carriers charge prices that, taken as a whole, recover all of their costs and expenses plus a reasonable profit. The authorized profit is a fixed percentage of the carrier's "rate base"—that is, its capital investment in telephone equipment and facilities.

To make this system of regulation work, regulators must approve the carriers' capital investments. Otherwise, regulators would be simply deciding a rate of profit for the carriers, who could then increase their total profits by investing in more equipment, whether needed or not. Regulators try to balance the benefits of upgrading facilities with the costs that must be borne by the customers. Consequently, rural communities trying to encourage investment in modern telephone equipment may need to persuade both telephone carriers and regulators of the value of new investments.

In this system of regulation, prices correspond to costs only in total, and not necessarily for each particular service. For example, regulators may choose to keep long distance prices higher than long distance costs so as to subsidize local service. Similarly, business service prices may be kept higher than the actual costs of business service, to subsidize residential phone service.

Because prices for some services are artificially higher to subsidize other services, many large businesses and state government agencies opt out of the public network and establish their own private lines and networks for less than telephone carrier prices, particularly for long distance services. This practice is called "bypass," because the private network traffic bypasses the public switched telephone network.

One result of bypass is that prices may go up for the remaining users of the public network to compensate for the revenue lost from the bypassers. The large fixed costs of the public switched network must now be borne by fewer users, since rate-of-return regulation allows the local carriers to recover all of their costs plus a profit, no matter how many subscribers they have. When state governments bypass public exchange networks taxpayers may save money but, as telephone ratepayers, they may pay for the "savings" through higher phone bills.

Many large businesses bypass the public switched telephone network because they need services not available through the network, such as data and video services. Small businesses do not have the resources or the volume of traffic necessary to justify private bypass networks. They have no choice but to communicate through the public network. Any rural economic development strategy that hopes to help small businesses must ensure that communication services needed by small businesses are available on the public switched network at affordable rates. As discussed in chapter 7, this goal can be advanced through both state telephone regulations and state government network procurement policies, usually without cost to taxpayers.

In the post-divestiture environment, telephone carriers and regulators find it difficult to maintain the traditional system of pricing (and its social equity goals such as universal service) because competition has become so widespread. Local carriers face many more competitive challenges than bypass of the network by government and large corporations. Manufacturing telecommunications equipment for customer premises is a flourishing new market. (As recently as ten years ago, local carriers provided telephones as part of their service.) Mobile (cellular) telephone service companies have sprung up in recent years to build a huge new market. With the fall of telephone company prohibitions against the resale of telephone services, scores of "value-added" communication and information services (for example, BT Tymnet, CompuServe, SprintData, Prodigy, Dialog and many others) rely on the right to lease facilities from regulated carriers, which they use to sell specialized services to their own customers.

As competition increases, telephone prices in each segment of the market (basic service, long distance calls, customer equipment, specialized services) inevitably are driven closer to their underlying costs. These forces threaten the subsidy mechanisms that traditionally have helped sustain rural telephone services, keeping them available, affordable and reasonably modern. The transition to cost-based pricing may take longer in some states than others, depending on how aggressively telephone carriers and regulators respond to the competitive pressures. Market conditions and technological advances have already wrought such sweeping changes in telecommunications that a return to the prior system is unthinkable. In grappling with the quandaries raised by competition, the FCC has abandoned traditional rate-of-return regulation of large telephone carriers in favor of a new system of "price-cap" regulation that directly limits prices.

Regulators in many states have established or experimented with various "incentive regulation" programs in which they give carriers more pricing flexibility. The purpose of many incentive regulation programs is to give telephone carriers incentives to reduce their costs. This differs from rate-of-return regulation, which was a form of cost-plus contracting that passed higher costs on to customers through higher prices. Under incentive regulation, regulators let carriers keep some of the additional profits they can achieve through cost reductions. Properly structured incentives can stimulate cost reductions sufficient to achieve both lower prices and higher profits.

The Threats and Opportunities for Rural Development

The telecommunications industry is currently navigating through a regulatory transition, a period during which old pricing subsidies are changing and market forces are driving prices closer to the actual costs of each specific telephone service. This transition poses daunting challenges for rural communities. The previous system of internal subsidies within telephone prices, designed in part to support rural telephone service, is threatened. As telephone carriers struggle to cut costs, service quality may deteriorate and rates of investment in modern equipment may slow, especially in rural areas.

In this difficult transition, rural America faces great risks to its economic well-being if it leaves policy decisions entirely in the hands of the telephone carriers and their regulators, who often are more concerned with the more lucrative and competitive urban markets. Rural leaders must mobilize to prevent rural areas from being hurt in the transition. This transition is also a time of genuine opportunity for rural America, if it seizes the moment to seek a modern telecommunications infrastructure that can help revitalize troubled or stagnant rural communities.

In metropolitan areas, vigorous competition, including the proliferation of dedicated private networks, is the engine for major service improvements. In rural areas, it is difficult to bring together enough demand to establish even one network of new telecommunications services. A recent report from the Congressional Office of Technology Assessment (OTA) proposes one solution. In an age of Local Area Networks (LANs), Metropolitan Area Networks (MANs), and Wide Area Networks (WANs), the OTA recommends combining the telecommunications demands of government, business and residential users to develop shared Rural Area Networks (RANs) (U.S. Congress, 1991). The multiple needs of education, health, government, business and consumers would be aggregated and served through a single network. Innovative organizational arrangements and regulatory flexibility would be required for such a scheme to succeed. Innovative rural cooperation is worth pursuing because it could help bring a modern telecommunications infrastructure to rural America, thereby creating new economic development opportunities.

A fruitful new dialog between rural development advocates, the telephone industry, and telephone regulators is already under way. Unlike many political debates in which the gains of one group come at the expense of another, this dialog can lead to cooperative strategies that yield benefits for all parties. Three key issues must be addressed:

1. **The transition from telecommunications monopoly to telecommunications competition.** Competitive market forces in telecommunications are too strong for a return to the "good old days" of regulated monopoly. The question now is: How can we protect those rural users of telecommunications who do not yet (or may never) have the benefits of competition? If regulators abandon the universal service goals of the prior regulated monopoly system in favor of a "let the market decide" policy, rural users will be the first to suffer—through higher prices, antiquated technology and inadequate service. If rural communities are to benefit from the new infrastructure, services and economic opportunities that competition is already bringing to urban America, regulators must decide which of the subsidies inherent in the prior monopoly structure should be retained or modified. Regulators also will need to devise transitional strategies to smooth the inevitable disruptions that accompany change.

2. **Spurring investment in rural telecommunications infrastructure to support economic development.** Recent and continuing advances in telephone technology are helping slash the underlying costs of telephone service. Just as cost-saving technological advances in computing made a wealth of new information processing services economically feasible, so technological advances in telecommunications networks will open the door to new information transmission and access services. Recent innovations such as facsimile and data transmission will soon be

supplemented by new voice, data, and image transmission and information access services. Just as the new services made possible by
computer technology have contributed to a global competitive advantage for the U.S. economy, so the new telecommunications services can
contribute to future economic advancement of both rural and urban
regions of the country.

The regulatory question is: How can the initial investments in this
newer, lower-cost communications technology—which can do much to
fuel economic development—be paid for? The initial capital is available
from private investors and the profits generated by prior telephone
company investments. This issue becomes one of devising regulatory
incentives that can leverage private investment to achieve public economic development goals.

One obvious option for regulators is simply to lower prices for
existing telephone services. This reduction would divert telephone
company profits to consumers and thereby reduce the funds available
to invest in new telecommunications facilities, especially in rural areas.
Alternately, regulators could provide incentives for investment in
newer facilities that could help stimulate both rural and urban economic development. This is a unique and unusual choice. Unlike the
development of transportation infrastructure, which requires a substantial investment of taxpayer dollars, major upgrades to the telecommunications infrastructure can be made *without* taxpayer dollars or
raising telephone rates! The resulting productivity gains for industry
and (given appropriate regulatory incentives) economic development
gains for rural communities make this a rare "win-win" opportunity
that development advocates should not miss.

3. **Exploiting the existing and future telecommunications network to
   achieve development goals.** This may be the most critical priority of all.
   The network infrastructure is necessary for development; it does not
   guarantee it. What generates development is the various applications
   that use the network to improve delivery of information services and
   increase the operating efficiencies of business and government. Technology is not enough. Distance learning networks can bring improved
   education to rural schools. Telemedicine applications can improve
   rural health care delivery. Enhanced telephone service options can
   improve productivity for small rural businesses. None of these pro-
   spective benefits can be achieved unless telecommunications applications serve specific user needs. Training may be needed to teach rural
   businesses (and small businesses generally) how best to use new
   information technologies and services. To help ensure that the infra-

structure will be appropriate to local development needs, a community must plan both the new infrastructure *and* its uses and applications. Consequently, a successful rural development strategy that relies on telecommunications will require cooperation among parties that have not traditionally joined to work for common goals. Rural communities, development agencies, state government telecommunications network managers, regulatory agencies, and the telecommunications industry have a unique opportunity to cooperate to mutual benefit.

CHAPTER 2

State Telecommunications Players and Policies

1. TWO CULTURES

The prior Aspen Institute book on rural telecommunications, *Rural America in the Information Age*, pointed out:

> There is no inherent technical reason for the historic "rural penalty" of geographical remoteness. Yet the rural penalty persists because policies affecting telecommunications and economic development have not kept pace with the times and taken sufficient account of changing rural economic needs (Parker and others, 1989).

One of the reasons why policies have not kept pace with the times is that the fields of telecommunications and economic development are like two distinct cultures that have little in common. The culture of the telephone industry and its regulators is different from the culture of rural development advocates and economic development agencies. They not only use different terminology, but are administered through different agencies, which often have little contact with each other. Historically, the two cultures have pursued their separate concerns in their two distinct worlds, never pausing to think that they have something in common.

Now, as the evidence in this book demonstrates, the cultures of telecommunications and development have a great deal in common. Yet this recognition alone is not enough to usher in a new era of constructive collaboration. We need deliberate strategies to foster communication, cooperation and coordination between the two cultures. Legislators and state agencies must coordinate telecommunications and development planning and policy; regulators must consider the role of telecommunications in social and economic development; telephone carriers, local governments, school systems, businesses and consumers must all recognize the benefits of modern telecommunications.

For these changes to occur, the states must take the lead. State governments regulate all intrastate telephone services, which account for approximately 75 percent of telephone costs. (The FCC regulates the other 25 percent.) State governments administer most rural development programs, including those using federal funds. State leadership is needed not only to build new bridges between the two cultures of telecommunications and development, but to reach out to rural communities. Rural development succeeds best when it is tailored to the unique problems and opportunities of individual rural communities. Whatever policy reforms are adopted at the state level must be closely coordinated with local communities and their leaders, businesses, schools and citizens.

This chapter provides an overview of the chief players in telecommunications at the state level, their levels of expertise, and their perceptions of telecommunications and development. We then examine telecommunications policies and initiatives state agencies have taken that could foster rural development. We hope that demystifying the telecommunications policy apparatus will help to bridge the gap between the cultures, and enable rural development specialists to influence state telecommunications policy.

To ensure that our description of the state policy making process for telecommunications was accurate, we conducted a survey to find out the roles played by state legislatures, regulatory commissions, telephone carriers, equipment suppliers, and others. In 1990, we sent a questionnaire to the 50 state regulatory commissions to gather information on state telecommunications players and policies. For many states, it was sent to a contact known to be concerned with development issues. For other states, we sent the questionnaire to the chairman of the commission with a letter explaining the purpose of the research and the type of information requested. Typically, a senior staff member of the commission completed the questionnaire or provided the information in a telephone interview. All 50 state regulatory commissions responded. Public utilities commission (PUC) officials supplied information on legislative committees responsible for telecommunications in their states; these committees were also contacted directly. Many additional sources identified by the respondents were contacted for follow-up telephone interviews.

We also sought information from the telecommunications industry through national and state telephone associations. Organizations representing REA borrowers and other rural telephone companies were particularly responsive and provided many examples of rural projects. We also interviewed representatives of rural telephone companies and equipment suppliers to augment information from recent studies and publications.

2. THE PLAYERS: STATE GOVERNMENT INVOLVEMENT IN TELECOMMUNICATIONS

Three different parts of state government all influence state telecommunications policy—the legislature, the executive branch headed by the governor, and the state regulatory agency. Each can assume leadership in different ways:

Legislatures enact state policies or delegate policy authority to executive or regulatory agencies. State legislatures usually have committees with responsibility for telecommunications, although these committees typically have additional responsibilities for utilities, transportation, commerce or consumer affairs.

At the executive level, a few states have an office of telecommunications in the governor's office. In most states, however, executive branch concern for telecommunications focuses almost exclusively on state government's internal telecommunications requirements, not public policy needs. This planning function is usually assigned to a state department of administration or government services. While the policy leadership of such agencies is generally minimal, their economic leverage for improving state telecommunications can be considerable because they are often one of the state's largest purchasers of telecommunications equipment and services.

Regulatory agencies are the major telecommunications policy actors at the state level. The primary regulator of telecommunications is usually a PUC, but is sometimes a public services commission or a commerce commission. It is generally responsible for regulating intrastate telecommunications. In all but two states, the commission that regulates telecommunications also regulates other utilities such as electricity, gas, water and, sometimes, transportation. The commission influences the quality and availability of rural telecommunications through regulations concerning prices, capital depreciation, and allowable investments of the carriers.

Telephone carriers make the actual investments in rural telecommunications infrastructure and provide telecommunications services to rural areas. When it comes to telecommunications infrastructure, state governments cannot directly finance the improvements, as they do for roads, bridges and waterways. They must work indirectly, using the levers of state policy, to encourage privately-owned carriers to make investments and provide services.

Telephone carriers have a direct self-interest in successful rural economic development because it will increase their revenues. It is not always necessary to change legislation or regulation to get them to help with rural development activities in their service areas. Sometimes all that carriers need to stimulate action is a direct request for help from local businesses, schools or residents.

Comparison with the Federal Level

Each state function has its analog at the federal level. Both the U.S. House of Representatives and Senate have telecommunications subcommittees. Congressional committees concerned with agriculture,* education, and science and technology, also address telecommunications issues. Within the executive branch, the National Telecommunications and Information Administration (NTIA) in the Department of Commerce sets national telecommunications policy for the executive branch, advising on pending legislation, regulation and government procurement policy. The FCC is responsible for regulation of interstate telecommunications.

In addition, various other federal agencies may from time to time examine telecommunications policy issues. For example, in 1991, NTIA, OTA, and the General Accounting Office (GAO) were each studying telecommunications issues as they relate to rural development. See, for example, OTA's study on *Rural America at the Crossroads: Networking for the Future* (U.S. Congress, 1991).

3. THE ROLE OF THE STATE LEGISLATURE

Executive and regulatory agencies receive their operating budgets from appropriations passed by the legislature. Executive and regulatory agencies make policy and administrative decisions within the framework of the legislation delegating authority to them. In most states, major policy changes—including a redirection of telecommunications policy to serve economic development goals—require new legislative authority. State development agencies wishing to increase their expertise and influence in telecommunications issues may need legislative authorization of budgets for such activities. Regulatory agencies may need legislative authority to use their regulatory powers to stimulate telecommunications infrastructure appropriate for economic development.

Much of the work of a legislature gets done in committees. None of the states currently has a legislative committee that deals exclusively with telecommunications. Typically, committees with responsibility for telecommunications also have responsibility for other utilities, such as electricity, water, and natural gas, or for transportation or commerce, in general.

* The Rural Electrification Administration, which supports rural telecommunications through low cost loans to rural telephone companies and cooperatives, is in the Department of Agriculture. For a list of agencies and organizations with an interest in rural telecommunications, see Appendix B.

Committees that consider both telecommunications and commerce or economic development often consider the issues separately. Some states do, however, try to bridge the gap between telecommunications infrastructure and development. Respondents from sixteen states reported that other legislative committees responsible for economic development, regional development, or rural development participate in state telecommunications planning or policy.

The Oregon legislature's approach is an example of such cooperation. In 1991 it passed a law requiring the state economic development department (in the executive branch) to prepare recommendations for a statewide strategic telecommunications infrastructure plan. The legislation originated in the committee responsible for telecommunications policy, but the committee responsible for economic development arranged for funding for the study. The legislation directed the economic development committee to prepare legislative proposals to carry out the plan.

Typically, state legislatures have little telecommunications expertise. Some 32 legislatures have no professional staff working on telecommunications. Most of the rest have only one or two telecommunications staff; no legislature reported more than six. With limited staff, legislatures must rely on other sources of expertise, usually the regulatory commission. The second most important source of expertise is not a state agency, however, but the telecommunications industry itself. (Telephone carriers, especially the Bell operating companies, usually influence state legislation through well-funded lobbying efforts.) Other sources of expertise for legislatures include other state government staff (such as state telecommunications administrators and public counsel), consultants, consumer representatives and the FCC (see Figure 2-1).

Figure 2-1   Sources of Expertise for Legislatures

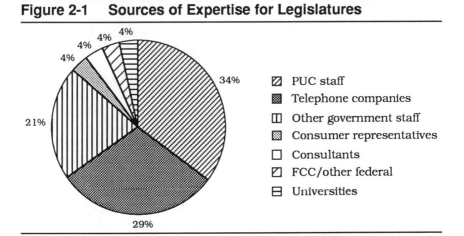

34% ☒ PUC staff
     ▨ Telephone companies
     ⊞ Other government staff
     ▨ Consumer representatives
     ☐ Consultants
     ▨ FCC/other federal
     ⊟ Universities

Despite the distractions of other political pressures and the scarcity of technical expertise, legislators do make the key policy decisions affecting telecommunications for rural development. (Chapter 5 describes the key role of a legislative committee in changing rural telecommunications policies in Washington State.) Rural development advocates who want changes in telecommunications policies need to be sure that legislative committees hear from them as well as from the telephone carriers.

4. THE ROLE OF THE EXECUTIVE BRANCH

The Governor's Office

Twenty-one states reported that the governor's office plays a role in telecommunications policy. The precise nature of these roles varies considerably, however, and often is indirect or temporary. The governor's most direct influence on telecommunications policy in many states is through appointments of PUC commissioners.

As the rest of this section explains, governors also can play a critical leadership role in several other areas of the executive branch: through state telecommunications agencies, the state government procurement process, and special task forces and studies designed to forge a consensus on new telecommunications policy. Governors also may get involved by participating in telecommunications task forces of the National Governors' Association.

State Telecommunications Agencies

In most state governments, a separate office manages the state's internal telecommunications facilities: assessing state government needs, purchasing new equipment, operating state-owned telecommunications networks, and providing technical guidance to other state offices. The telecommunications office is usually not a separate department, but a division of the state's administration or government services department. As such, it is an administrative office that plays no role in public policy making concerning telecommunications.

Better management of a state government's varied telecommunications systems could generate spin-off benefits for rural users and for businesses and citizens statewide. In some states, individual agencies such as the highway or police department manage their own telecommunications networks, resulting in a proliferation of specialized, sometimes duplicative, networks. Similarly, telecommunications networks for state lotteries and other government functions often reach rural communities but are restricted to internal government use. If consolidated and made available to local governments, school districts and health care facilities, these systems could serve as valuable development tools at minimal costs.

State Government Networks

An often-overlooked instrument for improving rural telecommunications is the state government's own telecommunications network. State governments can provide leadership in two key ways: creative use of the state network to reach dispersed rural users, and innovative use of the procurement process to leverage new telecommunications infrastructure and services into existence.

Many states have extensive dedicated networks linking offices throughout the state, including rural areas. These networks may be owned and operated by the state or leased from one or more carriers. Utah, for example, provides a data network (known as Digicom) to all state offices. Some states have recognized that their networks could be used for education and other developmental applications. Minnesota's STARS (Statewide Telecommunications Access and Routing System) is a statewide voice, data and video transmission facility designed to serve government agencies and educational institutions. STARS resulted from a joint planning effort of the Department of Administration and the Higher Education Advisory Council.

States are planning or building a variety of telecommunications networks. The state of Iowa has plans to build its own fiber optic network for education and economic development. The backbone would be 3,500 miles of optical fiber. Connecticut has invested in a state-of-the-art telecommunications network (StateNet) that will include 336 miles of fiber optic cable and seven digital switches to support voice, image, and high-speed data applications. The University of Connecticut, state agencies, and eventually municipal governments will all have access to the network.

The state of Maine has taken a different innovative approach to encourage extension of rural telecommunications facilities. The state provided access to rights-of-way along its highways for a carrier to install optical fiber, in exchange for extension of fiber to smaller cities and towns (Silkman, 1989).

South Carolina has a statewide video network, South Carolina Educational Television (SCETV), for both distance education and teleconferencing among state employees. SCETV officials report that teleconferencing has saved state taxpayers millions of dollars in state government travel costs, and that its training programs have helped to improve productivity throughout the state.

State financing of rural telecommunications for the general public is rare. One exception is the State of Alaska, which in 1976 appropriated $5 million for the purchase of 125 satellite earth stations to provide basic telephone service to Alaska villages. Alascom, the intrastate carrier, installed and operated the earth stations. The Alaska state government has also been an innovative user of the satellite network. Its Legislative Teleconferencing Network (LTN) enables citizens to testify in hearings in Juneau from their home communities. Government officials also can conduct statewide meetings via audio conferencing (Hudson, 1990).

The purpose of most of these state initiatives is to improve the quality of government services, from education to data services to videoconferencing. To achieve rural development objectives, the networks should be extended statewide, and not simply link major cities and government offices or research centers. When they do reach rural areas, state governments can increase the benefits by making them available for a wide range of state and local government services—such as high schools and junior colleges, hospitals, clinics, and rural development agencies.

State networks may be helpful for some rural development functions, including distance learning networks that improve the quality of rural education. They may be particularly helpful in bringing to rural communities video and data networking capabilities that are not now provided by the telephone carriers. Paradoxically, state telecommunications networks could serve to stifle rural development in the following manner. Government applications, including education, may be the first economically viable use of video or data networking in rural communities. If a dedicated network restricted to government use delivers these services, it may "skim off the cream" of the demand, making it even more difficult for other potential users of the system (businesses, nonprofit organizations, private citizens) to aggregate their demand and secure advanced telecommunications services through the local telephone carrier. Instead of acting as a cornerstone around which other users can build a telecommunications infrastructure (through the local telephone carrier), state government can unwittingly preempt new development by making it too difficult and expensive for local carriers to aggregate rural demand. Ironically, a government system for rural education could make it impossible for rural businesses to obtain videoconferencing, electronic mail and electronic data interchange (EDI), all of which could help them reduce their rural competitive disadvantage.

Some states are beginning to recognize the importance of using the state government's network procurement process as a policy lever to help rural communities obtain modernized network facilities. For example, a recent telecommunications task force appointed by the Governor of Oregon recommended that, "whenever possible, the procurement of Oregon state government network features and capacity should help ensure the availability on the public switched network of the features and capacities needed for the development of a modernized telecommunications system throughout the state" (Oregon Task Force on Telecommunications, 1991).

Task Forces and Studies as Catalysts for Change

As the role of telecommunications in economic development has become a more visible issue, several states have established task forces to help reach a statewide consensus to revamp state telecommunications policy. In different states, this process has been instigated by either the governor, a telecommunications carrier, the regulatory commission, or a citizens' organization.

The task forces usually bring together a range of participants who share an interest in either telecommunications or development—telecommunications policy makers, government users, educators, business and other users, and the telecommunications industry. It is important that telephone carriers participate in this process so they can provide technical expertise and learn about the development implications of telecommunications and the needs of these various constituencies. However, a study that is perceived to be too closely linked to telephone company interests will have limited credibility among users and policy makers.

The purpose of any task force should not simply be the production of a report, but the forging of a genuine consensus for a new telecommunications agenda. A task force that lacks broad-based citizen involvement or fails to publicize and disseminate its findings may have little effect on communities that may be seeking new models for development, or the telephone companies that serve them. However, a task force that is committed to spreading the word and working to implement its recommendations may catalyze innovative policies and projects to further the state's social and economic development goals.

It is worth examining how several states have used task forces to assess state needs and to formulate coherent plans for moving forward. Examples of the approaches used by ten states follow.

In 1988, Governor James Blanchard of *Michigan* established a Governor's Telecommunications Task Force that included representatives of the Public Service Commission and state departments of commerce, education, labor and management and budget. The panel also had advisors from private industry, telecommunications and education. The task force report, *Connections,* contained both policy and strategy recommendations to implement a telecommunications vision for Michigan that "focuses on technology as a means to ensure Michigan's children, workers, entrepreneurs and government officials have access to the high-technology tools of tomorrow—tools which will enhance the quality of life in the Great Lake State and assure the personal and economic success of its people"

(Governor's Telecommunications Task Force, 1990). The task force also commissioned a "Use Assessment of Michigan's Telecommunications Systems," prepared by Electronic Data Systems (Electronic Data Systems, 1990). The task force's chief recommendation was to develop an integrated statewide high capacity switched network.

A task force appointed by Governor Roberts of *Oregon* included representatives from schools and higher education, local government, large and small users, a telecommunications consultant, and the Oregon PUC. Its mandate was to review the existing telecommunications activities within state government and to determine what role state government should play in establishing an advanced telecommunications infrastructure that serves all Oregonians. The task force report, *Telecommunications: Oregon's Next Trail*, urged state leaders to develop integrated telecommunications and information technology policies. The report noted that telecommunications must be an integral part of any statewide development strategy, in particular: "Rural economic development and educational opportunities will ultimately depend upon the quality of telecommunications systems" (Oregon Task Force on Telecommunications, 1991).

The *New Jersey* Board of Public Utilities (NJBPU) initiated a study of telecommunications infrastructure funded by the state's three local exchange carriers, New Jersey Bell, United Telephone of New Jersey, and Warwick Valley Telephone Company. The study, conducted by the accounting and consulting firm of Deloitte and Touche, examined the economic impact of rewiring the state with optical fiber. The report concluded that an advanced telecommunications infrastructure is essential for New Jersey to create the number of new jobs desired for the state (Deloitte and Touche, 1991). It compared alternate plans for accelerating the investment in telecommunications infrastructure beyond the telephone company "business as usual" case. They found that an "aggressive" program could accelerate the replacement of analog telephone switches with digital switching by three years, and accelerate the deployment of fiber optics in various parts of the network by from two to twenty years. Such a program would require annual revenue increases in the range of 1 to 6 percent— amounts they said would allow New Jersey to maintain its relatively low prices for basic telephone service.

In *Washington* State, a Telecommunications Task Force with members drawn from GTE Northwest, US West, and Global Telematics examined future telecommunications services and potential benefits for the state of Washington, with input from consumers, academics, and government. (The formation and activities of this task force are reviewed in chapter 5.)

In *California*, the Intelligent Network Task Force, sponsored by Pacific Bell, brought together individuals representing California's diverse ethnic and public service constituencies. The group prepared a report explaining how new telecommunications technologies and services could benefit Californians, and recommending widespread access to new services (Pacific Bell, 1987).

The Information Age Task Force in *Alabama* was set up by the Public Service Commission and the Alabama-Mississippi Telephone Association so that a wide range of end users could explore current and future benefits of the intelligent network, issues raised by its deployment, and impacts on all Alabamians, urban and rural. The Task Force was composed of 17 individuals representing small business, the elderly, the disabled, agriculture, education, health care, social services, small municipalities and state government.

In *Tennessee*, the Information Systems Council is composed of several heads of state government agencies (finance and administration, general services, treasury), a commissioner of the Public Services Commission, six legislators and two private sector representatives. This council is examining options for investing in telecommunications and information technologies to help to diversify the state's economy. *North Carolina* also established a task force with forty representatives from the governor's office, education, business, and the telecommunications industry to determine how the state could use telecommunications to attract new businesses, enhance productivity, and upgrade education levels.

In *Minnesota*, the impetus came from the Citizen's League, which carried out a study called "New State Goals for Telecommunications" that looked into ways Minnesota can use new technologies to create opportunities for business and the public. The goals of the Citizen's League are to use Information Age technologies to provide improved public education and health, better government services, economic growth, political awareness, efficiency and productivity and reduce the need for transportation (Citizens League, 1989).

Hawaii's Department of Transportation established a task force consisting of private and public sector executives and university faculty to plan a Hawaii Telework Center demonstration project. Hawaiian Telephone and equipment donors supported the one-year demonstration project. The evaluation found that teleworking (also known as "telecommuting") was more than a travel and traffic reduction measure; "jobs near homes" (that is, satellite neighborhood offices) could improve the quality of life for employees and their families (Hirata and Uchida, 1990).

While none of these task forces or studies focused exclusively on rural requirements, collectively they made a number of recommendations that could help states better integrate telecommunications planning with development goals:

- Coordinate state government policy making in telecommunications: Michigan proposed establishing a Cabinet Council on Information Technology to coordinate state government efforts in telecommunications and information technologies;

- Obtain input from users in the policy process: Michigan proposed setting up a State Telecommunications Users Group to provide user input to telecommunications management, simplify user needs analysis, assist in standards selection and analysis, and promote shared services and applications;

- Measure progress: Oregon recommended adopting a set of performance measures for the state government's networks and the public telecommunications infrastructure;

- Coordinate planning for voice and data: Oregon proposed eliminating distinctions between telephone (voice) and information technology (data communications) in planning and management of state government networks;

- Try out new services and applications that support state development goals: Hawaii carried out a pilot project on telework to test the viability of reducing travel time and congestion by enabling people to work nearer home using telecommunications; and

- Upgrade telecommunications infrastructure: Reports from several states, including California, Michigan, and New Jersey recommended accelerated deployment of a reasonably priced high capacity network that would benefit business, education, and health care delivery.

These studies and task forces are so recent that it is still too early to assess their impact. Yet the process seems valuable, particularly when it involves broad-based participation from state government, carriers, and users, both business and residential. To be effective in bringing about change, they should formulate clear goals and plans for reaching the goals. Also, they should have high level support in state government.

Task forces can be particularly useful in filling in the "knowledge gaps" with respect to state telecommunications: What sorts of equipment and services are currently available, and to which localities? Could the state's educational system benefit from telecommunications? What are the current modernization trends? Are they ambitious enough? Armed with comprehensive and reliable data, task forces can propose ambitious yet realistic strategies that stimulate new telecommunications investment, which in turn can support state social and economic development goals.

As noted above, rural development was not a major focus of concern for most of these state task force reports and studies. This makes it all the more important that rural development advocates step forward in each state to ensure that their voices are heard and their views represented in future studies and plans.

5. THE ROLE OF THE STATE REGULATORY COMMISSIONS

State regulatory commissions have more influence on rural telecommunications than any other state agency. Regulatory commissions are independent agencies. Unlike executive branch agencies, they do not report to the governor, although in many states the governor does appoint the commissioners. Their function is quasi-judicial; they must adjudicate among the often competing interests of telephone carriers and their customers. The mandate of the commissions is to ensure that the utilities serve the public interest. They also regulate telecommunications because it has been considered a natural monopoly, that is, it made economic sense to have only one carrier for each area. Without competition, the PUCs use regulation to substitute for the marketplace forces that consumers would otherwise rely upon to keep rates reasonable and service quality high. As new technologies force us to redefine the limits of the natural monopoly, the regulatory role of the PUC may diminish.

How Regulatory Commissions Perceive their Roles

In our survey of regulatory commissions, we asked whether they considered their role to be exclusively regulatory, primarily regulatory, or both regulatory and policy making. The majority, 63 percent, saw their role as both regulatory and policy making. The other 37 percent saw their role as primarily regulatory, but also involved in some policy making. None saw themselves as exclusively regulatory (although one telephone association characterized its state PUC that way). See Map 2-1.

We also asked PUC respondents to describe their commission's approach to issues as strictly reactive (responding to issues raised by carriers or other agencies), somewhat proactive (sometimes initiating hearings or investigations), or strongly proactive (for example, initiating hearings or proposing regulations to deal with future issues or problems that have not been raised by the carriers). Eighty percent of commissions considered themselves strongly proactive, while 18 percent considered themselves somewhat proactive. Only one commission considered itself strictly reac-

62

Map 2-1   Role of Public Utilities Commissions

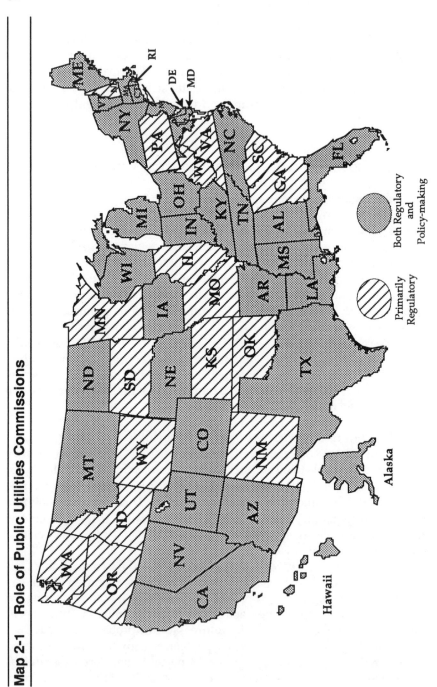

tive. The telephone associations generally agreed with the characterizations the commissions used to describe themselves. Only two associations disagreed (one characterized its commission as "somewhat" rather than "strongly" proactive, and the second labeled its commission "reactive" rather than "somewhat proactive").

While not unexpected, the results are interesting in that they show that the commissions see themselves as state policy makers in telecommunications. Regulatory commissions must be key participants in any effort to refocus state telecommunications policies to consider development goals. However, as we will see below, they generally do not have clear guidelines about how to develop policies to support economic development.

Importance of Decisions Made in Other States

In our survey, we asked commissions to assess the influence of decisions and policies made by regulatory commissions in other states, both across the country and in their region. Eighty percent of the states said that the activities of other commissions across the country were "somewhat important." A few said that decisions made elsewhere were "very important"; they tended to be looking for bellwether policies to study or emulate. States that found commission decisions across the country very important were California, Colorado, Maine, Michigan, Montana, Oregon, and Tennessee. A few commissions (Alabama, Florida, Indiana, Nevada and New Mexico) said that decisions made across the country were not important to them, primarily because they felt conditions in their state were either unique or at least atypical.

More commissions thought that decisions and policies made by other commissions in their region were "very important." About 18 percent of the states thought regional decisions were "very important," while 72 percent thought they were "somewhat important." Only 6 percent thought they were "not important." Many commented that they try to share information with other states served by the same RBOC. For example, many of the commissions in states served by US West exchange information on regulatory policies. (The territories served by the RBOCs are shown in Map 1-1.)

Criteria Used in Making Regulatory Decisions

Most commissions recently have made decisions that affect rural telecommunications. Forty-one commissions said they had made decisions in the past three years affecting access to telecommunications services in rural areas, cost of rural services or quality of rural services. These decisions included requirements for upgrading rural facilities, eliminating multiparty service, reducing costs of rural services through general rate reductions, extended area service rates, lifeline rates or installation assistance programs.

Even though they often set policies affecting rural services, the commissions generally do not consider rural development goals in their regulatory decisions. Most commissions do not have explicit legislative authority to consider economic development, although their authorizing legislation usually provides a broad "public interest" standard that could be used to justify development goals. Nearly all commissions said they consider the impact of regulatory policies on the telecommunications industry and on consumers. In assessing how their decisions affect the telecommunications industry, commissions said that they examine the financial soundness of the carrier, the likely impact on company earnings, and the carriers' opportunity to earn a reasonable rate of return. Some respondents added that their commissions also try to:

• ensure the financial viability of small telephone companies;

• foster competition;

• discourage uneconomic bypass;

• promote the sharing of costs between local exchange carriers; and

• ensure the practicability of proposed changes.

Some commissions appeared to limit their socio-economic analysis to consumer issues, with telephone rates as their primary consideration, particularly for residential consumers. The chief criteria used to judge the impact of regulatory decisions on consumers are rates and quality of service. Although a majority of commissions said that they also consider effects on the state's social or economic development, most of these respondents did not cite specific goals or techniques for measuring the effects; some said they considered the effect on development a secondary issue, albeit of increasing importance.

In considering the socio-economic effects of regulatory decisions, respondents said they tried to:

• promote the efficient use of telecommunications facilities;

• enhance the state telecommunications network;

• build infrastructure support for the state economy;

- assess impact on attracting and retaining industry; and

- provide rural access to the same services available in urban areas.

Regulatory Commission Expertise

Where do regulatory commissions get their information about telecommunications and development issues? The standard sources of expertise include state government economic development staff, commission staff, expert witnesses and special studies. Yet the strength of this expertise differs greatly from state to state, largely due to the varying number of telecommunications specialists.

Not surprisingly, the states with the highest populations have the most staff. Six states have more than 300 staff (California, Illinois, New York, New Jersey, Ohio, and Pennsylvania), while ten states report having 20 or fewer total professional employees. Invariably, the number of staff that deal with telecommunications is a fraction of the total professional staff. Only New York and California have more than 50 professional staff working exclusively on telecommunications. Thirty-two states have ten or fewer staff working exclusively on telecommunications; five states have no staff assigned exclusively to telecommunications (see Map 2-2).

Some commissions do not dedicate professional staff exclusively to telecommunications; their engineers and economists, for example, cover all utilities they regulate. Some states such as California rotate professional staff through various divisions so that they become familiar with all of the utilities under the commission's jurisdiction.

Implications for State Rural Telecommunications Policy

There are several implications of these findings. First, commission staff are likely to be overwhelmed by the volume of information that telephone companies file during a typical rate case. As a result, commissions generally do not have the time to analyze and verify much of the data provided by telephone companies, let alone to collect additional independent data.

States with lower population and large rural areas in the west and midwest may be at a particular disadvantage: not only do they have very small staffs, but they also have many telephone companies to regulate. On the other hand, rural areas in the more populated states may simply be overlooked if commissions rely on statewide data from larger carriers.

To help compensate for these deficiencies, rural development advocates should ask their commission to establish specific measurable goals for rural service. They should also request regular monitoring of progress toward those goals. Without such rural advocacy, busy commission staff members are likely to focus their attention elsewhere.

Map 2-2 PUC Staff Working Exclusively on Telecommunications

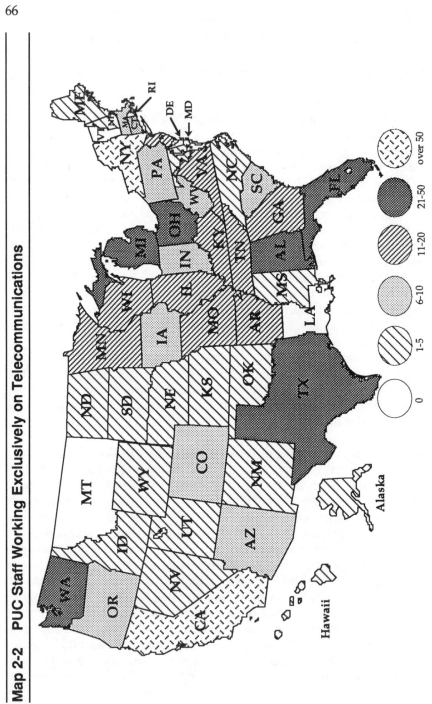

While many commissions philosophically agree that they should assess social and economic criteria as part of their regulatory decision making, few have any specific guidelines or indicators to follow beyond keeping rates reasonable, particularly for residential subscribers. Overworked commissioners and staff may scoff at the idea that commissions should broaden their horizons to include economic development issues. Yet this goal is neither far-fetched nor impractical if commissions build partnerships with other state agencies to share the burden of expanding their horizons to include economic development. Commissions could also require the telephone companies themselves to collect data or conduct studies that would monitor progress toward established targets and identify the developmental impacts of their services. (Suggestions for specific goals and measures are presented in chapter 7.)

6. REGULATORY POLICIES

As noted in chapter 1, changes in telecommunications technology and competitive pressures are forcing PUCs to explore new ways to regulate telephone carriers. To take account of these new realities, many commissions have adopted alternative regulatory frameworks to the traditional rate-of-return approach. For example, approximately two-thirds of the regulatory commissions now have the authority to establish pricing flexibility for individual services, many without the need for traditional regulatory review (Deloitte and Touche, 1991). States are exploring a wide range of innovative regulatory models which are outlined below.

At this point, the alternative regulatory models are too new and untested to provide a basis for solid conclusions. In any case, no single approach may be suitable for every state. An examination of the major alternatives may help the states identify the model best suited to their specific situation.

Five Regulatory Models

Traditional rate-of-return regulation. As described in chapter 1, the traditional regulatory model is a "cost-plus" pricing model in which regulators approve prices that recover all of a carrier's costs, plus a profit based on a percentage of the carrier's total capital investment. Carriers use the state-approved rules for cost and return on investment to calculate a total "revenue requirement." This, then, becomes the basis for the second "rate design" phase in which regulators review the carrier's proposed prices for different services. The prices are set so that the projected total revenue from these services equals the revenue requirement.

Perhaps the most notable feature of this model of regulation is that prices for each service need not correspond to the costs for those services; what matters most is that the total revenue requirement is met. Under this system, business rates and long distance rates traditionally have been kept high as a way to keep the rates for local residential phone service low. As competition emerges for the services that are priced well above their costs, pressures mount on regulators to revise the entire rate structure and rate-setting process.

Under rate-of-return regulation, major changes in telephone rates require a "rate case," usually initiated by the telephone carrier when it wishes to raise prices. Rate cases were frequent during the 1970s and early 1980s when inflationary pressures required price increases to keep up with rising costs of labor and materials. More recently, costs have actually declined because of new technologies that move and switch voice and data traffic faster and require less maintenance; as a result, some telephone carriers have earned profits that exceed their allowed rate of return. When regulatory commissions suspect such "over-earnings," they may initiate a rate case to propose adjusting the carrier's revenues or allowed rate of return. If the commission finds that earnings have exceeded allowable levels, it may not only require a reduction in rates, but may also decide what to do with the excess revenue that the carrier has collected.

Commissions may order that excess earnings be returned to customers in the form of credits on their monthly bills. But commissions may also take a different approach, by requiring that the companies use the excess profits for specific purposes such as upgrading their facilities in rural areas or introducing services for the disabled. Given the urgent development needs of states, particularly in rural areas, we believe that these funds can be best spent to help modernize the telecommunications network.

Deregulation. There has been much talk of "deregulation" in the telephone industry, but total deregulation in the literal sense of removing all regulation has not happened. Deregulation usually is advocated by free market economists who doubt the conventional wisdom that local telephone service is a "natural monopoly." They believe that the greatest good for a state will result from letting an unregulated, competitive marketplace determine prices. High prices for some services or some locations may be harmful to users in the short run, but will encourage more competition and better service over the long run. According to this theory, a state with a deregulated telephone industry would have an excellent telecommunications infrastructure at competitive rates over the long run. So far, no state has been willing to conduct that experiment to find out if the theory is correct.

Nebraska has come closest to deregulation. In 1986 the Nebraska legislature removed the power of the Nebraska Public Service Commission to control local telephone prices, except in special circumstances. Services other than local phone service were deregulated. Competition was restricted, however, by keeping local monopoly telephone franchises in place. This drastic shift in Nebraska policy apparently has not led to major changes in the availability or price of service. Perhaps the reason is that taking advantage of the opportunity to raise prices excessively would undoubtedly lead to reregulation in Nebraska; it might also discredit attempts to reduce regulation in other states. In rural Nebraska, the change has not made a noticeable difference because these areas are served primarily by customer-owned telephone cooperatives.

In many other states, competitive services were distinguished from monopoly services, with competitive services becoming deregulated. In North Dakota, for example, "nonessential" telephone services were deregulated in 1989; "essential" telephone services are still subject to regulation. Many states such as Indiana have deregulated telephone cooperatives on the theory that consumers, as the direct owners of coops, are able to make the coops responsive. Idaho is considering deregulating small investor-owned telephone companies. Small, privately-owned telephone companies in rural areas (often called "mom and pops") tend to be more responsive to local needs than large telephone companies that have little rural presence. For that reason, small companies may need only minimal regulation.

Social Contract. The "social contract" model requires building a consensus among the state government agencies, consumer representatives, the carrier, and other interested parties. The goal of the social contract usually is to stabilize rates for basic exchange service and set minimum service quality standards and modernization criteria for consumers. In return, the local exchange carrier receives greater marketing flexibility and relief from rate-of-return regulation.

This innovative model was formally adopted in December 1988 when the Vermont Public Service Board approved a five-year agreement with New England Telephone that altered the regulatory framework in Vermont. The Vermont Telecommunications Agreement (VTA) is neither an instance of deregulation nor a rate case settlement, but a modified regulatory approach that responds to both cost and competitive pressures. Vermont views the social contract model as a controlled experiment because the agreement can be renegotiated, and because the enabling statute expires in 1992. Extension of the contract will require further negotiation.

This creative model is appealing, but reaching a policy consensus in states much larger than Vermont could be difficult. Even so, the model has many features worth emulating. It started with a set of goals and involved all the interested parties: government agencies, carriers, and consumers. Through a longer and more iterative process, Washington State, larger in population and area, also sought to set goals based, in part, on development needs. The Washington state approach is the subject of the case study in chapter 5.

Incentive Regulation I. The most common alternative to rate-of-return regulation is a form of financial regulation designed to give carriers a profit incentive to reduce costs and offer new or improved services. Such "incentive regulation" schemes give carriers some pricing flexibility, within limits, particularly for fully or partially competitive services. The most appealing feature of incentive regulation, however, is its ability to encourage carriers to reduce costs by permitting higher profits, provided such profits do not result from higher prices. In a typical scenario, carriers are allowed to keep a portion of the profits above the prior rate-of-return allowance, while the remainder is returned to customers in the form of lower prices.

The simplest form of incentive regulation is "price cap" regulation, in which carriers are expected to achieve cost-reducing productivity gains each year at a specified rate, for example, 3 percent. Carriers may raise prices only when the rate of inflation exceeds the negotiated "productivity gain" rate. In exchange for their productivity gains, carriers are allowed to keep the additional profits they can achieve without raising prices.

The FCC has adopted this form of incentive regulation for the largest telephone companies. But federal price cap regulation applies only to the portion of telephone carrier costs allocated to interstate service; intrastate service is unaffected. Yet federal price cap regulation is putting pressure on state regulators to implement similar changes, because they fear that carriers will find ways to allocate more of their costs to the state jurisdiction—generating higher profits on the federally regulated portion of their business at the expense of intrastate users.

New York was the first state to introduce incentive regulation, in 1986. The California Public Utilities Commission (CPUC) has approved an incentive regulation structure for Pacific Bell and GTE California that will peg prices of the carriers' monopoly services to a productivity-based inflation index.

Many of the incentive regulation plans are purely financial. They give telephone companies flexibility in setting rates and opportunities to keep more profits if the companies improve their productivity. However, some states have also tied incentive regulation of the carriers to agreements to upgrade infrastructure—that is, to make new capital investments. In Michigan, the Public Service Commission (PSC) has implemented an incentive regulation plan requiring Michigan Bell to invest a portion of any earnings above 13.5 percent return on equity in network improvement projects not covered by the company's normal $520 million annual construction budget. The balance of the excess profit will be split between the company and ratepayers. Michigan Bell has proposed to the commission enhancements totaling $55 million: $29 million for digital switches on Michigan's rural upper peninsula, $12 million for fiber optic deployment, and $14 million for upgrading residential multiparty service to single-party service.

Other PUCs have tied incentive regulation to increased investment in infrastructure. The Tennessee Public Services Commission has adopted a master plan that makes regulatory reform contingent on technology deployment. The plan gives local telephone companies earnings sharing (a plan to share "excess profits" with consumers) and pricing flexibility, provided they commit to meeting a ten-year investment plan. The master plan includes deployment of Signaling System 7 (SS7) and eventually Integrated Services Digital Network (ISDN), fiber trunks and switched broadband services. In Texas, as part of a settlement in a rate case before the PUC, Southwestern Bell will replace its electromechanical switches in rural Texas with digital switches over a four-year period. Extended Area Service also will be introduced in some regions.

Incentive Regulation II. In the form of incentive regulation described above, performance is measured by examining the carrier's financial records. Critics charge that large companies will be tempted to cut corners on service and quality in the less profitable regions of its service franchise, particularly in rural areas. Even when the regulatory commission stipulates statewide benchmarks for service quality as a condition for incentive regulation, poorer rural areas may suffer worse service because the declines might not show up in statewide averages.

These fears have given rise to a still-untried variation of incentive regulation that can be characterized as "management by objectives." Under this model, proposed here by the authors, carriers are required to achieve state telecommunications policy goals in exchange for a higher profit potential and greater flexibility in their investments, technology choices, and overall management. Traditional regulation was designed to prevent financial abuses by monopoly utilities. Financial incentive regulation attempts to fine tune that process to benefit users and providers, but it is still financial regulation substituting for marketplace forces. As an alternative, instead of stipulating specific investments, regulatory commissions would set positive state telecommunications infrastructure goals. For example, a state could propose the statewide goal of universal single-party touchtone service with quality standards sufficient for reliable voice, data and facsimile transmission—and a schedule of interim benchmarks. Upon achieving the designated goals, carriers would be allowed to retain a higher percentage of their profits.

The advantage of this alternative form of incentive regulation is that it is a healthier incentive structure. Instead of being tempted to reduce the quality of rural service to reap higher profits, carriers would be rewarded for improving rural service. Instead of making detailed decisions concerning what specific investments should be allowed and what services can be offered at what prices, regulators could oversee a less burdensome "management by objectives" program. Regulators would set the overall (measurable) policy objectives; carriers would be duly rewarded upon meeting them. Public needs would be satisfied yet carriers would be permitted greater discretion over the means used to achieve them.

At present, there are no actual examples of this type of regulation. Yet it is a relatively minor variation from current incentive regulation schemes that could, with careful crafting, lead to the faster achievement of development goals.

Subsidy Issues and Rate Structures

The traditional subsidies within the telephone industry, implemented through prices approved by regulatory commissions, are threatened by competition. Even without competitive pressures for change, they should be re-examined in the light of changed circumstances to determine whether the present system of subsidies is best suited to assist rural development. Traditionally, the price for each service was not based on the cost of that service. Only in the grand total of all services did prices have to correspond to costs. To achieve the policy goal of universal service, a general subsidy mechanism kept the prices low for all subscribers to basic local residential telephone service. The source of the subsidy was the higher prices charged to business users and long distance callers. Rural users have benefited from subsidies for rural local service received from long distance rates that were above the cost of long distance service. At the same time, those artificially high long distance rates have been a barrier to rural development by magnifying the economic penalty associated with rural distances.

Another mechanism used by regulators to keep basic telephone prices low for all residential users was to defer costs into the future. In this way, future users subsidize present users. The specific technique used by regulators to defer costs into the future is to require particularly long depreciation periods for capital equipment. For example, when telephone equipment is depreciated over 20 years instead of ten years, only one-twentieth of the cost, rather than one-tenth, is included in the rates charged to users each year. Interest charges and profit (rate of return) are paid for 20 years instead of ten, however, leaving larger total costs for ratepayers over the 20-year period. Lowering the depreciation period saves money, just as paying off a consumer credit card balance saves money by reducing interest charges.

As marketplace forces assert themselves through competition in many telecommunications services, prices move toward costs, which is more economically efficient than artificially pricing services to meet regulatory goals. More than 93 percent of U.S. households now have telephone service. We have passed the point of diminishing returns by continuing to pursue the universal service goal through general subsidies for all users. Universal service is now more likely to be achieved through subsidies targeted to those most in need, rather than by maintaining an economically inefficient pricing structure for all users.

Targeted subsidies are now offered through federal and state programs both for installation of telephone service and basic monthly service fees for low-income subscribers. Link-Up America is a federal program designed to preserve and promote telephone subscribership among low income households. The program provides a maximum of $30 per subscriber to offset up to 50 percent of the charges for connecting a subscriber to the telephone network. Link-Up America is available in both urban and rural areas, but may be particularly important to rural residents who must travel long distances to get help or exchange information if they lack a telephone. Several states also have programs to subsidize installation in high-cost rural areas. For example, in Wyoming, where the rural population is small and widely scattered, first-time telephone service is provided for an installation fee of $375 if costs are under $10,000; the customer pays half the costs in excess of $10,000.

Another direct subsidy program is the Lifeline Service Fund, authorized by the FCC to help make telephone service affordable to low income subscribers. Federal support requires state regulators to order matching funds from state sources. Most states offer special monthly rates for basic telephone service to low income customers. Some states such as Arizona, Idaho, and New Mexico are making special efforts to publicize these programs in rural areas to increase participation by the rural poor.

As competition in telecommunications increases, and states move to give carriers more regulatory flexibility, targeted subsidies will become even more important because it will no longer be possible to subsidize rural and low income subscribers by lowering prices for all residential subscribers. States will have to continue to ensure that subsidies are available for disadvantaged customers, although they may need to shift from general to narrowly targeted subsidies in order to improve economic efficiency.

Rural Issues

Three state regulatory issues are of particular concern to rural users of telephone services: service availability, service quality, and a set of two closely related pricing issues, extended local calling areas and reduced intrastate long-distance charges.

Service availability. In many states, telephone carriers are introducing new services to urban areas, including the controversial caller ID (caller identification) feature which displays the phone number of the calling party. Other new services include voice mail and electronic mail services. New services are likely to be introduced first in urban areas where there is greater demand, although the services may be equally valuable to rural users. Meanwhile, many rural users still do not have services that have long been available to urban users, such as single-party touchtone service. Rural development advocates should pay particular attention to how quickly carriers offer new services to rural users.

Service quality. It will be important to monitor the quality of telecommunications services in rural areas under the new incentive regulation plans, because carriers seeking to maximize profits may pay more attention to their urban and interurban networks than to rural facilities. The most basic rural need is for telephone line quality that is sufficiently reliable for facsimile and data transmission as well as voice communication.

One of the chief impediments to monitoring rural service quality is statistical: telecommunications data are often aggregated for an entire state or service area and thus may mask differences between rural and urban areas. To ensure that all areas served by a carrier receive service that meets the established standards, regulators should obtain data on quality of service by exchange, individual community, or district. For example, this approach was recently adopted by the Massachusetts Department of Public Utilities, which required New England Telephone to include district level data in addition to regional and statewide data (Massachusetts Department of Public Utilities, 1990).

Extended Area Service (EAS) and intrastate long distance rates. In major cities most telephone calls are local. Businesses can reach customers and suppliers elsewhere in the city with local calls. Residents can make appointments, call the school, talk with merchants, call government offices and otherwise conduct their personal business with local phone calls. They also can access many national information services through a local number. In rural areas, however, a much higher percentage of calls for the identical purposes are long distance. Businesses in outlying areas are also at a disadvantage if their customers must make long distance toll calls to reach them.

The appropriate, financially feasible response is EAS, a tariff that lets rural residents make unlimited calls within an extended area for a flat monthly rate. This policy helps reduce the disparities between rural and urban subscribers.

Several varieties of EAS have been adopted by different states. The Colorado PUC ordered a plan for county-wide EAS, thereby creating the largest local calling areas in the United States. Costs will be shared by all Colorado telephone subscribers through slight increases in monthly rates. The Georgia PUC ordered a county seat calling plan whereby all residents can make free calls to government agencies in the county.

The Louisiana Commission established a Local Optional Service (LOS) Plan that caps rates on toll calls within twenty-two miles of a parish (county) calling area. The plan resulted from a rate case proceeding in which the commission ordered a rate reduction of $36 million, half to be achieved through a reduction in access charges and half through the LOS plan. In West Virginia, local calling areas are also being established within a twenty-two mile radius of home exchanges.

In 1990 the Washington Utilities and Transportation Commission (WUTC) adopted rules to identify and expand local calling areas where customers must rely excessively on toll service to meet basic calling needs. Telephone companies must identify exchanges in which the average customer can complete less than 80 percent of intraLATA calls toll free. For exchanges that fall below the 80 percent threshold, telephone companies must evaluate possible EAS routes, and propose EAS additions and rates to the Commission.

Hawaii has not implemented EAS, but has taken steps to reduce intrastate toll rates that will benefit rural customers. A study commissioned by the Hawaii Public Utilities Commission, in response to a request from the Hawaii Legislature, recommended a reduction in intrastate long distance charges by restructuring rates to reduce first minute charges from 40 cents to 11 cents. It also recommended increases in local residential rates. However, the combined result should be a reduction in overall monthly charges for business customers and residential customers of the most rural islands, Lanai and Molokai. The lowering of inter-island toll rates could have the effect of reducing the barriers for businesses to locate on islands other than Oahu. In addition, it may help to draw the islands together by making inter-island calling more attractive for residential customers (Hartman and Schoonmaker, 1991).

Will Policy Reforms Make a Difference?

As the states amend their regulatory policies, it will be particularly important to monitor the effects of any new regulatory schemes. These new regulatory initiatives can contribute to improved access to rural telecommunications by providing more equipment, more services, and more equitable prices. It will be important to monitor them to find out not only what changes occurred in facilities and services, but what effects, if any, these changes had on rural life. Policy makers should take advantage of the changing regulatory environment to take stock of progress toward telecommunications goals. For example, has reduced regulation led to upgrading of rural telecommunications facilities?

If the intended results never materialize, the credibility and energy of any campaign for telecommunications reform may well dissipate. Ongoing evaluations of new policies can help ensure that the telephone companies meet interim targets, that the anticipated indirect benefits for rural communities are occurring, and that any necessary modifications to new policies are made. Has the number of rural households without telephone service decreased? Has the number of party lines decreased? Has the number of lines served by digital exchanges increased?

The more fundamental question is: What difference did these changes make? Have rural customers benefited from the improved facilities and new services? If so, how? Have the facilities helped attract new businesses or residents? Have schools and clinics actually begun to use the network? Here, we are looking for the indirect benefits of telecommunications investment, or what economists call externalities—the benefits derived from better telecommunications that are not reflected in the telephone companies' revenues.

For policies such as EAS that adjust the price of rural services, we also need to find out whether usage increased, and if so, to what effect. First, were the new rate areas designed to include the "communities of interest," that is, the towns that people need to call to reach businesses, banks, doctors, and government agencies? Washington has mandated an approach based on community of interest, which is easily discernible from an analysis of telephone traffic data. Flat rate county wide calling may be useful if people need to make a large number of calls to towns within their county; however, if calls go to regional centers across county lines, county EAS plans may be less effective. Assuming that calling volumes do increase, what are the effects of these added calls? Do they increase productivity? Provide greater access to information? Strengthen regional ties between communities?

Rural development advocates should ensure that the results of regulatory changes are monitored to ensure that the intended benefits are obtained. If there is little change, research may be needed to find out where the problems lie. Do the flat rate areas include communities of interest? Are business and residential customers aware of the changes in rates and services? Do rural businesses and social services understand how to take advantage of these new telecommunications opportunities? Regulators are familiar with the rate-setting issues, but may not take into consideration the need for publicity and education about the new prices and services. Rural development advocates may be able to help ensure that rural residents are aware of the changes and equipped to take advantage of them.

7. A GROWING ROLE FOR THE TELEPHONE COMPANIES

Although the primary focus of this chapter has been on state agencies responsible for telecommunications, telephone carriers themselves are one of the most critical "telecommunications players" in a state. As noted in chapter 1, telephone carriers serving rural areas range from the large Bell operating companies, many of which serve several states, to major independent companies to small rural cooperatives and mom-and-pop companies. These carriers play many roles, from initiating and supporting rural projects to participating in joint ventures and activities with local businesses and community organizations.

Despite the lack of coordinated development strategies, many rural telecommunications projects are under way across the country. The survey respondents identified 82 rural telecommunications projects in their states implemented in the last two years or currently planned. This number does not include distance learning projects, which are discussed in chapter 3. Initiatives for these projects have come from many sources. Some are the result of government commitments to improve services or reduce rates to rural communities. In other cases, public pressure has resulted in extension of services or rate reductions. However, the telephone companies themselves often have been initiators.

The PUC respondents indicated that 60 percent of the rural projects they knew about were started by telephone companies, while 33 percent were started by a government agency. The other 7 percent were initiated by users. Of course, the total number of telecommunications projects in the rural United States is considerably greater, and the telephone companies may be involved in many projects that were not identified by PUCs.

Why are the telephone carriers involved? They may see new services as a way to increase use of their networks. Telephone carriers in rural areas are also interested in installing new fiber networks to position themselves to offer distance learning and other high capacity image and data services. They also may implement pilot projects as test and demonstration activities for new services.

Paradoxically, the trend toward deregulation has created new incentives for telephone companies to upgrade rural facilities in return for flexibility in pricing or other concessions. Thus companies may propose upgrades of rural facilities as a "good citizen" commitment in return for concessions on regulation or rates. The result of these incentives has been not only new investment in rural infrastructure but new partnerships between telephone companies and state or local governments in pilot projects.

These approaches of using rates and incentives are more prevalent than government funding for new or improved services. However, small phone companies may apply for REA loans to upgrade facilities. As we have noted above, state governments also may fund rural projects either through direct investment in facilities or through leasing capacity from telephone companies to offer educational and other services. Innovative approaches to using telecommunications for distance education are reviewed in chapter 3.

Expanding Services By Aggregating Demand

Another approach that small companies have used to expand services available in rural areas is to aggregate demand. Rural areas often lack economies of scale that would make it attractive to provide new services such as equal access to alternate long distance carriers. With the approval of regulators, small companies may aggregate their demand through pooling traffic to provide a viable market for new services.

The leading example of rural demand aggregation is Iowa Network Services (INS), a consortium of small independent telephone companies established to concentrate traffic as a means of offering their customers equal access to competing long distance carriers. Long distance carriers now have a single point of access for some 150,000 subscriber lines of the INS member telephone companies through the INS Des Moines switch. This centralized switch provides inter- and intraLATA equal access to 128 rural telephone companies. Iowa is the first state to implement 1+ presubscription for intraLATA long distance services.

In a similar vein, 90 independent telephone companies have created Minnesota Equal Access Network Services (MEANS). Using digital technology and optical fiber, MEANS intends to offer centralized equal access and other competitive services currently unavailable in rural Minnesota. A consortium of 26 South Dakota independent telephone carriers, Express Communications, Inc., has selected Sioux Falls as a central point from which to offer long distance carriers cheaper rates to reach rural exchanges than the cost of doing it themselves. Express Communications hopes to begin construction in 1991.

Kansas Independent Network, Inc. (KINI) was formed by 29 independent telephone companies and cooperatives. KINI was established to enhance the independent telephone companies' ability to obtain cellular telephone licenses, and is building rural cellular systems in nine areas. It is considering carrying long distance traffic and offering its customers equal access to long distance carriers.

This form of demand aggregation may be attempted in other states with many small telephone companies. Such an ambitious enterprise, however, requires dedication, organization, and persistence—to gain necessary regulatory approvals, raise capital, and attract customers. In other states customers themselves have persuaded an interexchange carrier to install an access point to its network (called a point of presence, or POP). Successful examples of demand aggregation by users in Kearney, Nebraska, and Pullman, Washington to obtain a POP, are discussed in chapters 3 and 4.

8. CONCLUSIONS

If rural America is going to obtain a modern telecommunications infrastructure, its most daunting challenge will be to build new bridges between the "two cultures" of telecommunications and development, which in the past have had little contact with each other. This lack of communication means that, apart from meeting the internal management needs of state government and traditional regulation of carriers, telecommunications is a largely neglected sphere of state policy. The roots of the problem are lack of awareness of the importance of telecommunications for regional development and lack of mechanisms for coordination among state agencies and between them and the telecommunications industry.

How, then, can the seeds of change be planted and cultivated? Most legislatures do not have the expertise—or perhaps the vision—to link telecommunications issues with broader development concerns. State agencies tend to focus on their specific mandates rather than seeing how interdisciplinary approaches and interagency coordination could help to achieve their goals. Some governors have had the vision to establish task forces or to work with colleagues through the National Governors' Association to identify goals and strategies for enhancing telecommunications in their states. With visible political support and a broad-based membership, task forces can help remedy the numerous "knowledge gaps" that plague state telecommunications policy and forge a genuine consensus for change. They can mobilize the key players in state telecommunications policy and educate them, as well as local officials and businesses, and the public at large.

Paradoxically, the trend toward deregulation may give regulators the opportunity to create incentives for carriers to upgrade rural facilities in return for pricing flexibility or other concessions. Competitive pressures have led regulators to seek alternatives to rate-of-return regulation, and created incentives for telephone companies to increase investment in rural facilities. Telephone companies now find themselves in the role of rural economic developers. Many are interested in installing new central office switches and fiber networks to offer distance education and other video and data services. The result of these changing incentives has been not only new investment in rural infrastructure but also new partnerships between telephone companies and state or local governments in pilot projects.

If states are going to harness the new telecommunications for development purposes, their regulatory commissions must begin to take a broader perspective on the significance of the technologies. State regulators and other policy makers must begin to appreciate the larger economic and social context in which modern telecommunications operates, and explore new regulatory approaches that can unleash new applications and benefits that will contribute to economic development.

The Challenge

The challenge facing state regulators and policy makers is to provide the telecommunications infrastructure that will support statewide and community-specific development goals, including rural development, while keeping telephone service affordable for residential consumers. Fortunately, costs are declining in the telecommunications industry. Given proper incentives, continuing quality and cost gains can be achieved. In most states it will be possible to stimulate substantial telecommunications investment in support of development goals without raising taxes or prices to consumers.

Yet recognition of the importance of telecommunications for rural development needs to be matched by action—to encourage new forms of investment, joint projects with communities, and aggregation of demand to make up-to-date services viable in rural areas. In states with extensive rural and remote areas, these issues may require creative initiatives by policy makers from both telecommunications and rural development. Chapter 3 examines the "development culture," the state and local agencies concerned with rural development, and their roles in telecommunications initiatives.

CHAPTER 3

Rural Development Players: State and Local Initiatives

1. THE CULTURE OF RURAL DEVELOPMENT

If development experts must learn more about the culture of telecommunications, as the previous chapter argues, it is equally important that telecommunications experts learn more about the culture of rural development. A constructive collaboration can transcend many of the barriers that now stand between the two cultures and help build new models of development for rural communities.

One of the first barriers that both cultures must surmount is the lack of understanding about how policy in the two respective areas is forged. In telecommunications, policy is established at state and federal levels; local communities have little direct influence. Development, on the other hand, is primarily a local process guided by the elected officials, businesses, banks, schools, and others in individual communities. State and federal initiatives can help this process, but the chief responsibility is local.

Perhaps the biggest challenge, therefore, is building new bridges between the state-oriented players in telecommunications policy and the locally-oriented players in development policy. With new linkages to each other, participants in both areas can contribute a great deal to the other's goals. State development agencies, for example, can provide considerable support and incentives to communities, from the funding of demonstration projects to the offering of expertise. Local leaders, in turn, can help state development officials see the value of more locally responsive assistance and of telecommunications as a development tool.

Communities need to cultivate better ties not only with state officials and agencies, but with telecommunications carriers. Even though they may succeed in mobilizing their community and in reaching out to state

81

officialdom, local leaders may still have trouble obtaining the telecommunications services they seek. The task may not be so formidable when the community is served by a local telephone cooperative or a small, locally-owned telephone company. But when the community is served by a large telephone company with offices in a distant city and no local manager, local leaders may find it harder to get the company's attention. The company's bureaucracy may be more oriented to state regulators and urban issues than to rural customers. Local leaders may need to work with state regulators to get the telephone company's attention and to ensure that the company receives regulatory approval for investments in their community.

Here again, cultural differences must be overcome: the telephone carrier's management may base its decisions on a five-year capital investment plan, while community leaders may want to pursue new development initiatives within the next year. Such mismatches between the telecommunications and development cultures—in the arenas of policy making (state versus local) and the time-scale of planning (short- versus long-term)—may appear to hinder cooperation and progress on telecommunications initiatives.

The task is not impossible. Both cultures are changing in ways that reduce their differences. Increasingly, community development leaders are discovering that they must operate at a state or regional level to achieve local goals. Telephone company managers are realizing that they must look beyond matters of technology and regulation and adopt a more customer-oriented marketing approach to their business. Community leaders should be able to find allies in both the more marketing-oriented groups in the telephone companies and in their regulatory commissions.

2. STATE AND LOCAL AGENCIES WITH LINKS TO RURAL DEVELOPMENT AND TELECOMMUNICATIONS

State Agencies

State rural development responsibilities are spread across many departments and agencies, several of which may have some connection with telecommunications. The respondents to our national survey of state regulatory commissions identified 90 state agencies that have some involvement in telecommunications policy, planning or projects. They include agencies directly involved in rural development such as agricultural extension, forestry and fisheries, and parks and wildlife. They also include state and county commerce or economic development agencies and social service agencies providing emergency services, health care, welfare and other community services. Educational institutions for preschool through adult learners are particularly important for rural development.

Most of these diverse agencies have little expertise or experience in exploiting telecommunications for rural development. In our survey, therefore, we selected agencies that have already participated in rural telecommunications projects. We interviewed staff members to find out how the agencies became involved and whether their participation is ongoing or only project-specific. Besides administration or general services departments responsible for the government's own telecommunications requirements, these agencies fall within the following categories:

Commerce or economic development: Many state agencies concerned with improving and diversifying their economies have identified high-quality telecommunications as a key tool for attracting information-intensive industries and for providing popular services in recreational and retirement communities. Examples are discussed in section 3, below.

Emergency services: Many state and local agencies have worked to extend 911 services statewide. Some of them are now trying to extend "enhanced 911" into more rural areas, so that operators can learn the location of the caller automatically and alert the nearest source of emergency assistance. See section 4, below.

Education: Distance education, using telecommunications to reach rural students, has become an important means of reducing disparities between rural and urban schools. Students now take courses offered from another school in their district or from a teacher across the country. Innovative applications of telecommunications for distance education are discussed in section 5 below.

Agriculture: Farmers equipped with personal computers and modems can now obtain information on crop diseases and new farming techniques directly from agricultural extension services operated by state agriculture agencies and the federal Department of Agriculture. They also can access specialized databases to obtain detailed weather forecasts, price information and market analyses.

Parks and recreation: Satellite terminals and radio transmitters are used for remote monitoring of fire danger, while mobile radios are important for coordinating search and rescue operations in wilderness areas. Data communications services that support state recreational facilities include traffic monitoring, weather reports, and reservation systems for campgrounds.

Consumer affairs: State consumer affairs agencies may be involved in identifying consumer needs for affordable telecommunications, and in presenting needs and concerns of both urban and rural consumers to state planners and regulators.

Local Agencies

Small rural communities feel the economic gap between rural and urban areas most keenly, as their shrinking populations erode the tax base, forcing local officials to consider closing schools and hospitals. As they search for solutions to such problems, many community and county development agencies realize that telecommunications may hold some answers. An advanced infrastructure can help economic development councils attract new service businesses that require good telecommunications facilities. Local school boards may look to distance education via telecommunications as a way of providing specialized instruction. County or regional emergency and health service providers may see telecommunications as a way to extend the reach of their services to smaller communities.

However feasible these plans, the majority of state and local development agencies do not consider them. With little expertise in telecommunications, agencies often depend on telephone company officials, individual businesses and consumer organizations for advice. However, each of these constituencies has its own agenda, which may not reflect the development agency's goals. In addition, agencies must recognize that using telecommunications to serve development goals requires two steps. First, the telecommunications facilities and services must be put in place. Second, those services must be used in ways that lead to development. Many communities are unaware of what services could be available or how to make their needs known to regulators and carriers. Even when services are available, many communities are unaware of how they can use them to achieve local development goals.

Our survey identified two additional reasons why state and local development agencies are seldom involved in telecommunications planning and policy. First, they typically do not have a formal mandate for telecommunications planning or policy, even if they are involved in telecommunications projects. Second, the agencies usually are not perceived by the regulatory commissions as having any ongoing role in state telecommunications planning or policy.

Exceptions are beginning to appear, however. For example, in 1991, the Oregon Progress Board (a unit affiliated with the Oregon Economic Development Department) issued a report, *Oregon Benchmarks*, which set forth a series of measurable standards for progress toward state development goals. The Progress Board had worked with the PUC to establish two telecommunications goals for the state: to install single-party touchtone telephone service in 98 percent of Oregon households by 1995, and to install telephone lines that could provide medium-speed data transmission for 100 percent of the state by 1995. Oregon's Progress Board provides a good model for other states to emulate.

Conferences and Seminars

One of the best ways to help build cultural bridges between telecommunications agencies and carriers, on the one hand, and educators and development agencies, on the other, is through conferences and seminars. By convening representatives of all the interested parties—telephone companies, government officials, consumers, schools, businesses—these gatherings can help a state develop a common vision and collaborative plan for improving the telecommunications infrastructure. To date, conferences and seminars exploring the role of telecommunications in state development have been held in Alaska, Indiana, Iowa, Missouri, Oklahoma, Pennsylvania, Texas and Utah, among other states.

Such conferences and workshops are usually well-received by local community development officials. For example, a rural county official attending a panel on telecommunications and rural development in Oregon urged the sponsors of the conference to find some way to package the panel and send it out on a six-month tour of the state to get their message out to every rural community (Oregon Independent Telephone Association, 1991). It may not be feasible to send a "traveling road show" to every rural area, but it may be possible to prepare a written report or a videotape that could be circulated. Experts could be available by telephone for conference calls to discuss issues with local officials. A recent example of a practical and readable report is *Lifelines to Rural Indiana: The Role of Telecommunications in Rural Economic Development*, prepared by the Indiana Economic Development Council (1991).

3. TELECOMMUNICATIONS AND RURAL EMPLOYMENT

Why Businesses Are Attracted to Rural Areas

As noted in chapter 1, information-intensive industries are often attracted by rural locations with high-quality telecommunications, reliable transportation, lower labor costs and stable workforces. The nature of this attraction is well documented in The *New Jersey Telecommunications Infrastructure Study*, cited in chapter 2, which examined the potential benefits of telecommunications through interviews with business and economic development officials. Economic development managers from major U.S.

cities were nearly unanimous in their belief that advanced telecommunications services are important to a company's ability to compete. They also believed that technologically advanced telecommunications services positively affect a state's ability to attract and retain businesses. Executives of relocating companies confirmed this assessment by ranking telecommunications fourth in New Jersey and sixth nationwide among more than twenty relocation criteria. Good telecommunications services, although necessary, are not sufficient to guarantee economic development. Other highly rated factors in the New Jersey study were access to airports and highways, labor costs and proximity to major markets (Deloitte and Touche, 1991).

There are many examples of companies that have chosen to decentralize their operations or to move to regions where these factors make a new location attractive. The best known case of decentralization by an information-based business is the relocation of Citibank credit card services to Sioux Falls, South Dakota. A prime reason for the relocation was South Dakota's favorable tax structure and relaxation of interstate banking prohibitions. But the move would not have been possible without a well-developed telecommunications infrastructure. Another often-cited example of decentralization through telecommunications is Omaha, which is now known as the "800 capital of the world" because of the huge volume of toll-free calls routed to or through Omaha.

The reasons motivating these business relocations to midwest cities also apply to relocations to rural areas. Breda, Iowa, a town of 500 people, was able to attract a branch office of Sitel, one of the nation's largest telemarketers, after the local telephone company linked the town to the fiber optic network of a major long-distance carrier.

Rural areas with adequate telecommunications may also attract a new breed of "footloose" entrepreneurs who enjoy rural living. Guides for All Seasons, a tour operator that specializes in treks in Nepal, operates out of Quincy, California, a small town north of Lake Tahoe. The business relies primarily on catalog distribution and word-of-mouth referrals. The company's owners found that, with an 800 number, fax machine, modem and telex terminal, they could operate successfully from the California Sierras (*Guides for All Seasons*, 1990). Similarly, Linea Casa, an importer of fine Italian linens, chose Tunbridge, Vermont, a rural community of 1,100, because of its quality of life and reasonable labor and operating costs. The company relies on telephone, fax, telex, and computer communications to place orders with Italian suppliers and respond to requests from U.S. retailers.

Urban entrepreneurs may also find rural areas attractive because of labor shortages and high wages in major cities. For example, Northspan Group, Inc. of Minneapolis matches needs of Minneapolis-St. Paul employers with labor and resources of small northern Minnesota communities.

Northspan recently placed a remote data processing center for an insurance company in International Falls, a town of 6,000 on the Canadian border. Also in Minnesota, the state government decided to use telecommunications to bring jobs to a depressed region. The Minnesota Department of Revenue opened a data processing center in the Iron Range town of Ely (population 5,000). The center is linked via telecommunications with St. Paul, 200 miles away.

Atlanta-based ANBC relocated its circuit-board assembly operations to rural Waynesboro, Georgia, because of lower labor costs and availability of a state of the art telecommunications network (Deloitte and Touche, 1991). Appalachian Communication Services (ACS) has located in rural London, Kentucky, from which it provides credit card processing services for several large banks located on the east and west coasts. It also provides computer services to the federal government and major corporations, including IBM and Federal Express. ACS reports that 85 percent of its clients are connected to them via data networks. ACS uses image processors to digitize documents, and then transmits them electronically to its rural field offices, which employ 2,500 workers.

Besides helping recruit new businesses, modern telecommunications can increase the efficiency of traditional rural occupations such as handicrafts. The Rochester Folk Art Guild in rural Middlesex, New York, is using Centrex services provided by the local telephone carrier to improve communication between customers and its artisans. The artisans are located in many workshops, most of which are at a considerable distance from the central farmhouse (Rochester Telephone, 1991). Centrex-based voice messaging is not only useful for communication within an organization, but also for rural schools wishing to keep parents informed about their children's homework and student attendance. Such facilities also can be used to provide weather reports, farm reports, and town events calendars.

Incentives to Attract Information-Based Businesses
The traditional way that state and local governments have recruited new businesses is through various incentives: reduced income tax, wage subsidies, reduced rent of buildings, and similar inducements. While relocation incentives may work in the short term, they may be controversial, not least because existing local businesses may resent not receiving the same advantages. Also, while incentives may generate short-term job gains for a given state or community, they may start a bidding war among states and communities, diminishing tax revenues for everyone. The effects will be particularly acute if there are too few relocatable businesses and too many bidding communities. More critically, incentives are unlikely to spur sustained long-term economic development, and they may do little to improve

the quality of life for most community residents. For all these reasons, development strategies that seek to nurture and expand existing local businesses and entrepreneurs are likely to yield greater long-term benefits than strategies that seek only to recruit new businesses.

Whether the local development plan is to recruit from outside or expand local businesses, there is no magic formula to guarantee success. Just as communities differ in character, resources and aspirations, so the strategies they pursue must vary. Yet one element common to most successful community development efforts is strong local leadership committed to mobilizing the community's resources and obtaining the facilities it needs. To diversify local economies, particularly into information-intensive industries, a modern telecommunications system is a critical strategic asset.

Many state and county economic development agencies are trying to diversify their economies by attracting businesses that are information-intensive such as telemarketing, customer support, mail order fulfillment and data entry. By upgrading the local telecommunications infrastructure, these agencies can make attractive overtures to businesses that require sophisticated services such as diverse routing of 800 number calls and improved data transmission services. Such upgrades can enable rural areas to exploit new opportunities from the federal government as well. For example, the Internal Revenue Service (IRS) now requires access to optical fiber as a qualification for sites wishing to be considered for an IRS information center.

Rural communities are not helpless in their quest for improved telecommunications. With skill and persistence, many towns have prevailed upon regulators and carriers to improve their telephone network. The Economic Development Council (EDC) of the County of Marquette, Michigan, for example, persuaded Michigan Bell to upgrade the local telephone switching equipment to modern digital facilities earlier than originally planned. The EDC staff organized local support, made contacts with the PUC, and made a strong case for the importance of improved telecommunications for the region. Not only did this advocacy bring about a digital switch sooner than otherwise, it saved the county $500,000 in the implementation of 911 services because most of the necessary features were already built in. (Providing 911 features using the older switch would have required substantial additional expense.) The improved telecommunications service also helped to forestall the relocation of the administrative offices of a regional air carrier, saving several jobs (Manto, 1990).

Local advocacy also proved indispensable in 1990 in eastern Washington State, where AT&T was building a major fiber optic route. Disturbed that the new line would not have a local "point of presence" (POP)—the "on-ramp to the electronic superhighway"—the Palouse Area Economic

Development Council and Washington State University persuaded AT&T to locate a POP in Pullman in exchange for right-of-way commitments. A similar bargain was struck with carriers by the State of Maine. In exchange for rights-of-way along state highways throughout Maine, the state government obtained major telecommunications links to several remote northern communities.

Some organizations offer assistance to rural communities interested in attracting "back office industries" such as data entry, order taking, customer service, operator assistance, and telemarketing. For example, National Consulting Systems Inc. (NCS) of Omaha produces a *Guide to Attracting Small Office Industries*. NCS's founder, Jim Beatty, calls this strategy a form of "teleconomic development." The Corporation for Enterprise Development, based in Washington, D.C., helps rural regions and communities assess their strengths and learn how to "get smarter" in upgrading their workforce and developing strategies to attract more highly skilled jobs, including information-based jobs (Ross, 1990).

One rural town that is planning its future around improved telecommunications is Bloomsburg, Pennsylvania. In 1990, the town completed a report, *Telecommunications Opportunities for Bloomsburg*, which sketches a comprehensive community strategy for enhancing existing businesses and organizations and attracting new information-intensive businesses (Depo, 1990). The community was unable to persuade the major long-distance carriers to provide POPs in Bloomsburg, because there were already POPs in nearby Harrisburg. Therefore the community plans to construct and operate a 4.5 megabit digital "electronic highway" to connect their town with the long-distance carriers in Harrisburg. By thus improving their town's "on-ramp" to national and international "electronic highways," Bloomsburg hopes to attract businesses dependent on modern telecommunications facilities that might otherwise locate in communities that have better facilities and direct access to the long-distance networks of AT&T, MCI and Sprint.

Whether Bloomsburg will receive all the necessary approvals from state and federal regulators without opposition remains to be seen. Sometimes, the development of a credible alternative itself encourages telephone carriers to invest in needed facilities. By taking the initiative, Bloomsburg officials are making it more likely that, one way or another, they will get the facilities they need.

Many more of these local initiatives will be needed. Few communities are fortunate enough to have local expertise in both economic development and telecommunications. They will need information about models tried in other communities to plan their own strategies. Using whatever outside help they can get, communities should assess their telecommunications needs and work with their telephone carriers and regulatory commissions to obtain needed improvements. Most importantly, they should plan to use upgraded facilities in ways that will help to achieve their own development goals.

The Telephone Company Connection

Telephone companies have a direct interest in stimulating economic development, particularly in information-intensive industries in their service areas, because it means more business for them. Sometimes the telephone companies themselves have become partners in bringing information businesses to rural areas. Several such ventures involve telemarketing. In Aurora, Nebraska, for example, the Hamilton Telephone Company established Aurora Telemarketing Inc. (ATI) to help encourage local economic growth and diversify the economy. Today ATI employs about 60 people in the community of 4,000. In Ruthven, Iowa, the Ruthven Telephone Company established a telemarketing subsidiary employing ten people in a community of 300 (Beatty, 1988). In Victoria, Kansas, a telemarketing service company called Intellisell and the Rural Telephone Service Company plan to construct a telemarketing center that will contribute to the economic development of northwest Kansas by employing 55 people.

North Central Telemarketing Services (NCTS) operates a chain of 11 telemarketing services in towns of 1,000 or fewer people in Iowa and South Dakota. Several independent Iowa telephone companies are participating in partnerships with NCTS including Prairie Telephone Company, Ruthven Telephone Exchange, Breda Telephone Corporation and Heart of Iowa Telephone Cooperative. As part of their contractual responsibilities, the telephone companies locate a work site, undertake its renovation, and assist in hiring local telemarketing management staff. (These telephone companies are also members of Iowa Network Services.)

C&P Telephone has pioneered a creative use of rural workers by transferring its operator assistance services from Washington, D.C., to Beckley, West Virginia. C&P, a subsidiary of Bell Atlantic, said it decided to locate in Beckley because of the availability and stability of the West Virginia workforce as well as the availability of a fiber optic network linking West Virginia and the District of Columbia (EMCI, 1991). By mid-1991, C&P employed 125 people in Beckley. C&P is encouraging other uses of rural telecommunications by working with the West Virginia Governor's Office of Community and Industrial Development and its "Office of the Future" project, which hopes to attract telecommunications-based businesses to the state. Already, a number of information-intensive businesses have located in West Virginia, including several Bell Atlantic offices, and branches of Chilton Research, Atlantic Financial and Blue Cross/Blue Shield (Fowlkes, 1990).

Efforts by the local telephone company to offer state-of-the-art facilities can make a difference in attracting a new business. Choice Hotels International selected Minot, North Dakota, over 22 other telemarketing locations, in part because the telephone company installed optical fiber to the proposed site (Rochester Telephone, 1991). Before moving into a rural area in Ohio, a large warehousing and distribution company required a letter of intent from the local telephone company stating that it would upgrade its switching facilities from analog to digital technology. In Warren, Maine, the availability of Centrex service offered by the local exchange carrier helped to attract new businesses and a new state prison. Sometimes, a promise by the telephone carrier to upgrade facilities quickly may be sufficient to keep a community from being disqualified as a relocation site, although, obviously, the community's recruitment task is much easier when facilities are already in place.

Beyond installing and marketing advanced telecommunications, carriers can help themselves and their communities by becoming active advocates for development. They can improve their own expertise on development issues, actively participate in local economic development councils, and even help finance certain forms of development. One strategy, adopted by General Telephone of the Midwest, headquartered in Carmel, Indiana, has been to establish an internal office of economic development to work with communities to foster telecommunications-related growth. In Orange County, New York, representatives of Highland Telephone are active participants on the Partnership Board, a particularly successful development group. Highland Telephone's digital switching technology, including Centrex, has been an important factor in attracting more than 20,000 jobs to the region (Rochester Telephone, 1991). In New Richmond, Wisconsin, St. Croix Telephone is a member of BiCEP (Business/Industry Community Education Partnership) which was formed to address the community's education and employment needs. The committee was pivotal in developing an industrial park which has attracted several new companies. And in Clintonville, Wisconsin, Urban Telephone helped attract a high-technology plastic mold business that now employs 45 people. The business makes camera parts in a building financed by Urban Telephone's pension fund (Rochester Telephone, 1991).

Telephone companies also may contribute to community development by sharing their knowledge and skills. The Germantown Telephone Company in New York spearheaded the development of the Countryside Computer Alliance (CCA), with the goal of increasing computer literacy in rural areas. CCA offers free computer literacy courses to improve the skills of the workforce and indirectly help create more jobs.

At the national level, OPASTCO, the Organization for the Protection and Advancement of Small Telephone Companies, has established the Fund for Rural Education and Development (FRED). FRED has created a database listing the rural development activities of its member companies and is providing support for pilot projects. State telephone associations also can educate their members about the importance of their services in rural areas and how they can contribute to community and regional development.

These examples show how telephone companies can stimulate economic development in the communities they serve, and thereby increase their own revenues. Indeed, they ought to view rural development as a new marketing frontier. Support for community development is different from traditional marketing to large corporations, but the principles are the same: find out what problems your customers are trying to solve, and help devise effective solutions.

4. APPLICATIONS FOR HEALTH CARE
AND EMERGENCY SERVICES

A healthy, educated workforce is critical to economic development. Indeed, investment in human capital, in the form of health and education services, may be the single most important strategy for long-range rural economic development. Communities without good schools and good health care will have a difficult time recruiting new businesses or expanding existing businesses—for the simple reason that people prefer to live in communities with better health care services, emergency services and schools.

This section reviews how telecommunications can help rural communities improve the quality of rural health care and emergency services. Section 5 reviews a particularly promising role for telecommunications, in rural education.

Rural Health Care Delivery

Many rural regions face a critical shortage of physicians. For example, Idaho, a primarily rural state, has the lowest number of physicians per capita in the United States and the oldest average age of practicing physicians. Loyd Kepferle, director of the Idaho Rural Health Education Center, sums up the importance of health services to rural communities: "If a community doesn't realize the value of its health care system and loses it, it doesn't just lose the health care system. It loses a great big piece of the economic machine of that community" (Lyons, 1991).

As in so many other segments of the rural economy, telecommunications and information technologies can do much to reduce costs and improve quality of rural health care services. Many hospitals already use EDI to communicate with their suppliers for ordering and billing. Hospitals also use health care information systems internally to maintain hospital records, improve decision making, do billing and manage schedules. In Connecticut, a statewide network is used for integrated insurance claims processing.

One promising way to address this shortage of rural health care providers is through innovative applications of telecommunications known as "telemedicine." Through a system of data networks and videoconferencing linking rural hospitals to university medical centers, rural general practitioners can consult with specialists in major urban hospitals. Physicians and other health care professionals can use the system for remote diagnostics, video consultations, in-service training and continuing education. In Massachusetts and Nevada, experiments in digitized transmission of X-rays are being carried out. In Minnesota and Nevada, physicians and hospitals are communicating over digital networks (Deloitte and Touche, 1991). Rural health care providers in Texas participate in "grand rounds" offered over an audio conferencing network operated by the Teleconferencing Network of Texas. Where there are no doctors, rural paraprofessionals can communicate with physicians for assistance in diagnosis and treatment of their patients. In Alaska, for example, village health aides talk with doctors at regional hospitals over a dedicated satellite radio network (Hudson, 1990).

As the scarcity of funding and physicians worsens at rural health hospitals and clinics, there will be even stronger incentives to turn to telecommunications networks to control costs and obtain needed medical expertise.

Emergency Services

In most of the country, we take for granted the value of 911 emergency service in saving lives. Good emergency services, when they are available, improve the quality of life in both rural and urban locations. In a very real sense, emergency services are a major development issue, and are a significant factor in the recruitment of "footloose" businesses. Regrettably, some rural areas are still without 911 service, and all rural areas have special needs in providing quick and accurate emergency responses.

In the standard 911 service, a central dispatch center takes emergency calls and routes them to the appropriate emergency service jurisdiction. One problem with this system is that dispatchers must learn the location of the emergency from the caller in order to decide which service to dispatch. If the caller cannot provide the address quickly, valuable time and possibly lives may be lost. The problem may be greater in rural areas with several service jurisdictions, than in a single city with only one police and fire department.

The solution to this problem, now available in some parts of the country, is enhanced 911 (E911) service. With E911, an automatic number identification feature in the telephone system shows the dispatcher the calling phone number and the location of the telephone, using a computerized data base. The dispatcher can then send help even if the caller cannot speak or describe the location. The advantages of E911 service may be particularly significant in rural areas where there are many different emergency service providers, distances are greater than in urban areas, and the 911 dispatcher may be many miles away from the caller and unfamiliar with the local place names and the service jurisdiction where the caller is located. An E911 database can help the dispatcher locate the caller and identify the appropriate emergency service.

Access for the Disabled

Some social services are important as a matter of social equity and fairness, while others are important because they help to rehabilitate people or compensate for their disabilities in ways that enable them to become, or continue to be, productive contributors to the economy. Providing services for the disabled is important for both reasons. Tools to help disabled people communicate are essential. As the percentage of jobs dealing with information increases at the expense of jobs requiring physical labor, there are more job opportunities for people with physical disabilities.

The Americans with Disabilities Act, enacted in July 1990, requires the FCC and the states to arrange for relay systems so that speech or hearing-impaired people using teletype or equivalent keyboard terminals can communicate with people using regular voice telephones. A relay operator acts as an intermediary to type oral messages to the impaired party and to speak typewritten messages to the unimpaired person. Without a relay operator, the disabled can reach only others using similar terminals. (Computerized speech recognition and speech synthesis may one day replace human operators, but such applications of "artificial intelligence" are not yet sufficiently developed for this purpose.)

Some states have also introduced policies to meet goals of statewide access to these important services. Nebraska, for example, has implemented a dual-party relay system for deaf and hearing impaired persons using 800 numbers statewide.

5. DISTANCE EDUCATION AND RURAL DEVELOPMENT

As noted in chapter 1, education is vital to rural America. Rural young people need to be prepared for information-related jobs. Many rural work-

ers need retraining or more advanced job skills. Even though rural education needs are as great as or greater than those in urban locations, rural
schools usually lack the tax base that more affluent urban and suburban
locations enjoy. They also lack the student population needed to be able
to afford a full range of course offerings. The scarcity of funds and students makes it particularly difficult for rural schools to attract specialty
teachers, especially in advanced mathematics, computing, science and
foreign languages.

Rural communities, with good reason, work hard to keep their schools.
Rural students already ride school buses for long distances because of past
school consolidations. Community leaders correctly perceive that the loss
of their schools means their community is dying. People will not want to
live, work and raise their children in communities without schools.

Consequently, rural educators have been among the most innovative in
harnessing telecommunications technologies to meet the needs of rural
Americans. Their experiences provide valuable insights into the potential of
rural telecommunications and the issues that must be addressed to put
these technologies to effective use. Many of the issues they face in using
telecommunications apply also to rural health care, other social services,
and business applications.

Why Distance Education?

Many states and communities are undergoing a crisis in school financing. Taxpayers are rebelling at high property tax rates. Poorer school
districts usually have an insufficient tax base to support needed programs.
Many rural communities are desperately trying to avoid additional consoli-
dation of school districts and longer school bus rides for their students.

Despite tight finances, educators are trying to maintain and improve
the quality of education. Students need to meet higher educational standards to be able to perform the more complex jobs in today's economy.
Mathematics, science and language skills are particularly important,
but good teachers in these subjects are scarce. Rural schools, with
smaller enrollments than urban schools, cannot offer all of these desirable
classes to their smaller classes. While urban schools offer their students
a choice of foreign languages, rural schools are lucky if they offer any
foreign language.

Since the early days of television, innovative educators have recognized
the potential value of that medium for instruction. Some promoted the
"master teacher" approach of using the best teachers to instruct students at
schools throughout the country. Others favored the enrichment approach
whereby audiovisual materials could be delivered electronically to supplement the classroom curriculum.

Yet despite many trials and pilot projects, there were few successful ongoing programs. A major problem was a lack of sufficient incentives to overcome differences of class size, accreditation and teacher preparation. Teachers tended to view educational technology as at best, an extra burden, and at worst, a threat to their jobs. Rural schools in particular were conservative about adopting new technologies.

Two major challenges in recent years have forced rural schools to reconsider. First, as the rural economy declined and residents moved away, rural taxpayers faced unbearably high costs to operate their schools. Second, many states revised their curricula and introduced tougher new standards for high school graduation, including requirements in foreign languages, mathematics and sciences. Many rural school districts do not have the necessary expertise on their faculty, and are unable to attract or afford the specialized teachers.

Telecommunications offers a welcome alternative to school closings. High school students may now study Japanese or calculus via satellite, and interact with their teachers via audio conferencing. In Kansas, Minnesota, Oklahoma, Vermont and other states, students take courses electronically from other regional schools over fiber optic networks.

Various state and local agencies have supported trials of new telecommunications technologies to test their suitability for various purposes such as distance education, social service delivery, and new enterprise development. These projects often involve partnerships between the school district or department of education and the telephone company. In some cases the telephone carriers have provided the equipment and reduced-rate access to a network for a trial period. Sometimes carriers have initiated the projects by approaching educators about using their facilities.

Frequently, carriers see pilot projects for education as a way to stimulate a broader demand for telecommunications services or to install facilities that could attract new business. Some educational fiber optics projects, for example, are designed to provide high-capacity telecommunications for business and government as well as schools.

Types of Distance Education

There are two major types of distance education services—broadcast video instruction from a master teacher, and curriculum sharing among schools. The use of broadcast video instruction from a master teacher—with audio feedback from remote students—is currently used in many school districts and universities around the country. In urban locations, this is generally accomplished through a special microwave frequency allocated by the FCC for instructional use, called Instructional Television Fixed Service (ITFS). This option is more suited for urban than rural locations, because receiving sites must be directly visible from the transmitter, which is usually located on a hilltop or mountain.

Rural locations are more likely to receive video transmissions from communication satellites, which are like tall microwave "towers" located 22,300 miles above the earth, and can transmit to any location in the United States. Whether the broadcast video transmission is from a hilltop microwave transmitter or a communication satellite, telephone lines are used to let students ask questions of the teacher and participate in class discussions.

Broadcast video instruction of this sort enables rural school districts to purchase courses they are not able to offer themselves from outside suppliers—most frequently advanced math, science or foreign language classes. The Texas TI-IN network began offering classes for rural Texas schools by satellite and now provides classroom instruction by satellite to 700 school sites in 32 states. Oklahoma State University offers special courses to secondary and middle schools via satellite. Many of their courses are "advanced placement" science courses designed for high school students who are ready to get a head start on their college education. Others are high school mathematics, economics or foreign language courses. One of their course offerings is a "non-traditional" basic English and reading class designed for grades seven and eight.

The second major type of distance education service is curriculum sharing, which uses telecommunications cables to share teachers in different schools via an interactive bi-directional video network. This system permits students to take classes not offered in their own school but available in another school in the region, without travelling to that other school. Curriculum sharing arrangements are popular with rural schools because they do not require the purchase of new course materials. The schools pay the transmission costs, but do not need to pay for instruction. The content of the classes is often provided on a "barter" arrangement, with each participating school providing special teachers as part of their arrangement with the other schools.

Curriculum sharing has grown in popularity as fiber optic cables have become more available. Fiber optics have high-transmission capacity, which is required for multiple video signals. Because this capacity is also valuable for business, telephone carriers that are cooperating with schools to install fiber optic networks can exploit business applications of the technology.

There are many current examples of telephone carriers and school districts cooperating to use fiber optic technology for curriculum sharing applications. The state of Minnesota appears to have made the greatest commitment to curriculum sharing. One-third of the state's school districts have some form of interactive distance learning capabilities (U.S. Congress,

1989). The Mid Minnesota Telecommunications Consortium is a group of five technical colleges connected by a fiber video network in and around St. Cloud. The video network is used not only for sharing courses between schools, but also for a variety of other purposes such as school district administrative meetings, training, and programs for senior citizens.

In northwestern Wisconsin, Urban Telephone installed a fiber optic network for the Educational Telecommunications Cooperative, linking seven schools. The phone company asked the Wisconsin Public Service Commission staff to consider regulatory implications of the distance education project. The phone company's goals were to maximize deregulated investments while minimizing risk to its existing fiber and electronics base, and to maximize pricing flexibility (Rochester Telephone, 1991).

The Oklahoma Panhandle Shar-Ed Video Network is a two-way digital fiber optic network linking fifteen rural schools. Panhandle Telephone Cooperative installed the network, which was funded by the state Department of Education, the state legislature, and foundation grants. In North Dakota, the Souris River Telephone Cooperative installed a fiber optic network to deliver advanced courses to five rural schools. In another project, the University of North Dakota used the fiber optic network of the Dakota Central Rural Telephone Cooperative to deliver instructional programming to dispersed rural sites.

Other telephone companies are installing optical fiber and digital switching facilities which they hope will be used by educators as well as commercial customers. Eastern New Mexico Telephone Cooperative has installed SS7 (the latest version of digital signaling) and has installed almost 1,000 miles of optical fiber. A subsidiary of the cooperative has embarked upon a campaign to convince schools to take advantage of the fiber network for distance education, and to encourage health and public safety agencies to take advantage of the network for continuing education and training.

The Mid-Rivers Telephone Cooperative in eastern Montana plans to replace all of its trunk cable and microwave with optical fiber. It also has proposed that four high schools and a local community college (which are from 15 to 112 miles apart) use the fiber to share courses and faculty (Schmandt and others, 1991).

In Maine, a fully interactive video and audio network links the seven branch campuses of the University of Maine system using facilities leased from New England Telephone. The University of Maine also plans to transmit courses to more than 200 high schools, technical schools and university centers throughout the state.

South Dakota LiveNet is a proposed interactive educational TV network to be used mainly by rural school districts. The fiber optic network will ultimately provide a statewide system for interactive education for all levels: kindergarten through twelfth grade (K–12), technical colleges, universities, state government and industries. Initial funding came from the local school district, state development fund and federal grants (U.S. Congress, 1989).

Although fiber optics are well-suited for distance education applications, they are not essential. Similar services can be provided on the coaxial cable systems used by cable television networks, provided they have bidirectional links connecting the cooperating schools. Instructional video also can be transmitted on data networks, using the same compressed digital video techniques used in business teleconferencing applications.

This is the approach used by the Distance Learning project in Gibson County, Tennessee, which interconnects five school systems to provide two-way interactive instruction in specialized subjects for which there is a shortage of teachers. Video equipment is installed in classrooms, and transmission is over high-capacity data links provided by the phone company. The pilot project began in August 1990, and is to be evaluated after one year to decide whether it should be expanded to other areas. Funding is from Bell South and South Central Bell.

Schoolink in Texas is a high-speed audio-video system that will link public schools and provide multi-site continuous networking to three to four sites. Schoolink is funded by Bluebonnet, a private nonprofit consortium funded by Southwestern Bell and information technology companies including Apple, IBM, and Texas Instruments.

Special Types of Distance Education

Besides these two major types of video education services—the imported curriculum and the curriculum sharing models—there are several other special types of distance education. One popular model is based on correspondence schools. Instead of sending print materials by mail, however, the system sends audio cassettes, compact disks and video cassettes to distant locations. The same lectures featured in broadcast video instruction by master teachers or in curriculum sharing can be used again, as "stored media" instruction. These videos (or audio cassettes) can be useful as a supplement for students who missed a classroom lecture or wish to review it again to prepare for examinations.

Stanford University found that videotapes of classes previously transmitted over its local ITFS network could be used successfully with motivated students who did not have direct access to the network. When used as primary instruction, rather than as a supplement, the taped classes worked best in a group setting monitored by a tutor or teaching assistant. While students could not ask questions of the video instructor, they could stop the tape and play it again to listen carefully to what was said.

They could also ask the tutor for help and discuss together the points they did not understand.

Other education projects rely on audio or data networking, usually using telephone lines. The Buddy System in Indiana is a home education project designed to explore the impact of placing personal computers in homes of third and fourth grade students in selected trial schools. Telephone companies and private donors support the project. Students use packet switching technology to get homework assignments, access electronic mail and data bases, and chat with other students online (U.S. Congress, 1989). The Teleteaching Project in Pennsylvania is a form of distance education to bring otherwise inaccessible courses to students in rural areas. Students use standard dial-up telephone lines for audio lectures and for access to computers and electronic chalkboards. More than 30 institutions are now participating.

The Big Sky Telegraph network in Montana began as a data network linking Montana's many one-room schools. The purpose was to provide in-service training and support for isolated rural teachers. The success of the project led to expansion of the network to include electronic mail and electronic bulletin board access for a variety of rural community development efforts in Montana and nearby states.

Within the next ten years, as computing and data networking become more common in schools, we can imagine rural distance education programs using computers in schools and homes. Advanced computer capabilities will be used for a variety of multimedia learning programs such as on-demand access to audio and video instruction, and access to encyclopedias, atlases and other library materials stored on compact disks. Meanwhile, importing courses by satellite and sharing courses by fiber optic cable are the two major techniques of proven value in rural schools.

To date, most distance education projects have concentrated on improving or extending educational opportunities for students in school (although a handful try to reach students at home via electronic mail networks or local cable television systems). But if the economy and quality of life in rural America are to be truly enhanced, another key priority should be "lifelong learning"—educational programs that help adults gain new work skills and enrich their leisure time. Given the proven appeal of lifelong learning through evening and weekend classes at schools and community colleges, there is obvious value in building upon this trend through the use of telecommunications.

Research Evidence

The research evidence proving that students can and do learn from video and other distance-spanning media is overwhelming. Of course, just as in classroom instruction and in textbooks, the quality of some presentations is better than others. Even with less than top-quality presentations, however, the research evidence is consistent and easily summarized: Students learn. Motivated students learn particularly well.

Years ago, Wilbur Schramm, summarizing a large body of research evidence, pointed out in *Big Media, Little Media* (1977), that motivated students can learn from virtually any medium, from television to chalkboards, radio to duplicated worksheets. Today, we could add computers and laser disks to the list. We do not need to reinvent the wheel by asking whether students can learn using new telecommunications technologies such as satellites and optical fiber, although evaluation should be built into new projects to ascertain student attitudes to distance learning and to fine tune content and delivery.

The evidence that is most needed today has to do with cost effectiveness and feasibility. For example: What is the cost per student of various types of distance learning? How does this compare with the costs of hiring specialized teachers, or sending students to distant schools? What is the break-even number of pupils to justify the costs of various delivery systems such as microwave, optical fiber, and satellite? What factors determine which projects continue after a trial period and which stop once grants are completed? Similar questions need to be answered for other applications of telecommunications, whether they are to link rural clinics with medical centers or to train rural employees at their workplace.

Educators should seek answers to these questions concerning the total costs and the relative cost efficiencies of the alternatives available to meet their particular objectives. As the costs of transmission networks and terminal equipment decline, the costs of distance education are declining. Many programs can be justified with today's costs. Other distance learning applications that are not economically efficient today may be so tomorrow.

Fifty Distance Education Projects

To get a better understanding of the trends in rural distance education projects in the United States, we identified 50 current rural education projects that use telecommunications and gathered information about each of them. This set of 50 projects does not include every distance education project currently operating in the United States, but represents the wide range of different approaches now being pursued. No other single category of rural development makes greater use of telecommunications than distance education, and the numbers are increasing.

Population Served

Most projects (58 percent) deliver instructional materials exclusively to rural schools, while some serve colleges and adult education programs. Some 34 percent offer programming for a variety of educational levels from elementary through high school, while 24 percent are for high school only (see Figure 3-1). The high school projects provide rural students with access to courses such as foreign languages and advanced mathematics and science that may otherwise not be available. Programming for elementary schools also may be used to supplement the basic classroom curriculum. Many school projects also include in-service training for teachers.

Project Initiators

Not surprisingly, educators were the originators of most of these projects. Local school districts and universities together initiated 70 percent of the projects. State governments, through departments of education or administration, originated many of the rest of the projects. While the telephone companies are not frequently cited as originators of educational projects, they have often worked jointly with educators to provide fiber optic links.

Sources of Funding

State governments have been the major sources of funding for educational projects, although the federal government also funds projects. Two major sources are NTIA's Public Telecommunications Facilities Program (PTFP), and the federal Star Schools Program. The PTFP provides

Figure 3-1   Level of Instruction in Rural Distance Education

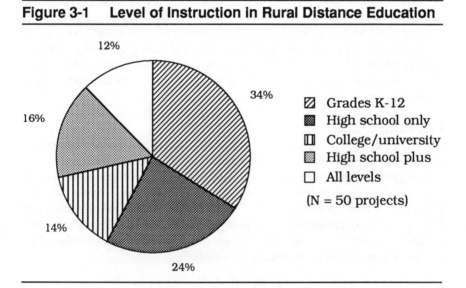

funds for hardware such as microwave and satellite equipment, and for project planning.

The Star Schools Act, passed by Congress in 1988, has two major emphases: to create multistate, organizationally diverse partnerships to prepare and deliver curriculum, and to create opportunities for disadvantaged students to receive remote instruction. To foster cooperation between institutions, all partnerships must include education agencies such as state agencies, higher education agencies and local authorities, or organizations already formed to develop educational networks. All partnerships must be statewide or multistate (U.S. Congress, 1989).

Private sources, including telephone companies, funded about a quarter of the projects for which we were able to learn the funding source. The phone companies also may provide other support for educational projects, typically by installing or extending links to schools, or by providing free or subsidized access to the networks for a trial period. Many smaller telephone companies obtain REA loans for upgrading their telephone systems by installing digital switches and optical fiber. According to a recent study, integrated planning between schools and telephone companies can pay off in savings of up to 75 percent when installing fiber during an upgrade of the telephone network. The cost of installing fiber to a school during an initial trunk line installation may be $1,500 to $2,500 per mile, while the cost of laying the fiber later may be $8,000 to $10,000 per mile (U.S. Congress, 1989).

Choice of Transmission Technologies

Optical fiber and satellite are the two technologies most frequently selected for distance education projects (see Figure 3-2). Interactive video projects, which use motion video originating at both instructor and student sites, typically use optical fiber. Courses distributed nationwide or across a large state typically use communication satellites. Satellites usually deliver one-way motion video. Students use telephone lines for interactive audio to ask questions and participate in discussion.

The selection of technology should depend on the type of communication needed for learning to take place. Full-motion interactive video in which students can see the instructor, and the instructor can see the students at each site, comes closest to face-to-face classroom instruction. Optical fiber is the most likely choice for such a network, although coaxial cable and microwave can also be used. Satellite and broadcast technologies are excellent for one-way video.

Although full-motion interactive video may be the ideal, projects in different parts of the world have used many other solutions effectively. Audio has been used for extension education in Wisconsin, continuing education for health care practitioners in Texas, and in-service education

Figure 3-2   Primary Transmission Technologies Used

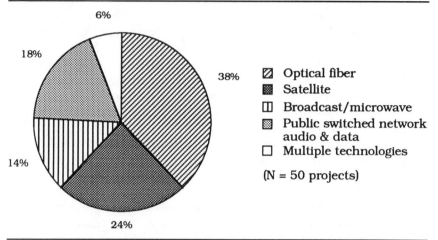

6%

18%

14%

38%

24%

☒ Optical fiber
▦ Satellite
⊞ Broadcast/microwave
▩ Public switched network audio & data
☐ Multiple technologies

(N = 50 projects)

for health aides in Alaska. Educational audio networks also have been used for isolated students in many regions of the world including Australia, Latin America, the Caribbean, and the South Pacific. These earlier projects (not included among the 50 current U.S. projects examined here) have relied on a variety of technologies including over-the-air radio broadcasting, dial-up telephone lines, two-way radios and satellite audio channels (Hudson, 1984).

Computers also can be linked to enable students to transmit assignments to instructors and interact with others in their "class" via computer conferencing. The Buddy System in Indiana, Big Sky Telegraph based in Montana, and Penn-Link in Pennsylvania are examples of projects linking students with computers over telephone lines. Some instructors have also used enhanced audio instruction by transmitting text and graphics via computer or information from other sources such as an electronic blackboard.

All these technologies work well. The choice should be based on the type of distance education program to be offered and on the costs at the particular sites. Not all technologies are available at all locations. Satellite costs are usually independent of distance and terrain, while longer distances and more difficult terrain will increase costs of fiber optic and other cable solutions.

Institutional Arrangements

The choice of technology is often less important than the institutional arrangements used to obtain service. There are five different choices to consider.

Dedicated Networks. One option for educational institutions is to install, own and operate a specialized "private" network dedicated solely to distance learning. Examples include fiber optic networks for distance education in Minnesota and instructional television networks used by several universities.

Shared Government Networks. Sometimes state and local governments share network capacity on a "private" network used for several different government applications, but not available for use by the general public. Sharing a government microwave, fiber optic or coaxial cable network often can be less costly than building a dedicated educational network. However, administrative arrangements and scheduling may be more complicated than with a dedicated facility.

Leased Capacity from Specialized Carriers. Educational institutions can lease transmission capacity for a monthly charge. The advantage is that they do not have to bear the capital costs of building their own network. Communication satellite capacity usually is obtained this way, although the school districts may own the earth stations they use. Private commercial microwave or fiber networks sometimes have capacity for lease.

Leased Capacity from Telephone Carriers. Besides offering "on-demand" switched voice telephone services, telephone carriers lease network capacity that is reserved for a particular application. Leased telephone facilities often are used for data and video networks. Schools might want to lease the capacity of one or more telephone voice channels for full-time access to a dedicated network connecting specific locations for audio or data applications. Leasing may be the only way that many telephone carriers offer access to fiber optic facilities for video distance learning applications. Educational institutions also may lease data capacity in units from 56 kilobits (thousands of bits) to 1.5 megabits (millions of bits) per second for transmission of data or digitized video images. Such networks do not require fiber optics and may be more readily available in some areas.

On-demand, "Dial-up" Networks. Audio or data circuits required only for occasional use may be accessed as needed. In some locations, 56 kilobit-per-second data circuits are available from telephone carriers on a "dial-up" basis. Commercial videoconferencing equipment called "codecs" (for coder/decoder) digitize and compress a motion video image so that it can be transmitted through such channels. Users may "dial-up" two or more circuits, depending on the quality of picture they require. The cost savings may be well worth the slight degradation of picture quality.

When choosing among these alternatives, rural educators concerned with the economic development of their communities should consider more than the direct costs involved. As noted in chapter 2, rural areas may not be able to afford more than one modern high-capacity telecommunications network. Whatever the merits of competitive approaches in urban areas, cooperation may be preferable in rural locations. A single modern network could serve education, health care and state and local government applications, as well as business applications that help the local economy.

The politics of achieving such a shared "rural area network" inevitably will be more complicated than arranging a dedicated network. Many communities select dedicated or shared government networks because they have lower costs than the tariff prices of the telephone carrier. Others select dedicated networks because the telephone carrier does not offer all the features needed for the educational applications. Some telephone carriers may not understand the urgency of getting facilities and services in place and tested before the start of the school year. These are cultural barriers that usually can be bridged with a little effort and goodwill from both sides.

Educators should develop detailed specifications and cost estimates for a dedicated network, and then use those requirements and cost estimates to negotiate with the telephone carrier for comparable services and prices. If only as a negotiating strategy, a credible plan for a dedicated network can give educators bargaining leverage to obtain the same services at a comparable price from a telephone carrier. Telephone companies could reap their own benefits in the process, of course, because the new equipment also could be used to serve broader community development goals.

About half the 50 distance education projects used private networks, while the other half used telephone carrier facilities. As shown in Figure 3-3, most of the private networks used satellite technology. Most of the projects using the public telephone network were on high-capacity leased channels used for video transmission. The rest used low-speed voice and data lines.

Cost Elements

Educators planning video distance education programs need to consider carefully four major cost elements. In the process, they need to consider the tradeoffs among different options in each category and across categories:

• The cost of the curriculum itself, whether paid for through local teachers' salaries or payments to the organization providing the curriculum.

Figure 3-3   Use of Private and Public Networks in Rural Distance Education

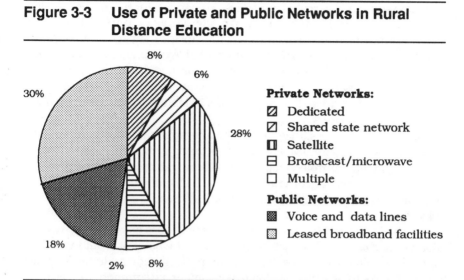

Private Networks:
- ▨ Dedicated
- ◨ Shared state network
- ▥ Satellite
- ⊟ Broadcast/microwave
- ☐ Multiple

Public Networks:
- ▦ Voice and data lines
- ▦ Leased broadband facilities

* The cost of the equipment needed at the school locations. These costs include satellite earth stations, cameras, video monitors, and "codecs" (short for coder/decoder) used to digitize the originating video pictures and to recreate the video image after digital transmission.

* The cost of the transmission channels, whether purchased or leased.

* The administrative cost of operating the distance learning program, including the operation and maintenance of the network and classroom equipment. Lease prices often include operation and maintenance, which constitute additional costs if facilities are purchased.

System Choices

Educators planning distance learning programs and projects face several choices. All options can lead to good quality instruction, but the costs may be quite different.

The major choice is between broadcast video (with audio feedback) and interactive two-way video. The transmission costs are almost certain to be higher for two-way video than for broadcast video. But the savings in curriculum cost resulting from using available teachers in the school district, or sharing courses with nearby districts, may compensate for higher transmission costs.

Video comes in different forms. Analog full-motion video may offer top quality with lowest terminal equipment costs for cameras and classroom television screens. The cost of transmission channels for full-motion analog video may be very high, however. An alternative is to use compressed digital video, which requires much less transmission capacity, but requires codecs at both ends of the transmission channel. A common data rate is 1.544 megabits per second, called a T1 rate in the telephone industry. With reasonable quality codecs, the resulting picture is indistinguishable from full motion analog video. This data rate is available in leased channels from most telephone carriers.

Some newer codecs, meeting a new international video compression standard, require only 384 kilobits to provide a quality picture. Using such equipment, multiple video signals can be transmitted on a T1 carrier. Some telephone carriers offer a "fractional T1" tariff under which educators may lease capacity in increments of less than T1 capacity, including 384 kilobits.

At the lower end of quality and cost are codecs using one or two 56 kilobit data channels. The picture quality is not what you would want for watching downhill ski races, but may be perfectly adequate for "talking head" classroom instruction. Such equipment is common in business videoconferencing applications. Data capacity is readily available from telephone carriers in 56 kilobit increments for leased lines. Many telephone carriers are beginning to offer "switched 56 kilobit" services on an as-needed, dial-up basis. The costs of codecs that can use such channels is declining rapidly, while the quality of video images is improving.

Educators also may need to arrange for facilities for transmission of charts, slides or documents, including examination papers. Facsimile transmission of documents may be sufficient for some applications. Some conferencing includes elaborate facilities for transmission or display of charts or other instructional materials. With two-way video, the audio usually is transmitted on the same channel as the video. For one-way video networks, separate audio channels are required for voice feedback. In some applications, data channels are also needed for computer links. Educators also may want to arrange for administrative channels to collect and return homework assignments or for other administrative functions. Sometimes a telephone in the classroom can provide an important administrative channel.

Pricing of Network Services

There are several different ways carriers price network transmission services for distance education. Tariffs designed for other services may be inappropriate. Price revisions by carriers require regulatory approval, so there is often a long regulatory delay associated with any price negotiation. Several alternatives should be considered, however.

Existing Tariffs. Telephone carriers do not sell network services under agreements between buyer and seller, as other businesses do. They file a price schedule, called a tariff, with their regulatory commission. Once the regulatory commission approves, the services are offered at those standard prices to any user. Most tariffs in use today were designed primarily for voice or data transmission and may be inappropriately high for the capacity required for video transmission. Some tariffs do provide for high volume discounts, off-peak discounts, or government discounts. Educators should not assume that they have to pay standard rates under existing tariffs, if they can allow enough time to negotiate appropriate rates with their carrier and wait for the regulatory approval of the negotiated rates.

"Dark Fiber" Rates. Some telephone companies have offered special rates for access to fiber optic capacity that would otherwise be unused ("dark"). Educators should ask if the carrier has ever offered such rates. If so, the regulatory commission may require it to be offered to others requesting comparable access.

"Free" Project Access. Sometimes, carriers may offer use of their facilities free of charge for a limited duration trial or demonstration project. Educators should look carefully at such offers and, if they accept, plan for the transition to paying the full rates when the free period is over. They should be careful not to get locked into a situation that may be costly in the future, despite the attraction of free service at the beginning.

Special Reduced Prices. To show their commitment to the community or region, or to showcase their technology, carriers may agree to offer educators access to their facilities at reduced rates. Two models are used now:

Waiver: The state's regulatory commission approves a waiver of the existing tariff for educational applications, based on the benefits to the community or state that would otherwise not be obtained. The waiver is generally approved on a case-by-case basis, and may apply only to some carriers or for a limited period.

Special tariff: A special tariff may be approved for educational applications. For example, in Maine, the carriers provide access to educators at cost, in an agreement negotiated between the state and the telephone company (Silkman, 1991). In Kansas, the Kansas Corporation Commission (KCC) created a special class of "Economic Development Rates" based on incremental rather than fully allocated cost accounting. These rates are determined on a case-by-case basis, and are designed to recognize the unique circumstances and economic development potential of a particular project or service (Davidson and others, 1990). This special rate has been applied to an educational interactive video project in Kansas involving three telephone companies.

Dedicated versus Metered Use. Prices differ depending on whether capacity is obtained by the minute or by the month. Monthly leased-line charges allow unlimited access for a fixed monthly charge. Especially during a start-up phase, when the amount of use is low, it may be more appropriate to negotiate a rate based on the amount of use. Usage-sensitive tariffs for video or high speed data channels are not yet common in the industry, but there is no reason why the carrier could not offer and get regulatory approval for such a tariff, if requested by users. Switched 56 kilobit capacity for compressed digital video use is the kind of "metered" use tariff most commonly available today. Others could be offered.

"Virtual" Networks/Volume Discounts. A hybrid form, halfway between metered use and dedicated leased channels, also may be explored. The telephone carrier may agree to make the channel capacity for video distance education available whenever needed, but reserve the right to sell any unused capacity to other customers. Prices may be based on a steep volume-discount price that is attractive, compared to dedicated leased lines, but with the convenience of on-demand access. These network arrangements are called "virtual" networks because they are available when needed without requiring the customer to pay a full leased channel price.

Fractional T1 Tariffs. Many telephone carriers offer leased lines for 56 kilobits or for 1.5 megabits (T1 rate) per second of data transmission, but no capacity in between. Some carriers offer "fractional T1" tariffs for channel capacities between these two extremes. In order to get an appropriate channel capacity at a reasonable price, it may be necessary to work with the telephone carrier to get regulatory approval for a tariff offering exactly what is needed for the distance learning application.

6. BRIDGING THE GAP

If there is one common denominator to the success stories of projects using telecommunications for rural development, it is that new bridges have to be built—between rural communities and state government, between rural development experts and telecommunications experts, between "the experts" who speak in technical jargon and the lay public whose future is being decided. Traditionally, each of these groups has worked in relative isolation from the other, with little professional interaction. Now these groups are finding ways to bridge the barriers they once separated them. They are gaining a better understanding of rural development needs; users are learning about the options available to them; policy makers are learning more about the communities and businesses their policies affect; and the interdisciplinary, intercultural discussions are unleashing the real potential of telecommunications—perhaps best illustrated by the Washington State experience (see chapter 5).

In times past, much of the telecommunications industry was slow-moving and bureaucratic. Carriers had a "one-size-fits-all" approach to customers. Now they are beginning to become more marketing-oriented. They are learning that services need to be developed and priced in response to specific customer needs. As they continue their transformation into marketing organizations, they will become better able to respond quickly to the specific needs of their customers. Then they will measure success one customer and one community at a time. Of course, more regulatory changes will be required to change the incentives for the carriers so that they can make customers their primary focus and be rewarded when they provide the facilities and services needed by the communities they serve.

As the telecommunications industry and its regulators learn how important modern telecommunications facilities are for development, there is a danger that people will get the idea that telecommunications is *the* answer to rural development problems. Although telecommunications is one essential element of development, telecommunications, by itself, is not enough. Development does not result from putting the necessary infrastructure in place, but from the creative use of that infrastructure by people, businesses and communities. Improved quality of life and economic well-being do not result from telephone switches and cables; they result from the ways in which education, health care and social services are improved and businesses made more productive.

Ultimately, rural development is a community process. There is an old saying, "You can lead a horse to water, but you can't make it drink." State development agencies cannot make rural development happen. Development depends on local leadership, local initiative and local cooperation. Many of the projects described in this chapter relied on local leaders with the vision to imagine new economies for their towns or regions, and a commitment to bring about change. The projects often require cooperation between rural communities or development agencies and telecommunications carriers or regulators.

Although responsibility will always fall on local residents, state development agencies can at least ensure that every community has available the basic infrastructure necessary for development. Development agencies should work with the state regulatory commission to ensure that telephone carriers have appropriate incentives to put a basic "equal opportunity" telecommunications infrastructure in place for all rural communities. Every community should have universal access to single-party touchtone telephone service with quality sufficient for reliable voice, data and facsimile transmission.

Beyond putting basic infrastructure in place, state development agencies should "look for thirsty horses." They should help the communities that do have the leadership, initiative and cooperation to attempt development projects making use of telecommunications. Some projects, including distance education initiatives, require more advanced telecommunications than basic touchtone telephone service. State development agencies, including state education departments, can help "thirsty" communities obtain the advice and advanced facilities they need. The AgriTechnics project in Washington State, discussed in chapter 5, is a good example.

These efforts will not bear fruit without local commitment. Community development doesn't just happen; it is a process that depends on local people. Many of the projects described in this chapter relied on local leaders with the vision to imagine new economies or improved education for their towns or regions, and a commitment to help bring about change. The projects often required cooperation between rural communities or development agencies and telecommunications carriers or regulators. As the telecommunications and rural development cultures learn about each other, new patterns of cooperation will emerge. Local leaders, state development agencies, telecommunications carriers and regulators will bridge the gap by cooperating to achieve development goals in their state and local communities.

Local Perspectives on Telecommunications and Development: Four Community Studies

This chapter explores how four different rural communities and their nearby regions promote community development. The four sites— Glendive, Montana; Kearney, Nebraska; Demopolis, Alabama; and Eagle Pass, Texas—were selected because of their varying geographic, economic and population characteristics and because of their varying uses of information technologies, especially telecommunications. We discovered that each community faces unique development challenges, with distinctive opportunities for telecommunications to make a difference. By looking in depth at how different communities chose to view development and how, or whether, they considered the role of telecommunications in their development, we hope to shed some light on the complex and subtle dynamics of this process.

1. BACKGROUND

In selecting communities for this study, we deliberately focused on the context in which telecommunications and other tools are used (for example, a town's economic history, political tenor, industrial base, worker demographics, geographic location) rather than on particular types of telecommunications applications (for example, business uses, distance learning). This represents something of a departure from previous research in that our net was thrown wide in an attempt to understand the *relative* role of

This chapter is based on a longer research report by Sharon Strover and Frederick Williams, "Rural Revitalization and Information Technologies in the United States," prepared for The Aspen Institute and The Ford Foundation. Austin, TX: University of Texas, 1991.

telecommunications in the development equation. Our assumption, based on our earlier research, was that the community context for telecommunications systems greatly influences the types of telecommunications needed and the effectiveness with which they are used. In particular, we hoped to assess the role of community involvement and community leadership in rural development and in use of telecommunications.

An earlier research project, *Telecommunications and Rural Development: A Study of Business and Public Service Applications* (Schmandt, Williams, Wilson and Strover, 1991), studied telecommunications applications and situations at 37 sites, with only the most minimal examination of community setting. The general conclusion of that study was that *telecommunications is a necessary but not sufficient condition for development*.

But what might constitute a set of "sufficient conditions?" This chapter attempts to answer that question. By conducting a holistic study of communities—and then comparing and contrasting them—we hoped to learn more about the interaction of telecommunications use and economic development (or lack thereof) at the rural grass roots.

We pursued a case study approach because other types of studies often do not capture the elusive human, social and political processes by which towns and regions grow and decline. Most studies do not adequately examine how specific people, leadership strategies, technology decisions and telecommunications policies—local, state and federal—affect the process of economic development. For each community's economy, therefore, we focused on both its historical and current characteristics, plus its employment patterns and trends. Over the course of multiple visits to each community, we developed case profiles that identify a matrix of rural characteristics, development trajectories and telecommunications systems and uses. Also, to understand better the interaction between state policy and local results, we looked at various state policy initiatives in the states (Texas, Nebraska, Montana and Alabama) where the four communities are located.

2. QUESTIONS RAISED BY EARLIER RESEARCH

The earlier study, *Telecommunications and Rural Development*, examined how telecommunications could overcome rural disadvantages of low population density and large distances. Did large and small businesses overcome these rural disadvantages in different ways? How are public services provided? What role if any did telecommunications providers and their systems play in more remote areas? This detailed inquiry into these questions convinced us that it was important to learn more about the community context in which new telecommunications technologies become adopted.

One finding of *Telecommunications and Rural Development* was that patterns of commerce and accompanying residential growth tend to vary according to the geographic location of small communities relative to larger ones, and to one another. For example, as illustrated in Figure 4.1, we could identify such patterns as "hubs," "partnerships," "alliances," and "adjacencies." A hub community might offer shopping and services to smaller rural towns—such as occurred in Demopolis or Kearney, which served as resource centers for even smaller nearby towns. An alliance might arise when small towns work together—as Glendive did with several of its small neighboring towns. (Spatially, however, Glendive is also somewhat of an isolate.) "Adjacencies" result when the economy of a small community feeds off that of a larger neighbor—as Eagle Pass does with respect to the large Mexican city, Piedras Negras, which lies across the Rio Grande.

These spatial patterns can influence greatly the types of businesses that may develop, the kinds of markets they can serve, and the types of telecommunications that can be useful. Spatial patterns of commerce and residential growth also affect the delivery of public services. For example, the sharing of educational resources among several towns is most feasible when they are configured in an "alliance" spatial pattern. A town with "hub" pattern has a better chance of surviving difficult times since its offerings are presumably more diverse or better developed than those in other local towns that rely on its resources.

Figure 4-1   Geographic Patterns for Rural Development

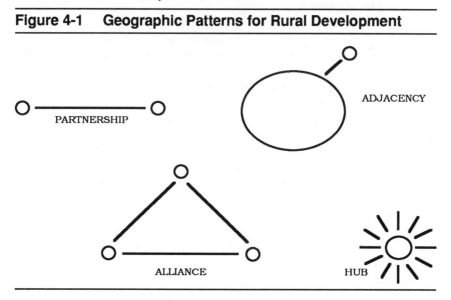

Telecommunications and Rural Development also revealed that the availability of telecommunications varies greatly from community to community. For example, we found striking differences between large and small businesses in rural locations. Large enterprises, such as the Wal-Mart discount stores, often have sophisticated telecommunications networks that bypass the public network. Some small businesses such as hardware stores or pharmacies may use computer-based systems for inventory and ordering. However, many rural small businesses rarely use even the most basic information technologies. Their knowledge of telecommunications services and equipment other than the telephone is generally limited to those offered by the local telephone company. With little exposure to such services as 800 numbers, alternate long-distance providers or value-added services, many small businesses in rural America never even consider the use of such telecommunications.

Ignorance about telecommunications possibilities has similarly limited rural demand for innovative public service applications. Rural regions often do not have the service providers or "pioneers" who have installed advanced telecommunications systems. This makes it difficult for local governments and schools to envision how telecommunications could help them. For example, the earlier study examined interactive television classrooms in Minnesota and satellite-delivered courses offered at various sites in the United States via the Texas-based TI-IN network (Schmandt and others, 1991). But many schools that saw the value of such services and wanted to install them often had no realistic way of doing so: they lacked the funds and the expertise.

Sometimes, a pioneering business that adopts a new telecommunications system opens the door for the rest of the community. That is what happened, for example, in Kerrville, Texas, when a resort owner bought the same computing and telecommunications package previously purchased by the local hospital. She saw advantages not just in the system itself but in sharing the talents of a local expert. These anecdotal examples prompted us to wonder if this diffusion process is common and how it might be accelerated.

Telecommunications and Rural Development also revealed the critical role played by the local telecommunications provider. A telephone company whose representatives live in and are personally involved in the rural community tends to be more responsive to local needs. They can readily offer needed telecommunications services and play an active role in community development. Such providers are typically locally owned or cooperative carriers. Although larger companies such as Bell operating companies or GTE generally provide acceptable service to their communities, they do not, by comparison, have as much personal contact with local businesses, schools and public officials. As a result, the staff of larger companies generally are not as involved in local rural development. Although large companies often express a willingness to help (by sponsoring a development workshop, for example), they have to be asked. Yet in most small rural communities, people rarely think to ask.

The *Telecommunications and Rural Development* study suggested to us that one of the most significant factors in rural telecommunications usage may be the community context. Armed with evidence about the role of a community's spatial characteristics, civic culture, local economic trends, and information needs, we decided to explore further.

3. THE FOUR COMMUNITIES

If telecommunications is a "necessary but not sufficient" condition for development, what can we postulate about the "sufficient" conditions for development? To answer this question, we identified rural towns in different parts of the country and then compiled a macroeconomic profile of the community and its changes over time. We next examined possible linkages between these changes and the community context, as gleaned from dozens of personal interviews with people representing a broad cross-segment of the community. We used this approach to identify the relative role of telecommunications in the development process.

The four communities were selected for their regional and economic differences, as well as for their varied applications (and potential applications) of telecommunications. (See Map 4-1.) These communities are:

Eagle Pass, Texas. This site is a rural border community of 28,000, with a population that is 90 percent Hispanic. In 1990, the Eagle Pass unemployment rate hovered at 35 percent. Its economy is in transition from agriculture to one based on trade and transborder manufacturing with the much larger Piedras Negras on the Mexican side of the border—an "adjacency" relationship. Not surprisingly, trade policies of the United States, Texas and Mexico are very important to Eagle Pass' economic development, particularly since it is a "maquiladora" (twin plant) center, with over 36 maquiladoras currently operating and more in the planning stages. (Maquiladora in Spanish refers to sharing proceeds from an effort, as when a person hired to harvest another's grain is given a share in payment. Here, it refers to plants taking advantage of a policy that allows foreign manufacturers to establish plants and use Mexican labor on partly finished materials in a zone along the Mexican border, and then to export them to the United States tariff-free.)

Map 4-1 Location of the Four Study Sites

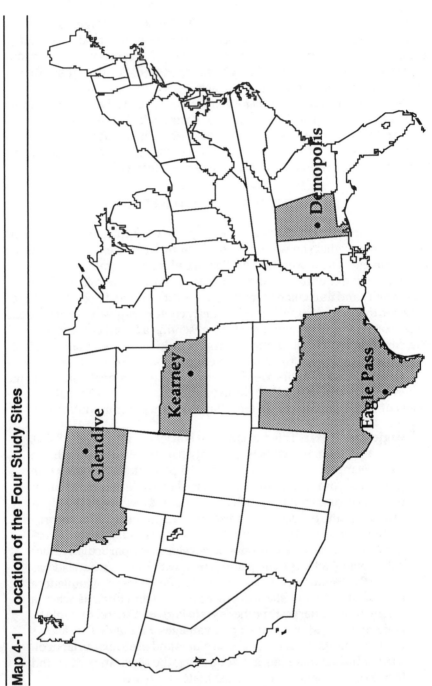

Transborder telecommunications play a vital role in the larger pattern of commerce in the region. Currently, differences in Mexican-U.S. technologies, telecommunications and trade policies, and cultural barriers make it difficult to use sophisticated transborder telecommunications. This, in turn, hinders certain commercial activities. Besides stimulating commerce, improved telecommunications could mean improved education in the Eagle Pass area, in part because enhanced educational offerings (via telecommunications) could help integrate young Mexican-Americans into the U.S. economy. Southwestern Bell serves the local Eagle Pass region; AT&T is the primary international long distance carrier.

Demopolis, Alabama. Demopolis is a community of 8,000 in a growing "hub" relationship with other nearby small towns. The regional population, about 25,000, is about equally divided between blacks and whites. Unlike other small towns in the South, the economy of Demopolis is fairly strong. Two large paper mills provide several thousand jobs. Local leadership, while emphasizing racial harmony and cooperation, has sought economic diversification. Until 1948, Demopolis was a conventional small town relying primarily on local sawmills for its employment opportunities. This changed in 1957 when Gulf States Paper built a large, modern paper plant nearby. A few years later, James River Corporation built another one further from town. Both companies have made a commitment to the local community that goes well beyond jobs.

Demopolis is now in transition from an economy based on agriculture to one based on light manufacturing and pulp mills. The town has enjoyed a significant spin-off benefit from the paper mills' heavy reliance on telecommunications, which the mills use for internal networking and to support geographically dispersed management. These improvements allow the mills to remain competitive and technologically advanced. Demopolis also presents several examples of small businesses struggling to acquire the telecommunications equipment and consulting services needed for advanced applications. Demopolis enjoys a relatively low unemployment rate, but it suffers from low wages and low educational attainment. Community leaders, aware of this latter shortcoming, are considering ways to improve the quality of local education. Demopolis is served by BellSouth. Several long distance carriers serve the area.

Glendive, Montana. Glendive is an isolated community of 8,000. Of the four communities we studied, Glendive faces the most extreme privation. Although near an interstate highway, it is quite remote from other towns. The nearest sizable population center is Miles City, with 8,000 residents, 80 miles to the west. Located in Dawson County in eastern Montana, Glendive is more culturally and geographically proximate to the wide, open spaces of North Dakota, 40 miles away, than to the mountainous regions of western Montana.

Glendive's remoteness from the population centers of the state—Helena and Butte, in western Montana—has resulted in a corresponding lack of political clout in shaping or taking advantage of the state's economic development policy. The larger cities in Montana are active adversaries in nearly every significant state-supported development initiative; tiny Glendive has little influence in these debates.

Agriculture, in the form of cattle ranching and grain farming, has been the traditional mainstay of the local economy. Oil and mining were once lucrative activities, but both the agricultural and natural resource base of Glendive's economy has severely eroded following the drought of the 1980s, insect infestations and plummeting world oil prices. The town lost half its population during the 1980s, and is now struggling to maintain itself. In its quest to replace its aging agricultural and oil-based industries, Glendive is examining the potential of various alternate businesses. Its prospects in this regard are enhanced by the presence of a very active local telephone carrier, Mid-Rivers Telephone Cooperative, which serves sparsely populated areas around the town. The town itself is served by US West. The presence of two companies serving the region has led to some interesting opportunities, such as Mid-Rivers' offering of distance education services in US West territory, and US West's later endeavors to do the same for the local community college.

Kearney, Nebraska. Kearney is a "hub" community of 24,000 on the western rim of Nebraska's most populous region. Kearney was selected for this study primarily because an interexchange carrier (AT&T) has installed a POP in a large, telemarketing-based firm there. The POP is the interexchange carrier switch that ordinarily connects the local exchange circuits to the long distance network. Normally, a customer's long distance costs include a payment (called an access charge) that goes to the local exchange company. In this case, the telemarketing firm, Cabela's, and other users piggybacking onto Cabela's technology could dial directly into the long distance network, thus reducing those charges and enabling them to take advantage of special software to make their calling easier. Kearney also was interesting because the town itself has a progressive, visionary plan for its development. One important priority in Kearney's development plan was to obtain an advanced telecommunications infrastructure, which the town has used to develop several telemarketing and "back office" telecommunications-intensive businesses.

Kearney has been part of the boom of telemarketing-oriented businesses, which spread throughout the Midwest in the late 1980s. Unlike many rural Midwest towns, however, the telemarketing and back-office businesses in Kearney operate alongside well established branch plant manufacturing operations that also use innovative telecommunications. The branch plants, which have been based in Kearney much longer than the telemarketing operations, give Kearney a diversified economic base. The local exchange carrier for Kearney is GTE, and the main long distance carrier is AT&T, although other long distance carriers also are available.

Of particular interest in Kearney are the spin-off benefits generated by the telecommunications infrastructure used by Cabela's, the area's largest telemarketer. This infrastructure is on the verge of serving several other local clients, who may gain new capabilities and reap new efficiencies as a result. Such efficiencies, however, will exact a cost. The local carrier, GTE, will certainly lose revenue from access charges as AT&T's capabilities are more fully exploited.

For the future, Kearney is systematically exploring ways to continue its economic diversification. Since Kearney functions as an economic, educational and service hub for the region, the town may exploit telecommunications for various public services, especially in elementary and secondary schools, and the local college and hospital.

Table 4-1 summarizes key aspects of each of the communities.

In studying Eagle Pass, Demopolis, Glendive and Kearney, we were most concerned with three major issues:

Economic development at the local level. The near-term view of each community's economic history was analyzed from county census data, community information and local interviews. Against this backdrop, we looked at current development projects and the relevance of telecommunications to them.

Table 4-1 — Community Comparisons

	DEMOPOLIS	EAGLE PASS	GLENDIVE	KEARNEY
Current Population:	7,600 (town)	21,407	6,000 (town)	22,000 (town)
Ethnic Composition:	53% Black; 45% White	90% Hispanic, 7% White	98% White	99% White
Major Industries:	Paper making and mill, lumber finishing, other food and chemical processing.	Cattle, farming, maquila, manufacturing, trade.	Cattle, grain; previously oil.	Cattle, crops, manufacturing, services (medical and education).
Unemployment:	11.1%	30%	6%	4.6%
Location:	West central Alabama, 50 miles east of larger Meridian, MS.	Border town on Rio Grande; larger Piedras Negras is trade partner.	Eastern Montana. Although off I-94, Glendive is remote from urban centers. Has experienced severe economic recession since late 1980s.	On the rim of the more rural part of Nebraska and off I-80, Kearney is a regional hub.
Important Features:	Local forests provide resource base; local high technology manufacturing plants provide bulk of employment.	Eagle Pass is an international trade area; it is a transitional place for both people and goods. Heavy influence of Mexican culture and Spanish language.	Population out-migration during 1980s. Diminishing tax base threatens schools. Newly organized economic development task force has had some success in recruiting a VA facility to locate in Glendive.	Basically a full-employment town, Kearney has a diversified economy and has taken a very active role in planning for its development.
Key Issues:	Economic development, desegregation, improving educational achievement.	Improving school system, economic development (jobs), poverty.	Economic development, improving agriculture.	Economic development, new telecommunications businesses.
LEC:	BellSouth	Southwestern Bell	US West serves the town; surrounding area served by Mid-Rivers Telephone Cooperative, a state-of-the-art telco interested in providing regional distance education.	GTE; AT&T, however, installed a point-of-presence (POP) in a local telemarketing firm.
Other Telecommunications:	Schools use Whittle and TI-IN; large businesses are developing private telecommunications systems with fiber and computers.	Infrastructure not integrated. Other broadband services important (cable, TV). Phone services for cross-border traffic important. Schools use TI-IN.	The schools' interactive television endeavors with Mid-Rivers may prove the broader utility of telecommunications to this community.	The POP may provide cheaper interexchange service to other business users and an incentive to other entities that may want to use it.

The demand profile. We wanted to know what telecommunications services were needed for the community's services and development. More specifically, what "demands" existed among large and small businesses, and among providers of public services? What infrastructure characteristics were important for economic and community development?

Cultivating the developmental view. We sought to generalize about how to stimulate a developmental view of telecommunications in these communities. We found that economic development, particularly if it includes using communications capabilities, requires the involvement of the widest variety of citizens and stakeholders. These include community development officials, regional development groups, the local telephone company and other telecommunications providers, local business and labor leaders, social service providers, elected and appointed officials, law enforcement officials, and health care administrators, to name a few. State utility commissions and development offices and sometimes education offices also need to coordinate their policies.

Each of these three issues is next discussed in more detail.

4. STRATEGIES FOR DEVELOPMENT AT THE LOCAL LEVEL

Over the past decade, development experts have come to realize that the most successful, enduring forms of development rely upon uniquely local resources and the activism of community groups and citizens. "Smokestack chasing" and other conventional development approaches offer industries incentives if they will invest or relocate in a town—a strategy that has often had disappointing results, especially in rural areas. When scores of industrial parks were built in the 1970s and 1980s, town officials often naively assumed that if attractive facilities are available, new industry would automatically come. These traditional approaches generally have not spurred revitalization in rural communities. In fact, spending public monies on unsuccessful development ventures often led to bitter disappointment.

In 1987, Nebraska authorized tax incentives for businesses that created certain numbers and types of jobs. The legislation, LB 775 (The Nebraska Employment and Investment Growth Act), was enacted partly because businesses threatened to leave the state if they did not get such breaks. Although the legislation did help to create new jobs, many Nebraskans came to realize that fundamental development goals were not really advanced.

Did the legislation truly change basic investment decisions? Did it alter business strategies? Did local economies gain greater long-term stability? Did rural areas benefit from the tax incentive? The answers to these questions are not always clear, but many state officials believe there are better ways to foster long-term development than to grant quick-fix tax breaks.

The problem with tax incentives, industrial parks and other conventional development strategies is that they usually do not address the core problems facing rural communities. Most rural areas in the United States have limited resources with which to attract new investment. (In our study, Kearney, with its diversified economy, is a notable exception to the rural norm.) Broad-gauged development strategies that are aimed at any and all industrial investment are not likely to succeed in rural regions. Instead, development plans should seek to cultivate directly a community's unique local resources.

A two-part strategy appears to make the most sense for rural development. First, the community itself must face up to its problems and opportunities. It must embark upon a deliberate review of its local resources—human, physical, business, geographical and otherwise—and devise a well-informed development plan. Secondly, the community must evaluate the nature and size of local demand factors (for example, labor, facilities, materials, supplies) and figure out how to achieve economies of scale.

The central consideration in rural development planning should be locational advantages. Could a town improve its opportunities through "hub" or "alliance" arrangements with nearby towns? Could new telecommunications systems be used to aggregate supply or demand? Could improvements in the school system or other public services make the town more attractive to certain types of businesses or employees? All these strategies are an explicit focus of development in Kearney.

Although "more jobs" is often the most urgent concern a town faces, no development plan is likely to succeed unless it takes a deeper look at a community's core problems and needs. New businesses, whether indigenous or recruited, will not flourish if a significant number of community resources—schools, health care, public services, physical infrastructure, telecommunications, and quality-of-life amenities—are dysfunctional. Success in securing "more jobs"—which is to say, jobs that are relatively secure over the long term and better-paying—generally requires a probing, holistic evaluation of the entire community and its unique resources.

In this process, cooperation among the town's leading businesses, citizen groups and government officials can yield impressive results. For example, in the 1960s, when faced with federal desegregation mandates, many local Demopolis leaders, black and white, agreed to work together in a positive, constructive manner to make the local school district the cornerstone of their efforts. They have been rewarded with a school district that routinely wins high achievement test scores for its part of the country, which is the chief reason that many families choose to settle in Demopolis. Today, business and community leaders in Marengo county proudly tell their story of racial cooperation—and point to the faltering economies of smaller neighboring towns which instead developed segregated "white academies" and let the public education system deteriorate. An educated workforce, Demopolis realized quite early, is an important foundation of economic and community well-being.

Cooperation can take many other forms: local businesses collaborating with the public schools, telephone companies working with the local economic development commission, and small retailers sharing telecommunications with large plants. In Kearney, the top executives of Cabela's, the large catalog sales firm, realize that its prosperity partly depends upon its ability to help the community. To ensure that the students it employs could stay in their dorms and continue to work during holidays, Cabela's worked out an arrangement with the local college. In exchange, the firm has given scholarships and other benefits to the college. When the firm deployed an AT&T POP switch in its plant, other telecommunications-intensive businesses in town realized they might have the option of "piggybacking" on Cabela's POP.

Eagle Pass offers a negative example: although its economy is briskly growing, many observers of the Mid Rio Grande Valley area feel that Eagle Pass could benefit greatly from imminent trade agreements with Mexico, but only if its constituency made a more orchestrated effort to take advantage of change. The lack of local cooperation and group planning may cause this community to lose some benefits from U.S.-Mexico free trade.

In essence, these cooperative efforts are methods of building upon a community's existing resources. Instead of waiting for the state or federal government to arrive with a revitalization plan that may or may not serve local needs, members of a community often can identify promising strategies simply by working together. Of course, new projects immediately raise concerns about risk and incentive: Who stands to benefit from initiating a risky venture? Who stands to lose? If a community can find ways to pool risks and rewards, and thereby build a spirit of trust, cooperative ventures stand much more chance of success.

The Role of Telecommunications

A primary appeal of telecommunications is its ability to bring people together and thereby stimulate new cooperation, new economic activity, and new bonds of community. Businesses can offer new services to customers; schools can offer new types of instruction to students; government services can be more responsive and efficient. From a more conceptual standpoint, telecommunications can overcome the traditional rural penalty of low population density by linking people or institutions together regardless of distance.

Despite these opportunities, many telephone companies are curiously indifferent. Kearney's local phone company, GTE, has been so wedded to conventional business and service offerings that the source of the town's telecommunications-based innovations has been users and competitive long distance carriers. In the past, GTE had helped in local business recruitment (to expand the customer base for its services), but it has done little more. Southwestern Bell in south Texas has shown a similar lack of interest in rural telecommunications. The large local exchange company has focused mainly on urban areas, upgrading its urban network and shifting its employees to more populous areas.

This sluggish attitude among telephone providers owes much to the traditional "utility mentality" among telecommunications providers. Immune from competition, telephone companies have had few incentives to improve service or be more responsive to the economic development needs of their communities. The Bell operating companies (BellSouth in Demopolis, US West in Glendive, and Southwestern Bell in Eagle Pass) offer what most people would consider "quite adequate" service. Yet none of the companies has much direct presence in economic development activities. Since divestiture of the Bell system in 1984, the local exchange companies have implemented cost-cutting programs that have replaced employees with equipment and eliminated local payment offices, sales persons, and in smaller towns, community relations employees. With fewer opportunities to "rub shoulders" with local business leaders, Bell company managers and workers are less attuned to community economic needs and less prone to mount their own development initiatives. Although large companies may be willing to help, community leaders would first have to ask, and they rarely do.

By contrast, community-owned cooperatives tend to be more responsive to their rural constituencies and more eager to innovate. In the Glendive, Montana region, the Mid-Rivers Telephone Cooperative is collaborating with local school officials to develop a distance education system. Beset with low population densities in locations dispersed across an area as large as West Virginia, the Glendive area school systems have struggled to offer the courses their few students need; sharing resources within the region is a logical answer. With partial financial support from Mid-Rivers for equipment and facilities, the schools launched an experiment in shared courses that could greatly enhance the quality of education in the Glendive region. (Similar projects also are found in several other states; see chapter 3.) Although the Glendive schools lie in US West's territory, the company has not objected to Mid-Rivers' activity here; interestingly enough, after Mid-Rivers' initiative, US West agreed to carry the community college's signal out to some adjacent communities on its lines.

Given the differences in developmental interests between Bell operating companies and community-owned cooperatives, it seems clear that policy changes should be considered. Current regulatory schemes affecting telecommunications carriers limit the incentives to invest in these regions. If telecommunications is an important infrastructure for rural economic development—and we believe it is—then the absence of incentives for local telephone company involvement hinders community development.

High-density urban areas are the most attractive markets for telecommunications because providers easily obtain economies of scale. Economies of scale in telecommunications, and the resulting user benefits of lower prices and service differentiation, are harder to achieve in rural areas. New regulatory policies may be necessary to create new incentives for telephone carriers to invest in upgrading rural telecommunications networks and providing new services to rural users. Recommendations for such regulatory incentives are discussed in chapter 7.

Apart from the responsiveness of the local telephone provider, there are at least two other factors that account for innovative telecommunications applications in the four towns we studied: entrepreneurial expertise from outside the locality and broad community support for a development project.

We observed that someone from another setting, with new ideas and different experiences, often sees possibilities that a town's natives do not. In Kearney, Cabela's long distance POP was devised by a newly hired telecommunications consultant and AT&T representatives, both from outside the community. Fortunately, Cabela's and community leaders were wise enough to see both the immediate and broader applications of the new technologies.

In Demopolis, the outside catalyst came in the form of new plant managers, who had lived elsewhere and been exposed to alternate ways of thinking about the relationship between technology and industry. In time, young executives working at Demopolis' paper mills shared their sophistication about computers and telecommunications with local officials, and the idea of introducing telecommunications to the local public schools was born.

Broad community support can be vital to the acceptance and success of an innovative development project. When interacting with new technologies or new applications of them, users want to have some decision making power and control. Technologies or technology applications imported from outside settings may or may not meet specific user needs. In any event, users must feel a sense of ownership and comfort with new systems if the technology is going to be used to meet genuine needs. Again, Kearney offers a good illustration. The town's businesses and development officials did not "parachute" the technology in, ignoring local needs and opportunities. They considered site placement, employment needs of local students and spin-off business applications, so that multiple, mutually reinforcing purposes could be served.

5. THE DEMAND PROFILE FOR RURAL TELECOMMUNICATIONS SERVICES

Generally speaking, rural business demand for telecommunications is growing. Large businesses generally obtain the services they need; they usually have the internal resources to plan and purchase the facilities and services. Sometimes they can get what they need through the local exchange network; other times they cannot. But a Wal-Mart or other large business usually has the means to get the telecommunications it wants.

For the larger universe of potential users, however—small businesses, local government, the schools, private individuals—demand for advanced telecommunications often is stymied by a lack of technical know-how, a fractured array of telecommunications vendors, disinterest among telephone carriers, and artificial barriers created by federal and state telecommunication policies. Small rural businesses tend to have few problems with routine telecommunications services. Their problems begin when they want to plan new services, obtain rapid installation of new equipment and, sometimes, when they want repairs. Most of these businesses do not have the resources to investigate innovative uses of telecommunications themselves. A host of interrelated factors can be blamed: the scarcity of technical expertise in rural America, the traditional barriers of distance and low population density, the "utility mentality" of many telephone providers, and outdated telecommunications policies.

Yet these barriers are not insuperable, as the Electronic Marketing Resource Group (EMRG) demonstrated. EMRG, an entrepreneurial start-up firm in Kearney that specializes in telemarketing and financial aid forms processing, did not receive technical support from local telecommunications providers. The company's founder, Dave Waldron, simply had the determination and expertise to do the job himself. As an entrepreneur who wanted to start a new business, Waldron taught himself what he needed to know about telecommunications and then went out and bought the necessary systems.

In Demopolis, Kim Mayton is another entrepreneur who used telecommunications to achieve a competitive advantage for his business, One-Stop Building Supply. Realizing that an important need in the building supply business is proximity to one's customers, Mayton speculated that his business could gain a competitive edge if he could open multiple retail outlets in the small towns of the region. It would not be necessary to have an office at every site, he reasoned, if he could centralize his administrative operations by linking the main computer in his Demopolis headquarters to terminals in three smaller outlets. It was an inspired business strategy. Yet Mayton faced an uphill struggle in dealing with a variety of vendors to get the system working.

Both EMRG and One-Stop Building Supply overcame a problem that defeats many small businesses: an inability to make informed technical judgments about the confusing array of equipment and capabilities that so many different vendors are selling. In Eagle Pass, customs broker Reymundo Gonzalez has been frustrated in upgrading his telecommunications linkages with his "sister" offices. No single vendor can serve his needs, so he must deal separately with the local exchange company, a long-distance company, a computer company, a software consultant, and still another consultant—just to get the system working properly.

Rural demand for telecommunications is also lagging due to a Catch-22 of supply and demand. Some telephone company executives shrug: "Why offer technology and services that people are not asking for?" But potential rural customers reply: "But how can we ask for something we have never had the chance to see and experience?" The knowledge void about telecommunications means that demand cannot arise to elicit supply nor can supply move forward with any assurance that demand will appear. This stalemate is exacerbated by the movement of large users off the public network. As telephone companies lose this potential demand for advanced telecommunications, they have even less incentive—and less revenue—to upgrade service for small telecommunications users.

Despite the large potential demand for telecommunications, current telecommunications policy generally does not sufficiently recognize its role in economic development, especially in rural areas. State utility commissions tend to ignore how strategic uses of telecommunications might help rural areas (see chapter 2). As noted above, large local exchange companies have reduced their presence in rural communities since 1984—a fact that makes telecommunications-based development all the more difficult.

Demand for advanced transborder telecommunications in Eagle Pass is stymied by a welter of jurisdictional and policy issues, which over the years have only made existing telecommunications equipment and practices more entrenched. Although federal policy encourages trade with Mexico, as a practical matter this transborder "center of commerce" must muddle through one of the most complicated and cumbersome telecommunications environments imaginable. To set up any transborder services beyond the most basic voice service, one must deal with at least three providers—local exchange carrier, international carrier and Telmex (Mexico's national telephone company). The inevitable frustrations sometimes resulted in some illegal jerryrigged "bypasses" across the Rio Grande. There appear to be no immediate solutions to this problem beyond businesses continuing to pressure Mexican authorities to allow bypass on the Mexican side of the river. In late 1990, however, Southwestern Bell purchased an equity interest in the newly privatized Telmex, which could lead to new partnerships with transborder long distance carriers or more responsiveness to transborder telecommunications needs.

The strong community of interest between Eagle Pass and Piedras Negras results in extensive pent up demand for transborder communications and efforts to bypass the public network. It is tempting to consider a "free trade telecommunications zone" along the border. In practical terms, the communities might propose a meeting with Southwestern Bell and Telmex to discuss possible solutions to bottlenecks, and tariff options such as a flat rate or reduced rate for local calls within the transborder zone. The community also might invite the major international carriers to propose a special border zone tariff.

If one primary purpose of the AT&T divestiture of the Bell operating companies was to spur competition in telecommunications, it generally has not achieved economies of scale that benefit small rural communities. As telecommunications service has fractionalized—among the local exchange carriers, outlying rural cooperatives, long-distance carriers, equipment vendors, and consultants—none seems to be able to find sufficient business to provide the range of services found in urban areas. Rural America has the latent or disaggregated demand for most of the services used in urban regions. Yet few if any policy initiatives, federal or state, have been launched to help aggregate telecommunications demand that will improve the rural delivery of both government and commercial services.

Although there have been some innovative attempts to use telecommunications for distance education, none of the initiatives in the four states we examined seems to have been propelled by policy changes. No PUC, state education agency or development entity seemed to promote uses of telecommunications for education. Some were entirely unaware of potential applications. Although Montana and Nebraska have new programs that may promote telecommunications applications, they are still in an experimental stage. Eagle Pass would welcome two-way distance learning but no entity or agency seems willing to help the district develop the possibilities.

The impetus for most distance education examples came from the grass roots, often because of a local champion.

National organizations such as the TI-IN network or Whittle Communications satellite networks can be credited with introducing distance education in some locations in the four states we studied. These services have often been introduced in the face of criticism or skepticism, and their services are not seen as fundamental. Yet in every community we studied, there were serious financial shortfalls in the operations of the schools, and in each there is great potential for expanding communication satellite use or the pooling of resources through linking adjacent school districts. Incentives for local telephone companies to develop fiber-based switched networks could in turn increase the economies of scale for educational activities.

The Whittle Communications distance education example has been especially controversial among educators, because in return for "free" equipment, a school district is obligated to show a daily TV news program that contains a brief commercial segment. The program, criticized by some for a breezy treatment of news (Kleinfield, 1991), is delivered to schools using 19-inch color TV sets that the company purchases for cooperating schools. When a school agrees to carry the programming, Whittle also provides VCRs and satellite dishes, representing an investment of up to $50,000 per site. Despite the Alabama school commissioner's warning against adopting the Whittle plan, the Demopolis school district joined the system, explaining that if the state would not help, it would help itself. The Demopolis schools seem to like the Whittle program; students have used the Whittle equipment to develop their own modest TV studio and produce an experimental local news program.

Sites like Demopolis and Kearney have a large potential for serving as educational hubs for nearby school districts. If hooked into an electronic network, the schools could reap better economies of scale, introduce worker training programs to serve technology-based local industries, and build new links with community colleges and other educational resources. A similar networking of health care services also could improve people's access to services and reduce costs.

Cable television providers also could take a more developmental approach. In all four sites, the cable companies were modest operations with little inclination to assist in community development. This raises the question of whether telephone companies should be able to move into the cable television business (they can now operate in towns with fewer than 2,500 households). An argument in favor might be that such entry could create competition, increase the local phone company's economies of scale, and thus perhaps increase the local presence of the telephone company. On the other hand, the result could be the demise of the cable company, resulting in a new, more powerful monopoly over both telephone and cable television service; the greater economies of scale could be offset by the reduced incentive to respond to customer needs.

6. CULTIVATING THE DEVELOPMENT POINT OF VIEW:
POLICY IMPLICATIONS

The four communities offer a range of perspectives on how telecommunications can foster rural development. Despite their differences, the experience of the four communities provided two related principles: development strategies must be based on vigorous local involvement; and state policies and programs should provide incentives carefully structured to stimulate community participation.

We conclude that economic development must be nurtured among all segments of the community, from citizen groups to business leaders, from elected officials to the schools. The very process of devising a development plan should draw these disparate parties together. Building a consensus for change is important not only as matter of democratic accountability, but to ensure that the telecommunications applications selected are indeed responsive to authentic local needs. Only if several constituencies are involved in the process can the full potential of the new technologies can be exploited. New partnerships for using telecommunications—among several rural communities or among segments of a single rural community—have a large, untapped potential. Partnerships help achieve economies of scale that are otherwise unattainable, creating new "win-win" situations for everyone. The participants all gain new telecommunications capacities, and the process itself helps build the civic culture of rural regions. Finally, the new development technologies are supported by existing marketplace incentives, and do not rely upon artificial subsidies that may not be responsive to marketplace need or local demand. The success of this model is most evident in Kearney, whose telemarketing industry worked with the local development office and local college to create highly productive symbiotic arrangements (the employment of college students and the use of the AT&T POP by other local businesses).

The energy for change must originate with the community. Solutions cannot magically rain down upon a town from the state capital or other outsiders. The reason for this is almost self-evident: every community has special attributes, including its location, natural resources, schools, and workforce. The community must decide for itself how it wants to improve its lot; then and only then can it seek out appropriate aid from state government, potential investors, and others.

The citizens of Glendive suffered through many years of drought, repeated crop failures and a declining oil industry before its civic leaders decided to mobilize themselves to formulate a long-term development program. The group's initiative and persistence is paying off. Through a concerted, coordinated campaign, Glendive's leaders came together to lobby the state to locate a new state-financed veterans' hospital in the area. The town's development task force is also working closely with the telephone cooperative as it puts together the new distance education project for the region's schools. Glendive's success at creating new development opportunities for itself has inspired the state government to promote the Glendive example. The state is now holding seminars for small telephone companies to educate them about how to organize communities to use telecommunications in economic development programs.

Demopolis is another good example of a community that came to a consensus about its future and took bold, deliberate steps to achieve a new development vision. Its development has sought to exploit existing resources and serve local needs, rather than "import" an industry or business that may not integrate well with the region's workforce, natural resources or physical infrastructure.

Of our four towns, Eagle Pass is the one with the most internal disagreement about its future. The older land owners still see Eagle Pass as an agricultural community. Young, well-educated and mostly Hispanic leaders want to attract different sorts of businesses, rezone land and invest in better utilities (especially water) in low-income areas. Planning a coherent future for Eagle Pass is complicated further by a consistently divisive local newspaper.

State governments and economic development. State governments in our four cases generally tailored their development strategies around specific industries rather than existing community resources. In state government's thinking, the condition of local markets and the regional economy did not rank as important development considerations. What merited attention were the "hot" industries which, for any number of reasons, were preferred targets of state-assisted development.

In Nebraska, state government has decided to recruit new businesses in the food processing industry. At one time, the state did emphasize telecommunications as a valuable development tool, to the extent of opening a special office in the Department of Economic Development (which was closed down when the unit's primary backer, then-Governor Bob Kerrey, left office). Now, Nebraska focuses on perceived business needs in a statewide manner. Individual communities are left to their own devices, and may or may not have the expertise or leadership to seek out state funding assistance.

Texas also targets industries, not communities, in its state development plans. Given its budget deficit and ongoing troubles caused by the collapse of oil prices in the mid-1980s, Texas has limited development resources. Individual localities rarely receive focused attention unless they organize and lobby for special treatment. This is a major reason why border communities, represented by the Middle Rio Grande Valley Economic Development Council, have gotten some attention. The state's public utility commission did give unusual recognition to the development potential of telecommunications in the 1990 settlement of an overearnings case against the state's dominant local exchange carrier, Southwestern Bell. Dubbed "Texas First," the settlement traded an earnings rebate to consumers for a promise by Southwestern Bell that it would invest in an upgraded telephone infrastructure, with certain guaranteed improvements for rural communities. (In January 1991, the commission voted to approve a rehearing to reconsider parts of the settlement.)

Montana resembles Nebraska in its fundamental fiscal conservatism and has even fewer resources to commit to development programs. To date, its most ambitious rural development efforts have revolved around agricultural programs such as those staffed by extension agents. To their credit, these programs increasingly focus on local business revitalization, youth-at-risk and other community problems. But these programs are not well-equipped to lead economic development programs for small towns, both because they remain understaffed and because the staff tends to be more expert in scientific matters (for example, animal sciences) than in economic development issues.

By and large, state development policies and programs do not take much account of local resources and needs. Nor do they generally consider how telecommunications could help a community exploit new opportunities. For state bureaucracies, there are certain efficiencies and conveniences in pursuing industry-specific development plans. Yet the long-term value of such approaches is dubious, since they do not address the distinctive local needs of specific communities. We believe that state development efforts could yield far better results by paying more attention to the existing strengths of local economies and to the existing interests, pockets of expertise and types of workforces in different regions.

Another shortcoming of existing state development is its oversight of needy towns that do not have the leadership or expertise to seek state aid. Under current approaches, the same towns repeatedly end up winning state aid; they have the technical expertise, political connections and savoir faire to win the grants. From a state's perspective, too, bestowing aid on towns with good records carries fewer risks than aid to new and unknown communities. Under this common arrangement, other needy towns may never break into the aid cycle. If state development programs are truly going to reach the most needy and less developed regions, they must undertake a more aggressive outreach program to inform communities about state aid programs and help them submit applications.

State development officials would do well to help build and expand existing industries rather than recruit entirely new and alien ones. That way, development can build upon existing investments and expertise, and thus have a greater likelihood of thriving. States also could help communities undertake their own self-assessments, so they could bring together civic leaders, help them formulate future goals, and forge a specific development plan.

We found no state economic development efforts that sought to use regional alliances or partnerships to exploit realizable economies of scale in rural areas. Although scale economies are more important than ever in the today's global economy, most state development authorities seem not to realize that aggregating demand through telecommunications may be an effective way to spur development in rural America. Aggregating rural demand through telecommunications creates new economies of scale where they are otherwise absent. Towns can be allied with each other and reap the benefits enjoyed by much larger towns and cities—lower costs, access to diverse information sources, a greater differentiation of products and services. The development potential of such telecommunications alliances needs to be explored, recognized by local and state authorities, and tested in different marketplaces. Given the current disinterest in such schemes by many state development offices, much of the burden for such innovations will fall on communities themselves.

State public utility commissions. The PUCs in the four states studied showed only occasional interest in promoting development through telecommunications. The Nebraska commission, with its deregulated telecommunications environment, avoids any social role for telecommunications (against the dissent of PUC staff) and follows an extreme laissez-faire approach legislated by its unicameral legislature. However, in Texas, two of the three PUC members who recently voted in favor of an incentive regulation package ("Texas First"), after 18 months of hearings, publicly cited economic development as the reason for their votes. (The dissenting commissioner also supported an economic development strategy, but felt that the proposed incentive package had not been sufficiently evaluated to be approved.) Utility commissions in Montana and Alabama have acknowledged the importance of development considerations, but have been more concerned with traditional regulatory issues such as rates and ratemaking.

On the one hand, it is easy to fault these PUCs (and most others across the nation) for not taking a more direct, aggressive role in fostering state economic development. On the other hand, as discussed in chapter 2, few PUCs have any specific mandate to pursue development goals or even give them explicit consideration. As a practical matter, however, the interrelationships between state regulatory policy and local development need to be more directly addressed, whether through governmental commissions or task forces. The PUCs are in a crucial position to create incentives for telecommunications providers to assist rural communities.

Our research suggests that commissions could accomplish a great deal by focusing on such issues as Extended Area Service (which can facilitate regional alliance-building), incentives for innovative service offerings to rural areas, and ways to foster educational and health-related applications in rural areas. Regulators also would do well to recognize that policies based on urban economies may be inappropriate for rural areas. Theoretical assumptions about competitive markets and consumer demand tend to fail in more rural, remote communities. Regulators could encourage rural revitalization by altering some of their rules so that they reflect the needs of consensual, precarious, and less competitive communities so characteristic of rural America.

Telephone service providers. One of the most important development players on the local level is the telephone carrier. Fortunately, cooperatives tend to provide responsive service to their local customers, who, not coincidentally, are also their shareholders. Some rural independents are eligible for REA loans that can provide the capital for such state-of-the-art services as Glendive's (Mid-Rivers Telephone Cooperative) distance learning network.

As mentioned earlier, the Bell operating companies have a less direct involvement in rural economic development than locally owned companies. US West, the BOC serving the largest rural area in the United States, appears to have focused its initial post-divestiture energies on upgrading services in its more lucrative urban markets, such as Phoenix and Denver. As a result, its facilities in rural areas are generally inferior to those found in urban areas. This was certainly true of Glendive.

The same service orientation probably applies to large independents such as GTE, the carrier for Kearney. It comes as no surprise that on a national level the rural facilities of the RBOCs are technically not the equal of most small independents serving rural areas (see Appendix A). In general, the smaller rural telephone carriers tend to have better facilities and to provide more development support for rural communities than the larger carriers that lack management presence in rural communities.

In all four communities, the local telephone carrier was a large company: an RBOC in Glendive, Eagle Pass and Demopolis, and GTE in Kearney—although Glendive's surrounding area was served by a progressive cooperative. In no case were the large telephone companies particularly aggressive in promoting new ideas about telecommunications or development in their service to rural customers. The larger carriers with large urban markets and a monopoly franchise protecting them from competition in their rural service areas, do not have much financial incentive to improve rural service.

Therefore, state policy makers should devise incentives for rural telephone companies both to upgrade their facilities and ensure their creative use in community development. This strategy could include incentive programs to help upgrade the information and communications infrastructure of rural towns and regions.

Our investigations of Glendive, Kearney, Demopolis and Eagle Pass prompt several general observations about telecommunications and development. We believe state policy should:

• Create incentives for telephone companies to be more responsive to users, both in providing existing and new services;

• Develop strategies for aggregating telecommunications demand so that economies of scale can be realized by providers and users;

• Foster a long-term, community-based approach to economic development by promoting the active participation of diverse constituencies;

• Identify the areas where the telecommunications marketplace works adequately and where it does not, and then forge new policies to spur competition or compensate for its absence; and

• Set priorities for the most important social services in rural areas, such as education and health care delivery, and identify how telecommunications might aid them.

How can we get there from here? Chapter 7 provides a more specific agenda of recommendations based on these and other policy goals.

Rural Telecommunications and Economic Development in Washington State: A Case Study

There is no single process by which a state comes to see how telecommunications can enhance rural development. So much depends upon a state's political culture, economic base, existing telecommunications infrastructure, and myriad other factors. That said, it is instructive to look at how one state—Washington State—developed its rural telecommunications services in the 1980s to stimulate economic development, ensure social equity and promote community stability in rural areas. Washington is a state that "got its act together" on the issue of telecommunications for rural development. This chapter tells the story of that process.

Between 1983 and 1990, the rural residents of Washington State received significantly improved telephone services after many people—university professors, rural advocates, entrepreneurs, telecommunications experts, legislators and regulators—began to focus on the problems of rural telecommunications. As initial interest in the issue grew, a critical mass of researchers and advocates propelled changes in people's expectations and in state policy. A new body of literature and a new network of experts emerged; regulators started new policies and programs; carriers made significant new investments in telecommunications; and new varieties of rural development ensued.

This chapter describes the fitful, unpredictable, synergistic process of change in Washington State. While we do not propose the Washington experience as a prototype for other states, we do believe it exemplifies some general factors needed to stimulate change elsewhere.

This chapter is based on a report by Don A. Dillman, "Rural Telephone Infrastructure and Economic Development in Washington State: A Case Study," Technical Report 90-103 of the Social and Economic Sciences Research Center at Washington State University, Pullman, WA, 1990.

1. BACKGROUND

Until the 1980s, rural residents of Washington State had one primary telecommunications concern: voice communications, via "plain old telephone service" or POTS. Basic telephone service met most rural needs and was affordable and widely available. Such federal laws as the Communications Act of 1934 (which made universal service a national goal) and the 1949 amendments to the Rural Electrification Administration Act (which established low-cost loans to rural telephone providers) advanced the goal of universal access to basic telephone service. For the most part, these laws have been effective in improving rural telephone service.

The complications to rural telecommunications policy began with the divestiture of the Bell system in 1984, which separated the RBOCs from AT&T. Under the new regime mandated by a federal court, AT&T and other national companies provide long distance service competitively while local service remains a regulated monopoly controlled by the Bell operating companies and approximately 1,400 independent telephone carriers in their respective service areas.

The severing of long distance and local service provoked new fears among rural Americans that basic telephone service might not continue to be as affordable and widely available in the new competitive telecommunications environment. Historically, regulators had kept prices to rural users quite low—despite the higher cost of providing service to sparsely populated areas—by using long distance rates to subsidize local service. Long distance rates were based on distance, but not on specific routes, even though rural routes were more costly to provide than heavily used interurban routes. People feared that the AT&T divestiture would lead to "deaveraging" of service rates, so that each household or business would pay the full costs of obtaining basic telephone service—a policy that seemed likely to hurt rural communities. In thinly populated areas of the western United States where distances between telephone customers are often great, people worried that the per-household costs for basic telephone service would soar.

The FCC introduced a new "access charge" nationwide, which required customers in local exchanges to pay about $3.50 a month for access to long distance carriers. (Previously, this access was "free" because long distance rates included these costs.) The access charge placed another cost burden on all local telephone customers, including rural residents, although all users of long distance services had a compensating benefit of lower long distance rates.

As the AT&T breakup was threatening new costs for rural America, many rural regions began to suffer a worsening economic decline that persists to this day. Traditional rural industries such as agriculture and natural resource extraction, as well as newer rural manufacturing businesses, all suffered, often because of intensifying global competition. As these industries contracted, rural communities stagnated, their populations declined, new investment dried up, and conventional manufacturing jobs fled abroad. It soon became apparent that new jobs would not be created by traditional rural industries such as agriculture, manufacturing and natural resources industries, but by the burgeoning information-intensive services industry of the 1980s (Dillman and Beck, 1988; Parker and others, 1989).

The rural communities of Washington State were not immune from these national trends. As the average income of Seattle-area residents rose in relation to the national average, the average incomes in *all* other regions of the state were decreasing (Lidman and Lyons, 1987).

In the midst of these wrenching economic changes, many rural people began to realize that telecommunications and computerization had important applications for them. Farmers in the 1980s found new uses for personal computers and on-line data services (for example, for tracking farm finances and monitoring commodity prices). Unfortunately, many farmers could not use on-line services because their telephone service was on a multiparty line. Yet single-party service was often prohibitively high due to "suburban mileage charges," a higher monthly fee based on the customer's distance from the closest telephone switching facility.

In the 1980s, it was becoming clear that the growth of global markets would require competitive companies to rely increasingly upon computerized networks. Business enterprises also would have to exploit the new efficiencies of advanced telecommunications technologies such as digital switching and fiber optic connections, both of which would require modernization of the nation's telephone infrastructure.

Given the economic decline of rural areas and the continued growth of large cities, it seemed plausible that most new investments in modern telecommunications infrastructure would occur in cities, where economies of scale would be most likely to yield greater returns on investment and where competitive pressures were stimulating early investment. In theory at least, it seemed likely that high quality telephone service would be provided within and between cities using fiber optics that pass through the rural countryside—without necessarily providing access to the businesses and residents of those rural areas.

For rural leaders of Washington State, this prospect naturally raised concerns. They worried that their participation in the information- and computer-dependent economy of the 1990s might be foreclosed before they even realized what was occurring. Yet those rural leaders who wanted to mobilize to change things immediately confronted a huge research void about rural telecommunications. At the time, for example, there were virtually no data describing differences in rural and urban telephone needs. Regulators who might be sympathetic to rural concerns were understandably reluctant to require new telephone technologies or more rapid deployment of them without reliable data confirming need. Many regulators suspected, furthermore, that what rural areas really needed were broader applications of existing technology rather than new technology. Without any research about what rural subscribers needed or would pay for, such decisions were risky and problematic.

It was in this context that several academics, rural advocates, telecommunications experts and legislators in Washington State began a series of *ad hoc* campaigns to bring advanced telecommunications to rural regions. Over eight years, from 1983 to 1990, they documented various rural telecommunications needs, assembled an inventory of the infrastructure, and showed how information technologies and advanced telephone services would be vital to rural economic development. Largely because of these people's research and advocacy, the state's public utility commission, the Washington Utilities and Transportation Commission (WUTC), decided to eliminate multiparty line service throughout the state and to expand rural local calling areas. Perhaps more significantly, the state's development agencies are actively exploring new ways to exploit telecommunications to foster rural economic development.

The following case study describes how Washington State came to recognize the importance of telecommunications in rural development. It would be convenient if there were a single event or leader responsible for the changes in Washington. As it happened, however, the telecommunications revolution in rural Washington State occurred through the separate yet loosely organized work of many individuals and institutions. It was an evolutionary process in which the work of several individuals—a professor, a telephone company official, a regulatory commissioner, and others—provoked others to action. One research report would trigger a regulatory inquiry. One conference would result in a personal friendship, which would alert a telephone company about rural demand for certain services. Although it is impossible to trace direct causalities in how change occurred, the critical mass of people actively interested in rural telecommunications was surely an important engine for change.

2. THE AT&T DIVESTITURE PROMPTS NEW CONCERN

Although state policy makers often discussed rural telephone service before 1983, the AT&T divestiture scheduled for 1984 promised to change the entire landscape of telecommunications policy. The prospects for rural residents in Washington were not bright.

The biggest fear, of course, was higher rates. Previously, the FCC and the Washington Utilities and Transportation Commission used two main criteria in major rate decisions—the cost to customers and the rate of return to telephone providers. Under this scheme, rural residents were traditionally able to obtain acceptable voice service at a low cost. Long distance telephone rates were used to subsidize local service, with rural users receiving the most subsidy, and low-interest federal loans helped subsidize expansion of the rural telephone networks.

Now, with divestiture beginning in January 1984, rural residents worried that they would have to shoulder the larger, actual costs of their telephone service. Also, new regulatory rules issued by the FCC would introduce new complexities. Consumers would become responsible for in-home wiring of their telephones and could own their own equipment. Installation could be performed by electricians and other non-telephone company employees. Various national companies could now offer long distance service of differing quality and cost. The new consumer choices would require new billing procedures, which would make telephone service more difficult to understand.

The prospect of these changes and a likely public outcry against them prompted the Washington State legislature to form a Joint Select Committee on Telecommunications in 1983. The panel had a two-year mandate, which was later renewed twice, to last through 1989. The legislature directed the Committee to study the likely consumer impact of the AT&T divestiture and FCC rule changes, and to recommend appropriate state policy responses. While the state legislature could do little to affect policy changes originated at the federal level, it could identify how Washington consumers might be hurt and suggest suitable state remedies.

The eventual impact of the Select Committee would owe much to its first staff director, Sharon Nelson, a consumer advocate familiar with the legislature and state politics, and Steve McLellan. In February 1985, both would resign from the Select Committee staff to accept appointments as the chair of the WUTC and director of public affairs/legislative liaison, respectively. Nelson and McLellan established a particularly knowledgeable linkage between the public utility commission and the legislature, facilitating the pursuit of new initiatives.

As one of its first inquiries, the Joint Select Committee began to examine how divestiture might affect rural areas differently than urban areas. Washington State is divided by the Cascade mountain range, which runs the length of the state. The Seattle-Everett metropolitan area and two adjacent counties, Pierce and Kitsap, lie just to the west of the Cascade range and contain more than half the state's population. In contrast, all of the region that lies to the east of the mountains contains less than one-fourth of the state's population and is quite rural. Towns and cities in eastern Washington are generally agriculture-oriented and separated by long distances.

Besides their economic and geographical differences, rural and urban areas of Washington State are generally served by different types of telephone providers. Rural regions are served primarily by small cooperatives and independent telephone companies, which tend to be responsive to their customers. Most of the state's large metropolitan regions, by contrast, receive telephone service from US West and to a lesser extent GTE—large corporations that tend to be more oriented to the telephone needs of urban dwellers.

Given the many east/west (and by implication, rural/urban) differences in Washington State, most legislative committees and state policy makers are careful to give special consideration to such differences. The Joint Select Committee on Telecommunications was no exception. At its first hearing on rural issues, held in Ellensburg, some 120 miles across the Cascades from Seattle, the Committee learned how the coming changes in federal telecommunications policy would affect the state's rural regions. The Committee would conclude, in its 1985 final report, that increased telecommunications costs could have a detrimental effect on the economy and social structure of eastern Washington (Joint Select Committee on Telecommunications, 1985).

Shortly after the Joint Select Committee completed its report, the WUTC adopted a new mission and goal statement that formally recognized the linkages between telephone service and economic development (WUTC, 1985). In its future decision making, the WUTC declared that it would seek to "provide a system of regulation that contributes to the economic development of the state," and would "identify and examine practices and policies that have economic impact on the state." Although it is impossible to find out how the Joint Select Committee's report influenced the WUTC's new mission statement, the two bodies were at least thinking along similar lines. For the first time, the WUTC made it clear that its policy interests were broader than monitoring telephone company rates of return and maintaining low telephone rates for consumers.

The WUTC underscored this shift of attention later in 1985 when it submitted a consultant's report to the legislature, *Telecommunications Industry in Washington State* (Ernst and Whinney, 1985), which noted that:

> ... to the extent that advances are greatest where population is most dense, the urban user is in the best position to reap the benefits

wrought by such progress. This situation has come to the attention of state policy makers who are concerned about the extent to which residents of rural Washington are able to access these improvements and participate in the technological and competitive revolution of the telecommunications industry.

Thus it became clear that not only was the WUTC linking telecommunications to rural development, it was broadly concerned about the social and human needs of rural areas. In the years to come, this early declaration of concern itself helped elicit new research and data about rural telecommunications, helping to define existing problems and formulate new solutions.

3. DEVELOPING A VISION OF RURAL TELECOMMUNICATIONS

In early 1986, after the legislature authorized another two-year term for it, the Joint Select Committee moved well beyond its initial assessments of rural telecommunications needs, as conventionally understood. In the next two years the Committee helped forge a compelling vision of what rural telecommunications could be. It marshalled the facts, anecdotes, statistics and quantitative analysis to show that telecommunications could greatly enhance the development prospects of rural regions.

This process began at a hearing on rural telephone issues held in Spokane, a city in far eastern Washington. One provocative witness at the hearing was Jon Ochs, a farmer and entrepreneur interested in developing overseas markets for products grown on his farm. Rather than relying only on traditional market outlets in the United States, Ochs was trying to identify and respond directly to potential purchasers abroad, using computerized access to crop price information, global weather reports, a telex network and agricultural trade information. Unfortunately, Ochs' attempts to use a computer modem on a multiparty line were both technically unsatisfactory and contrary to tariff regulations. Yet single-party telephone service turned out to be both costly and difficult to obtain. Ochs became a powerful symbol of imaginative, enterprising rural development thwarted by inadequate telecommunications.

Another witness at the 1986 hearing was Professor Don Dillman, a rural sociologist at Washington State University, located in Whitman County, where Jon Ochs resided. If Ochs provided some concrete examples of what rural telecommunications could do, Dillman offered a rich speculative, theoretical analysis. Drawing upon an article he had written, Dillman told the Committee that information technologies could provide an important boost for rural development at a time of great economic transition (Dillman, 1985). For that to happen, he warned, an adequate information infrastructure first must be built.

A few months after the hearing, the Committee decided to obtain a more rigorous, comprehensive research base. It gave a grant to Ochs and Karl Kottman, executive director of the Washington Farm Cooperative Association, to explain in greater depth how telecommunications could help farmers in eastern Washington (Kottman and Ochs, 1986). The Committee also funded Professor Dillman of the Washington State University Social and Economic Sciences Research Center (which he directed) to conduct a statewide survey of telecommunications problems facing Washington households. This survey would both identify problems caused by the AT&T divestiture, irrespective of place of residence, and find out how rural communities faced different telecommunications problems than cities and large towns. At the time such information did not exist. (A report financed by the Fred Meyer Charitable Trust, *Information Highways* [Murr and others, 1985], provided a valuable atlas of the Pacific Northwest's telecommunications infrastructure—from telephone service to cable television and libraries—but it did not survey consumer needs by region or evaluate the kinds of telecommunications equipment available.)

Upon learning of the planned survey, Stu Trefry, legislative director for the Washington State Grange, asked for permission to include questions from Professor Dillman's survey in his organization's newsletter. Trefry had been a 1984 witness at the Committee's hearings and he still kept tabs on rural telephone issues. By running the Dillman survey in the Grange newsletter, thousands of rural farmers learned that rural telecommunications was a matter of public interest—and Dillman himself received a fresh supply of primary data about rural telephone problems.

By 1986, when the Joint Select Committee issued its final report, rural telecommunications was listed as one of the top four priorities for the upcoming 1987 legislative session. The report declared: ". . . [The rural] community should not come late to the Information Age. It should have at its fingertips the same sophisticated information collection and transmission techniques as does the urban community."

4. REFINING THE RESEARCH, SPREADING THE WORD

While the Joint Select Committee had by this point assembled an impressive foundation of knowledge about rural telecommunications, more research was needed to justify concrete telecommunications programs or policy changes. Also, more rural constituencies and state policy makers needed to learn about how telecommunications could spur rural development. The next several years saw a remarkable expansion of research and the building of a larger network of people interested in the "telecommunications vision."

An important catalyst to this process was a set of hearings held by the Joint Select Committee in February 1987 at which the various research and data collection projects of the preceding two years were formally presented (WUTC, 1987). Kottman and Ochs, for example, gave a more detailed account of how telecommunications can help farmers. After overcoming the difficulties and costs of obtaining a single-party telephone line for his home, Ochs testified that he had used a computer modem in mid-February 1986 to discover the yield of garbanzo beans in India following that country's recently completed harvest. Using that information, Ochs decided to plant garbanzo beans on his farm starting March 1. Ochs also reported how he used his computer modem to obtain fertilizer test results and to identify Middle East markets for lentils that could be filled by Washington farmers.

Dillman's statewide survey documented people's suspicions about rural telecommunications deficiencies in great statistical detail (Dillman, Scott, and Allen, 1987). (For both urban and rural counties, the results distinguished between those residents who lived within city limits and who lived in the countryside.) A key conclusion of the survey was that over 95 percent of residents living in urban counties or within the city limits of towns in rural counties had single-party telephone lines. By contrast, only 76 percent of the rural countryside residents in rural counties had such lines. Furthermore, many residents with multiparty service reported that it would be prohibitively costly to switch to single-party lines.

The survey found that many rural residents faced additional burdens—in the quality and availability of telephone service, and in the lack of advanced technologies such as touchtone service. Rural residents also were more likely to incur long distance charges to call essential institutions and services, such as the "local" schools and the "local" insurance agency. The following percentage of households required a long distance call to reach the family doctor, 26 percent; to reach the community depended upon for most purchases, 26 percent; to reach an automobile repair garage, 32 percent; to obtain telephone repairs, 33 percent; and to reach an insurance agent, 37 percent. Spurred by these findings, the WUTC in 1988 appointed an advisory committee on extended area service to explore possible remedies (Local Extended Calling Advisory Committee, 1988).

The report published by Dillman's team suggested further avenues of inquiry that the WUTC and other state agencies might pursue to fill in the sketchy picture of rural-urban differences. The WUTC, after all, could obtain precise data directly from all telephone companies (rather than relying on sample survey data) and then compile a comprehensive inventory of rural telecommunications service. It could verify whether the problems in rural service were as serious or prevalent as suspected. By 1988, the WUTC staff, under direction from the legislature, was engaged in this process, compiling an inventory of equipment capabilities and types of services available throughout the state—for example, where party lines existed, where digital switching was used, where alternative long distance carrier service was available, and so forth (WUTC, 1989b). Although this effort resulted from legislative instructions originating in the Joint Select Committee, the WUTC was developing its own appetite for such information. In a rapidly changing telecommunications environment, an inventory would be a basic tool for developing appropriate policies.

Two of the earlier survey's authors—Dillman and Allen—spurred new interest in the state's rural telecommunications by surveying all businesses in three small towns in Whitman County, in a study supported by the Washington State University's Department of Rural Sociology. The purpose of the study was to identify the extent to which various information technologies were important to rural businesses, and how they may help create or eliminate jobs (Allen and Dillman, 1987). Using this business survey, the previous statewide household survey, and national data from the U.S. Department of Agriculture's Economic Research Service on digital switching and other services to rural communities, Dillman and Donald Beck published an article in *Journal of State Government* (1988) describing how telecommunications might influence rural development. The article became a benchmark document among the state's legislators and telecommunications policy experts, and was widely distributed and commonly cited.

Telecommunications and Education

As more research about rural telecommunications was generated, a wider circle of participants was attracted. New institutions stepped forward to assert their interests in better rural telecommunications. After a series of meetings in fall 1987 by the Spokane Region Partnership for Rural Improvement, a coalition of educational institutions and agencies serving northeast Washington, it became clear that certain telecommunications problems were preventing rural libraries from serving their patrons well.

David Gray Remington, director of the Pend Oreille County Library, reported that in Pend Oreille County there were multiple phone companies, and long distance charges for calls connected by different phone companies made it expensive for users to call the library. A second problem was the existence of a Local Access and Transport Area (LATA) boundary between the Spokane metropolitan area and Newport, the town in which the main county library was located. (LATAs were established as part of the AT&T divestiture to mark the limits beyond which the local Bell operating companies could not transport calls.) LATA boundaries separated telecommunications connections in tiny areas of northeastern Washington and southeastern Washington from the rest of eastern Washington. Remington found that it would cost several thousand dollars per year for a dedicated line to access information electronically from Spokane—located only 35 miles away but on the other side of the LATA boundary.

To help it better understand rural telecommunications needs, the Partnership for Rural Improvement hired Lois Irwin, a community development consultant with several academic affiliations, to investigate telecommunications issues. As part of that process, she convened a meeting in Spokane in January 1988 for representatives of various schools, libraries and colleges. The gathering gave new and broader exposure to the research of Don Dillman and his associates, and to the pioneering work of the Eastern Washington University and Educational Service District 101 in bringing satellite instruction to rural schools. (ESD 101 is an educational consortium dedicated to helping local school districts.) From Don Hanna, assistant vice provost for extended university services at Washington State University, the group learned how parts of rural Washington were using microwave transmissions and other electronic means to "import" various higher education classes. As interest in these issues grew, a consortium comprised of community colleges, rural libraries, Washington State University and ESD 101 was formed to improve rural access to education, technical assistance and other information via telecommunications.

The circle of interest in rural telecommunications kept expanding. Prompted in part by her academic department's interest in the issue, Lucy Burton, a Washington State University graduate student, decided to conduct a community case study exploring the implications of telecommunications for rural economic development. It asked, in essence: How could telecommunications in its many forms serve rural education, business and social needs? Burton's study established an empirical profile of rural people's exposure to and desire for various communication technologies such as computers, satellites, video, audio conferencing, cable television, and telephone service relating to business and education (Burton, 1989).

Developing a "Back Office" Industry

In southeastern Washington, meanwhile, two economic development officials began to explore how telecommunications could be used to spur economic development in their region. In the spring of 1988, Jim Weddell of the Port of Whitman County and Tom Kneeshaw of the Palouse Area Economic Development Council—with assistance from Lois Irwin—convened several county officials to discuss their ideas with them. They realized that economic growth in the region had stagnated, that agricultural production was not likely to create new jobs, and that a conventional industrial park development did not hold much promise either.

Through the Joint Select Committee's hearings in February 1987, Weddell and Kneeshaw had learned how rural communities in Minnesota used telecommunications to develop a "back office" industry by processing, and then returning, data transmitted from Minneapolis. Bill Blazer, an economic development consultant from Minnesota, had described this innovation at the hearings, and an article about his work was given by WUTC official Steve McLellan to Joint Select Committee counsel Debra Senn who passed it on to various legislators and policy experts. Now this seed was transplanted to Whitman County, as officials explored the idea of bringing back-office data processing into the region, probably from Seattle. This meeting led to a modest effort to inventory telecommunications capabilities and to identify potential problems.

Apparently, the state legislature was sufficiently intrigued by the Minnesota "back office" experience that it mandated a study into the feasibility of rural office development in Washington State. The modestly funded study focused on Wenatchee, Washington, a city of 20,000 just across the Cascade mountains from Seattle (Conway Associates, 1988). The main conclusions were that a modern telecommunications system is a necessary but not sufficient condition for office development in rural communities, and that the office sector represents a promising opportunity for economic development in rural communities. The study also brought together previous research on the special importance of service jobs (and therefore telecommunications and information technologies) in today's economy.

In striking out with telecommunications-driven development strategies, both the Partnership for Rural Improvement and the Whitman County effort exemplified a new consciousness about economic development. They recognized, first, that traditional "smokestack chasing" was not working, and second, that in the changing world economy information technologies, if deployed strategically, could play a vital role in reviving rural regions. Yet planners of these two efforts realized they were on a new frontier. They harbored uncertainty about whether the new technologies would spur development. The planners realized that development officials and citizens alike at least needed to learn more about telecommunications technologies and their potential for local development.

5. SUSTAINED MOMENTUM FOR CHANGE

The summer of 1988 represented something of a watershed for telecommunications progress in Washington State. It was a time when people with different sorts of training and expertise—regulators, community development consultants, state economic development policy makers, private development consultants, representatives of telecommunications companies and academic researchers—were researching, writing, meeting, debating and interacting in one fashion or another about telecommunications-based development. This heterogeneity of skills, focused on a common concern for the improvement of rural telecommunications, provided the real impetus for change. Now that a critical mass of experts had been achieved, knowledge of the subject was rapidly expanding, expectations for the future were soaring, and the political climate was quite hospitable to forward-thinking proposals.

Specifically, many state agencies were researching telecommunications problems and proposing solutions. The WUTC was preparing proposals to eliminate party lines and provide extended area service. The Washington State Economic Development Board was investigating whether inadequate rural telecommunications was impeding economic development. Community groups in far eastern Washington were exploring the telecommunications approach to rural economic development. Analysts at Washington State University continued to produce useful and insightful research. And various telephone companies were examining the costs and difficulties of improving rural telephone service.

In 1988 and subsequent years, there was much activity in three major areas: new development initiatives, new WUTC initiatives, and new regional and national interest in Washington's telecommunications policy.

New Development Initiatives

One significant sign of the new "telecommunications consciousness" was a 1988 report published by the Washington State Economic Development Board, a government body founded in 1985. This report was part of a larger Board project to formulate a long-term economic development strategy for the state. Because Washington's economy depends on exports more than most states, the Board sought to understand the interdependencies of the state and global economies, and of the rural Washington and the global economics.

Recognizing that telecommunications and information technologies are vital in the global economy, the Board appointed a task force to study how advanced telecommunications might help development. Two of the task force members, Vic Erickson of US West and Nancy Williams of

GTE Northwest, represented the telephone industry. The third member and principal author of the task force report, was John Niles, founder and president of Global Telematics, a Seattle consulting firm (Niles, 1989).

The task force report made a wide range of recommendations for deploying telecommunications in innovative, productive ways: to help mitigate an emerging urban traffic congestion problem in the Puget Sound region of western Washington; to develop a back-office industry in rural parts of the state; to create new jobs outside the Puget Sound region through telecommunications linkages with existing businesses in the region. Significantly, the report concluded that the existing telecommunications infrastructure in Washington was generally sufficient to support business incubation, retention and attraction, partly because of an aggressive program of US West, approved by the WUTC, to provide digital telephone switching capability throughout its rural territory in the Pacific Northwest.

Another important planning initiative was jointly launched in 1988 by the Palouse Area Economic Development Council and the Center for the New West, a policy institute. Together, these two groups determined that the existing telecommunications infrastructure was adequate for most kinds of services local businesses wanted to offer. Through focus group discussions and other research, however, they decided that providing back-office functions for urban businesses was *not* the most promising path for the region. Instead, they decided that regional development would be best served by adding value to existing businesses (primarily agriculture, food processing and related equipment) by using information and communications technologies to develop international export markets.

The cooperation of the Palouse Area Economic Development Council and the Center for the New West, which had first encountered each other at rural telecommunications conferences (see below), produced fertile new synergies. A development group with a grass roots constituency and an informed sense of local needs (Palouse) was able to exploit the broader knowledge and contacts of a regional policy institute (New West). Previously, members of the Palouse Area Economic Development Council were stymied in developing larger exporting business because of their difficulties in learning about opportunities and in developing contacts. Now, the Center for the New West found concrete, local applications for its broader policy sophistication and state and national contacts.

The initial result of this collaboration—under the leadership of Tom Kneeshaw, a development specialist with the Palouse Area Economic Development Council—was a proposal for an experimental office that would use telecommunications and computer linkages to help farmers and businesses in the Palouse region learn about international marketing opportunities. The office would determine the export potential of a given product or service, help locate target markets, identify trade leads, provide information on export financing and payment, and serve as an information clearinghouse, among other functions.

Eventually, the proposal was submitted to the state Department of Community Development, which was sponsoring an open competition for innovative community development proposals. Of 44 proposals submitted to the Department, the Council's project was one of two funded. (It is noteworthy that nearly a year earlier the Washington State Economic Development Board had recommended that the Department of Community Development explore a telecommunications-based project.)

With a $95,000 state grant, the new office, called AgriTechnics International, began to identify export opportunities for businesses in four adjacent counties and to provide information on export and international shipping documentation, letters of credit and all the mechanics of doing business internationally. By 1990, eleven counties in eastern Washington were participating in the program. By charging users for direct costs and levying finder's fees on successful transactions, AgriTechnics expects to be financially self-sufficient by the end of its third year of operation.

One success resulted when AgriTechnics connected a French distributor with a local company that was selling technology for moisture sensing in food processing. The company already had a small European market but the new connection increased sales to Europe by 500 percent within six months. In another success, a mailing of cooperative advertisements to Chambers of Commerce in New Zealand resulted in sales of farm implements.

An indispensable factor in AgriTechnics' success has been access to modern telecommunications networks and services, such as international facsimile transmission and remote access to electronic databases. Useful as these systems are, however, the most important source of success has been the skillful application of the technology to help local businesses add value and reach new markets. Basic telecommunications infrastructure is vital, but little will be achieved without the effective, strategic use of that infrastructure.

New Utility Commission Initiatives

Various WUTC initiatives reflected the new consciousness about telecommunications. If the citations in the WUTC's annual report are an indication, the WUTC was familiar with virtually every article and report written about telecommunications in Washington State. Given the growing body of literature and political consensus, the WUTC, with Sharon Nelson's leadership, proposed an array of its own initiatives.

During the summer of 1988, the WUTC sponsored a policy round table on telecommunications regulation, one section of which focused on learning more about the problems of rural telecommunications. A representative of the Washington State Grange reported that a farm family had been quoted a price of $23,000 to string 3.7 miles of telephone line to reach their home, a clearly unaffordable sum that led to their leaving the family farm. A representative of a rural telephone company argued in favor of single-party service to every home and the elimination of suburban mileage charges, which were making the cost of single-party service prohibitive for some people. At this meeting, US West reported on a pilot project in three rural towns (Edwall-Tyler, Ridgefield and Sprague) where the company had eliminated suburban mileage charges, frozen multiparty service and promoted upgrades (WUTC, 1989d).

Based partly on the testimony at this round table conference, the WUTC in the fall of 1988 formally announced through an "open letter" its intention to propose incentive regulation. One component of this proposal called for an upgrading of every exchange in Washington State to single-party touchtone service.

In 1989, the WUTC completed its inventory of the state's telecommunications infrastructure, which identified (among other things) the regions where multiparty lines and extended area service problems existed (1989c). Armed with these data, the WUTC recommended that the 1989 session of the state legislature declare a new, minimally acceptable level of basic telephone service: single-party touchtone service at affordable rates, without suburban mileage charges. The legislature instead ordered the WUTC to conduct a study to determine the feasibility of such a policy. In December of 1989 the WUTC completed that study and issued a report declaring that it was feasible to achieve such a goal within six years (WUTC, 1989a). Since no further legislative authority was needed, the WUTC established that policy, and expects to achieve the new goal by 1995 for all locations, with most locations upgraded to single-party touchtone service by the end of 1992.

After months of study, another WUTC project bore fruit in December 1990, when the Commission issued new rules for enlarging the boundaries for extended service areas (WUTC, 1990b). The chief goal was to allow toll-free calling to those areas where phone calling is consistently heavy. To this end, the WUTC ordered telephone companies to identify exchanges where an average subscriber paid long distance toll charges for more than 20 percent of the minutes of phone calls within the LATA. (This "80 percent rule" represents a rough equivalence with costs faced by urban telephone users, who generally do not pay long distance charges for at least 80 percent of their intra-LATA calls.) The commission ordered the carriers to prepare new extended area rate plans that would include 80 percent of intraLATA call minutes in flat rate EAS services. For exchanges falling below this 80 percent threshold, the new rules mandated criteria for deciding new call routes: areas where half the people made at least two telephone calls per month; adjacent exchanges; those exchanges most frequently called; and those areas called by many residential subscribers. Any increased costs for the new extended local calling will be recovered primarily from customers who directly benefit.

This significant step forward in rural telephone service represented the culmination of a process begun more than five years earlier. The issue had first been identified in the Select Joint Committee's statewide survey (Dillman and others, 1987) and had been given considerable elaboration at WUTC hearings and in other research reports.

Regional and National Interest in the Washington State Experience
A good indication of the success of Washington State's great progress in rural telecommunications is the regional and national interest it has attracted. A significant event was the formation in 1988 of the Northwest Policy Center at the University of Washington. Directed by David Harrison and supported with funding by the Northwest Area Foundation and The Ford Foundation, the Center seeks to stimulate thought and action on major policy issues facing the five-state region of Alaska, Washington, Oregon, Idaho and Montana.

An early focus of the Center's activities was to explore the essential interdependencies of urban and rural parts of the region. In Washington, this inquiry focused on the booming economy of Seattle and the stagnating economies of rural regions. In a report exploring these themes, *A Northwest Reader: Options for Rural Communities*, the Center devoted a chapter to telecommunications and rural economic development (Northwest Policy Center, 1989). Besides researching telecommunications issues, the Center became an important forum through which different policy players can discuss ideas and build connections.

The cross-fertilization of ideas and the building of a network of personal contacts was greatly enhanced in 1988 through two important round table conferences. The first, sponsored by US West for telecommunications faculty members at western colleges and universities, brought together Vic Erickson (US West), Don Dillman (Washington State University), John Niles (Global Telematics), and WUTC commissioner A.J. Pardini. Also attending was Phil Burgess, an employee of US West, who would soon become director of the newly created Center for the New West, which would provide vital support for the Palouse Area Economic Development Council's project, AgriTechnics International.

The second influential gathering was The Aspen Institute's first conference ever on telecommunications and rural development. Burgess and Dillman both participated in this conference as well, along with 25 other professionals from throughout the United States. The conference, an intensive three-day interchange, was to a considerable degree responsible for defining rural telecommunications as a coherent set of interrelated issues (universal service, elimination of party lines, provision of digital switching, quality of transmission lines, adequacy of trunk line connections, extended area service, alternative long distance carriers, and cellular service) rather than as isolated issues amenable to quick fixes. A resulting book funded by the Aspen Institute and the Ford Foundation, *Rural America in the Information Age* (Parker and others, 1989), offered a multifaceted perspective on rural telecommunications problems, which also found expression in the Northwest Policy Center's reader and the WUTC's 1988 policy round table.

The Washington State experience received still further national exposure through the OTA. In March 1990, an OTA delegation visited Washington State as part of its congressionally mandated study of the role of telecommunications in rural economic development. The OTA report, *Rural America at the Crossroads: Networking for the Future*, commented favorably on the developments in Washington (U.S. Congress, 1991).

With so many parties exploring the promise of telecommunications, new projects were reaching beyond the traditional corps of experts to the general public. In 1989, the Washington State Energy office sponsored a conference in Seattle on "Telecommuting: An Alternative Route to Work," which would lead to the funding of a Seattle-area demonstration project. Another attempt to popularize issues of rural telecommunications came in 1990, when the Partnership for Rural Development and Washington State University published "Telecommunications and Rural Development," a publication prepared by Lois Irwin (Irwin, 1990). This booklet demystified telecommunications technical jargon and policy debate, helping the public to appreciate the importance of the issues and play a more active role themselves.

By 1990, there was a consensus that the state had reached something of a midpoint in its telecommunications reforms. It was well on its way toward building a sufficient and affordable rural telecommunications infrastructure, yet it was still in the early stages of using that infrastructure in creative ways to spur rural economic development.

In a speech delivered in March 1990, Sharon Nelson, chair of the WUTC, summarized a central conclusion of her state's experience (Nelson, 1990): "Advanced telecommunications technologies by themselves will not revitalize rural America. Their prudent deployment, however, is a necessary condition for other rural development activities." The WUTC (1990a) elaborated on this theme in comments to the National Telecommunications and Information Administration:

> The potential for telecommunications infrastructure improvements to play a strategic role in reaching economic development goals is most clear in the rural context. Telecommunications can be used in rural areas as a means of improving commercial exchange facilitating social intercourse and more effectively delivering public services.

As the Washington experience shows, much of the change occurred through the happenstance of personal and professional friendships, the leadership of key individuals, fortuitous political circumstances, and other unpredictable factors. Are there more general lessons that might be gleaned from the rural telecommunications initiatives in Washington?

6. LESSONS LEARNED

An important lesson of the Washington experience is that change in the quality and use of rural telecommunications can be achieved through the cooperation of many individuals and organizations who together reach a consensus concerning what should be done. To achieve this consensus requires the involvement of many individuals and leaders with differing sorts of expertise and organizational affiliations. In Washington there were regulators and academics, legislators and development experts, citizen groups and local businesses, private consultants and entrepreneurs, among others.

Mobilizing the potential power of this array of players requires some means to bring them together in constructive ways. A *process* must emerge through which these individuals can forge personal relationships, discuss and debate new research, identify common concerns, develop political alliances, learn leadership skills, and so forth. Had there not been situations in which people could share their expertise with one another—through conferences, official hearings, research monographs, and community meetings—it is unlikely that the WUTC would have recognized the importance of telecommunications for rural communities or acted with such dispatch.

Once it became clear that there were many people interested in rural telecommunications, the beginnings of an interpersonal network took shape. People began to share information and provide mutual support, and this in turn created new ripple effects that reached a still wider group of interested professionals. For example, when the Joint Select Committee gave a forum to the entrepreneurial farmer, Jon Ochs, and to the academic researcher, Don Dillman, not only did the state legislature and WUTC learn a great deal more about rural telecommunications, a variety of development officials, farmers, and academics were also exposed to, and energized by, their research and ideas.

Within three years, the small, loosely connected network had expanded into a large network of people deliberately exchanging information to spur telecommunications-based rural development. At a certain point, the network reached a critical mass and developed an impetus of its own, greatly multiplying the impact of any single state agency or private organization. In short, active "networking" can greatly enhance the chances of success.

Yet the goal of networking is not to develop a unified corps of researchers and activists pursuing a monolithic, fixed vision of development. It is to provide a heterogeneous mix of fact and opinion, values and constituencies. Only through such a robust process of debate can action be tailored to serve genuine community needs. For example, the Palouse Area Economic Development Council, after conducting focus group discussions with its constituents, realized that the development of a back-office industry was not suited for its region, and instead pursued a development vision more suited to its existing agricultural capabilities and constituency.

This shift of focus could occur only because the participants were sensitive to changing conditions and grass roots concerns. Telecommunications policy was crafted to meet real needs; an external model of rural development (for example, back-office outsourcing) was not adopted wholesale. This very flexibility has allowed Washington policy makers to see that the telecommunications infrastructure is a means to an end, not an end in itself. Once they identified and resolved deficiencies in the infrastructure, policy makers and development experts could shift their attention toward *using* telecommunications in effective, strategic ways—that is, to spur enduring community development.

A vital instrument throughout the process of change in Washington State was rigorous research. Research on a state's telecommunications needs is often quite limited. With the introduction of thorough research and analysis—such as provided by the Dillman team's statewide survey in 1987 and the WUTC's 1988 inventory of the telecommunication's infrastructure—a persuasive case was made for specific policy reforms. Uncertainties were resolved and minds were changed, opening the door for action.

The early studies were commissioned by state legislators who wanted answers to specific questions (such as the prevalence of multiparty lines in rural regions). This research had a powerful multiplier effect. It highlighted the need for new research to fill gaps in knowledge about state telecommunications. As it turned out, graduate students, professors, telephone companies and private consultants were able to remedy this research void. The early research also led to interactions with other telecommunications researchers and policy experts, in other states and in Washington, DC. For example, Bill Blazer's research into Minnesota's back-office industry proved to be highly catalytic in Washington State, just as Don Dillman's research was quite catalytic within Washington State itself.

Important as research is, its vital partner is the real life experiences of rural residents. Much of the emotional and political power fueling telecommunications improvements in Washington State came from the concrete anecdotes and personal testimony of ordinary people. Jon Ochs and members of the Grange, for example, were both advocates and symbols of a revitalized rural economy. They personally embodied the demand for, and promise of, rural telecommunications. Their testimony, when combined with more generalized, systematic survey research, spurred the legislature and the WUTC more than either could have achieved alone.

Finally, it is worth pondering the reasons for the remarkable speed of change in Washington's rural telecommunications. One reason is that, unlike many legislative issues, improvements in rural telecommunications generally do not provoke serious opposition. The measures adopted by the legislature and WUTC focused mostly on costs (and moderate costs, at that)—and not ideology. Rural telecommunications is generally not a divisive, polarizing issue.

Since the telephone industry is one of declining costs, there are sufficient financial margins with which to undertake innovations, given the political and regulatory desire to do so. People's telephone bills are not so high, in absolute terms, that major improvements at modest costs cannot be pursued. Producing a greater measure of economic opportunity and social equity for rural residents can be achieved through investing in rural telecommunications funds that might otherwise be used to achieve minor reduction of telephone rates.

Above all else, the actions taken to improve rural telecommunications in Washington State from 1984 to 1990 show that significant state action is possible. Now that major advances have been made in the rural telecommunications infrastructure, attention is properly shifting toward the business, community and human applications of the technology, a process that remains in its infancy. The future will depend greatly upon such innovators as AgriTechnics, which must learn how to use telecommunications systems creatively to revitalize rural communities. Nationwide, many innovators are showing that telecommunications-based development can succeed. The next step is to build a critical mass of rural innovators on the national level, unleashing the same sorts of potent synergies that proved so effective in Washington State.

CHAPTER 6

Telecommunications and Rural Development: Quantitative Analyses

1. WHY QUANTITATIVE ANALYSIS?

Case studies help us to see how telecommunications can be important to rural development, and how it helps make development happen. But case studies alone cannot give planners and policy makers the quantitative evidence many of them seek. Indeed, some policy experts are skeptical of rural development proposals that are based solely on development theories and anecdotal case studies. This chapter provides quantitative statistical evidence that strengthens the argument that telecommunications can contribute to rural economic development.

The relationship between telecommunications and economic development does not fit a simple linear cause-and-effect model. That is to say, new investment in telecommunications infrastructure unaccompanied by complementary development activities will not automatically result in economic development. Telecommunications is a catalyst and facilitator, not a magic solution. Its success in stimulating development depends critically upon how well individuals, businesses and communities use telecommunications networks to improve their economic prospects.

Given this dynamic, any quantitative evidence of the role of telecommunications in development is likely to be indirect and statistical. Such evidence comes as data showing that, on the average, economic development is more likely than not to be associated with improvements in telecommunications infrastructure.

Recent quantitative statistical research, some of which we report here for the first time, confirms that improvements in telecommunications infrastructure have a significant relationship with economic development in the United States. The data reported in this chapter provide solid

161

arguments for development advocates attempting to persuade skeptical policy makers and policy analysts who insist on quantitative evidence.

Those who are leery of policy intervention to stimulate investment in rural telecommunications sometimes base their judgments on a familiar economic philosophy—that the forces of a competitive marketplace, not government, should decide rural development outcomes. Whatever the merits of that policy in other contexts, there are two reasons why a free market philosophy is insufficient here. First, the basic rural telecommunications infrastructure is provided by local telephone monopolies, which are not fully subject to competitive market forces. The economic theory of competition makes it clear that monopolies lacking the pressure of competition do not automatically make the investments that would be ideal for the economy as a whole.

Second, many of the economic benefits generated by telecommunications investments accrue to parties who do not make the investments. Business, government and residential users of telephones save time and money because they are able to gather and exchange information by telephone. Yet these economic benefits are not fully reflected in the prices charged by telecommunications providers; in economic jargon, the benefits are "externalities" to the marketplace transaction. (In other spheres, externalities may consist of such negative consequences as pollution.) Where significant positive externalities are present (as is true with most infrastructure investment, including both transportation and telecommunications), a competitive marketplace will not generate the amount of investment needed to achieve efficient economic growth. Hence the need for policy intervention.

How confident can we be that policy intervention to build better rural telecommunications infrastructure will yield higher levels of economic development than would otherwise be achieved? This chapter presents quantitative evidence to show that significant positive externalities accompany telecommunications investment. In general, quantitative evidence of externalities makes a strong case for policy intervention. With respect to telecommunications, the positive externalities suggest that policy changes that stimulate increased private investment in telecommunications infrastructure will lead to greater economic development than would otherwise occur.

2. GAPS IN EARLIER RESEARCH

In *Rural America in the Information Age,* Parker and others (1989) summarized prior research into the complex relationships between telecommunications and economic development. That research included both macroeconomic statistical studies and a variety of community case studies. Taken together, those studies showed that the availability of telephones contributed to economic development, particularly in rural areas. They also showed that there were significant positive externalities: that is, the general economic benefits (accruing to residential customers, businesses, government and others) were significantly greater than those obtained by the telecommunications providers.

There were two major gaps in the prior research, however. First, there was little evidence showing how improvements in telephone service *beyond the provision of basic voice communication* did or did not help rural economic development. It was not known, for example, whether upgrading rural multiparty phone lines to single-party service would result in measurable improvement in the economy of rural areas. Neither was it known whether upgrading old electromechanical telephone switches to modern electronic or digital switches—thereby allowing touchtone service, faster connection times and custom calling services—has a measurable impact on rural economic development.

Most of the prior research compared development in locations with and without telephone service. Now that more than 93 percent of U.S. households have telephone service (FCC, 1991), such comparisons miss the major point. In the 1990s, the most relevant telecommunications policy questions concern the benefits to be obtained from *upgrading* telephone services. Do the quality and variety of services affect economic development? If so, how?

The second gap in the research literature was the absence of reliable quantitative data comparing rural and urban locations in the United States. Most of the prior research data came from other countries, and the available U.S. data were national statistics that did not permit separate analyses for rural and urban locations. Furthermore, the earlier data suggested there may be diminishing returns from increasing investment in existing telecommunications infrastructure. Hardy (1980) found that the higher the level of pre-existing infrastructure (for example, the percentage of households with telephones), the less the incremental benefit from further investment. Therefore, given the widespread availability of basic telephone service in the United States, further analyses were needed to confirm a causal relationship between telecommunications and economic development in the United States.

This chapter describes two recent quantitative studies that go a long way toward filling these two gaps in the telecommunications research literature. The first is a national time series analysis providing definitive statistical evidence that investment in U.S. telecommunications infrastructure in earlier time periods generally "causes" increases in the U.S. Gross National Product in later time periods. These results show that, more often than not, when telecommunications investments are made, the resulting networks are used in ways that lead to economic growth. This report, prepared by Cronin and others for DRI/McGraw-Hill, represents a milestone in research into the impact of telecommunications infrastructure on the U.S. economy (DRI/McGraw-Hill, 1990; Cronin and others, 1991).

The second study analyzes recent data from both rural and urban counties in two Pacific Northwest states, Oregon and Washington. It concludes that counties with better telephone networks perform better economically. The results of this research, which was done specifically for this book, are presented in section 4, below.

3. NATIONAL TIME SERIES DATA

The history of U.S. telecommunications investment can be traced through aggregate national statistics; unfortunately, no separate figures for rural and urban investment are available. National time series data can shed light on the relationship between telecommunications investment in one time period and economic growth in a later time period. Such data can confirm that, on the average, including both rural and urban investment, the effect of telecommunications investment on the total economy is beneficial.

This section describes the DRI/McGraw-Hill study (Cronin and others, 1991), which confirmed that prior U.S. telecommunications investments resulted in growth in the total national economy. (Confirmation that the relationships found in the national data also occur in rural locations requires separate analysis. See Section 4, below.)

The DRI/McGraw Hill study of national data tested two hypotheses:

Hypothesis 1: In the United States, the amount of economic growth in one time period is a reliable predictor ("cause") of increases in the amount of U.S. telecommunications investment in a later time period. (This is the common sense prediction that the more an economy grows, the more telecommunications investment it can afford.)

Hypothesis 2: The change in the amount of U.S. telecommunications investment in one time period is a reliable predictor ("cause") of the amount of economic growth in a later time period. (This is the key prediction that increased investment in telecommunications networks and facilities stimulates economic growth.)

These two hypotheses were tested by examining 31 years of U.S. time series data (1958 to 1988, inclusive) using year-to-year changes in the Gross National Product as a measure of economic growth. These changes in economic performance were compared with year-to-year changes in national telecommunications investment. Using a time lag of two years, both hypotheses were confirmed after conducting rigorous statistical testing. For example, changes in telecommunications capital investment in 1986 were reflected in economic growth in 1988.

The results confirmed a "cyclical, positive feedback process": telecommunications investment stimulates economic growth, and economic growth in turn stimulates further demand for telecommunications investment.

Using an econometric technique called input-output analysis, a related study (DRI/McGraw-Hill, 1990) also measured the amount of savings for the U.S. economy resulting from telecommunications infrastructure production and utilization in the period from 1963 to 1982. The savings came in two forms. First, after adjusting for inflation, prices for comparable communications services were lower in 1982 than in 1963. Capital investment in more advanced technology was a major factor in achieving those lower costs. Second, the use of telecommunications increased as telecommunications substituted for more expensive alternatives, such as travel, or made the production processes of other industries more efficient. Partly offsetting this second form of savings is the cost of the additional telecommunications services themselves.

Detailed analysis of 29 industries responsible for 99.6 percent of the U.S. GNP showed that the 1982 economy saved $65.7 billion in labor and capital expenses, compared to the 1963 economy, as a direct result of improved telecommunications infrastructure. (These savings were measured in 1990 dollars.) Efficiency gains in the production of telecommunications in the nineteen-year period accounted for $46.5 billion in savings. The remaining $19.2 billion in net savings resulted from other industries using more telecommunications as a substitute for more costly inputs to their production processes. The $19.2 billion net savings figure resulted from $36.2 billion in actual savings in other industries less the $17.1 billion in additional resources required by the telecommunications industry to produce the additional telecommunications services.

Most of the $36.2 billion of telecommunications-related savings in other industries benefited those industries and their customers. Significantly, these benefits were largely "external" to the telecommunications industry. It is the confirmation of these external benefits that justifies policy intervention to ensure that regulated telecommunications carriers, especially local monopolies, provide the infrastructure that is necessary for growth in the rest of the economy.

On average, the 29 industries increased usage of telecommunications by 150 percent in the period from 1963 to 1982. The benefits of improved telecommunications were spread widely over almost all industries, with the most information-intensive industry—finance and insurance—increasing telecommunications usage by more than 800 percent. The service sector of the economy, which is now the largest and fastest growing sector, accounted for nearly three-quarters of the total increase in telecommunications utilization.

These national statistics provide convincing evidence that the economy as a whole benefits from increased investment in telecommunications infrastructure. The causal connection observed in the time series analysis is indirect, however; telecommunications was not the direct "cause" of economic growth but rather, a vital catalyst. The economic growth stemmed from the ways that other industries used telecommunications to make their production processes more efficient.

4. THE DATA FROM THE PACIFIC NORTHWEST

Although the national data confirm that telecommunications investment leads to overall economic growth in the United States, they do not *prove* that rural telecommunications investment will necessarily lead to rural economic growth. The national data could simply reflect the results of urban investment, for example. However, if similar effects are present in both rural and urban locations, then improvements in rural telecommunications infrastructure should lead to improved rural economic performance.

It would be ideal to repeat the national time series study using rural data. Unfortunately, comparable rural time series data are not available. The next best option is to use rural and urban data taken from a single point in time to confirm a positive relationship between the level of telecommunications infrastructure and the level of economic performance. Such evidence would support the case for state policies to foster investment in rural telecommunications.

To fill in that missing rural piece for this book, we gathered data on the telecommunications infrastructure in two Pacific Northwest states, Oregon and Washington. To permit comparisons between rural and urban counties and correlations with economic variables, we collected data for all counties in the two states.

One reason for selecting these two Pacific Northwest states was their progress, compared to the rest of the country, in upgrading the rural telecommunications infrastructure. For example, US West was just completing the replacement of its rural electromechanical telephone switches with digital switches in both states. As in other parts of the country, small independent telephone carriers supported by the Rural Electrification Administration were well along in upgrading their facilities. Furthermore, there were indications that the rural communities in these two states were finally beginning to recover from the nearly decade-long rural recession. Was there a connection? Given Hardy's (1980) finding that the largest economic payoffs resulted from investments in locations with least advanced infrastructure, it would be more impressive to confirm the relationship in states that already had a particularly well developed telecommunications infrastructure.

Thanks to two regulatory commissions, we were able to obtain the data needed for our analyses. The Washington Utilities and Transportation Commission (WUTC) had conducted an inventory of the infrastructure in their state as it existed in mid-1988. (See chapter 5, above.) Data from that inventory were available by telephone exchange and thus could be aggregated at the county level for comparison with economic data. In Oregon, we prepared a questionnaire, which the Public Utility Commission sent to all telephone carriers in the state. With appropriate follow-ups, the PUC obtained a 100 percent response rate. The Oregon data report conditions as they existed at the end of 1989.

Our research confirms for the first time that electronic telephone switching and single-party telephone service *are* related to rural economic performance. Since these data describe the situation at a single point in time, they cannot, by themselves, show that telecommunications investment is a *cause* of economic growth. The correlation between the level of telecommunications infrastructure and the level of economic development at a single point in time may have several explanations. A higher quality of telecommunications infrastructure in some counties may be a cause of higher economic performance in those counties. The correlation also may indicate that counties with higher economic performance are able to afford better telecommunications. Another factor, such as population density, may be a cause of both the economic performance and the quality of telecommunications. (The data failed to confirm this possibility.) The best explanation of the cause of that relationship comes from the national time series data. As discussed above, those data give a clear answer to the chicken-and-egg question concerning which comes first—telecommunications investment or an improved economy? The answer is: both. The national data confirm that in the U.S. economy as a whole, better telecommunications led to better economic performance, while better economic performance also led to better telecommunications.

A completely persuasive explanation of observed correlations requires time series data. Nevertheless, contemporaneous data can confirm that rural areas exhibit the same relationship between telecommunications and economic performance seen in the national data. Replication of the national results with rural data at a single point in time provides a strong indication that the causal relationship found in the national data is also the reason for the similar relationship found in the rural data. Data taken from a single point in time also can show that the relationship between telecommunications and economic performance in rural areas is not just a common result of the lower population density in rural counties.

The Hypotheses

There are 39 counties in Washington and 36 in Oregon. Despite this small number of cases, it was possible to conduct a number of statistical analyses. We tested four correlational hypotheses to clarify the relationship between telecommunications infrastructure and rural economies:

Hypothesis 1: More densely populated counties have better economic performance than less densely populated counties. (The chief rationale for policy intervention to stimulate rural economic development is that people in rural locations are economically less well-off than those in urban areas. Hypothesis 1 predicts the reconfirmation of that basic assumption.)

Hypothesis 2: More densely populated counties have better telecommunications infrastructure than less densely populated counties. (Assuming Hypothesis 1 is confirmed, this hypothesis suggests that one reason for poorer rural economic performance is poorer rural telecommunications.)

Hypothesis 3: Counties with better telecommunications infrastructure have better economic performance than counties with poorer telecommunications infrastructure. (If improved telecommunications contributes to improved economic performance, then this relationship should be empirically observable.)

Hypothesis 4: The quality of telecommunications infrastructure is a significant predictor of county economic performance after controlling for differences attributable to population density. (The results of Hypothesis 3 could be confounded by differences in population density. Therefore, it is necessary to confirm that the relationship is still observed after statistically controlling for effects attributable to population density.)

Unlike the time series analysis, which measured the *growth* in the national economy, these hypotheses consider the *level* of economic performance. If prior investments have created an above average telecommunications infrastructure, then we also should see above average economic performance in those locations. The two measures of economic performance available for both rural and urban counties are per capita income and unemployment rate. Of these two measures, unemployment rate was the better indicator for Oregon and Washington because of a statistical anomaly resulting from aggregating income data at the county level. (In some locations, such as California, high unemployment may coexist with strong economic growth because many people migrate there in search of opportunities that do not always appear for them. In the Pacific Northwest, however, unemployment rate is an appropriate indicator of county economic performance.)

The two measures of telecommunications infrastructure most relevant to rural locations are:

- the extent to which multiparty telephone service has been replaced with single-party service; and

- the extent to which older electromechanical telephone switches have been replaced with electronic switches.

In theory, single-party telephone service for both residential users and businesses should contribute to better economic performance in several ways. Single-party telephones provide the privacy important for many business transactions. Also, because a single-party line is not shared with others, it is more available for both incoming and outgoing calls. Single-party telephones usually provide a higher quality of voice telephone service, making transactions easier. Most importantly, single-party lines permit data and facsimile transmissions, both of which are increasingly important for business information access from both offices and homes. Reliable fax or data transmission is not possible on multiparty lines.

Electronic switching provides a variety of economic advantages over electromechanical switching. Service is much more reliable, as measured by fewer periods of telephone unavailability and by better quality of transmission for both voice and data. Electronic switches also reduce the time for call set up (the time between completing dialing and the beginning of the phone ring). One consultant attempting to work from a rural location found that his urban clients, who were accustomed to having a phone ring almost immediately after they dialed the number, hung up before the phone rang because they thought they had a dead line.

Electronic switches also make possible several new services that save time and money for businesses. These include call forwarding, call waiting and three-way (conference) calling. One promising mail order business in rural Iowa could not expand in its rural location because the local electromechanical telephone switch could not provide multi-line 800 number service, needed for the firm's catalog sales. Telephone carriers using modern electronic or digital central office switches can offer Centrex business services, which provide smaller businesses with many of the services available to larger businesses on their PBXs. The absence of modern telecommunications services leaves local businesses at a competitive disadvantage and therefore less likely to expand than similar businesses in locations with better telecommunications.

For firms looking to relocate, reliable modern telephone service may be fourth or fifth on the list of criteria. Yet rural towns without modern telephone services may be summarily excluded from consideration because acceptable telecommunications can generally be found elsewhere. Rural areas without a modern telecommunications infrastructure may find that they are less competitive in recruiting new businesses—and thus less likely to grow than competitors who have superior phone service.

We predicted that better telephone service for businesses would help the economy; we also predicted that better residential service would improve economic performance, as Hardy found in his study. In rural areas, residential telephones are commonly used for business transactions. Many rural residents are self-employed farmers, ranchers, fishermen, craftspersons or small business operators who take business calls at home. Many other residential calls are to businesses, are from employers, or are to or from others who can provide information useful for improving income or employment.

The key question to be answered by testing the four hypotheses was whether the benefits from improved rural telecommunications were sufficiently large that they would result in higher income levels or lower unemployment rates.

The results, summarized in the following figures and tables, give a clear answer: Yes, counties with telephone lines upgraded from multiparty to single-party lines and telephone switches upgraded from electromechanical to digital have better economic performance than other counties. The evidence from the national data show that the observed correlation is at least partly the result of telecommunications investment leading to better economic performance. If so, upgrading rural telecommunications infrastructure should help to reduce the "rural penalty"—that is, the size of the economic gap between more and less densely populated counties.

Population Density and Economic Measures
Figure 6-1 shows that the unemployment rates in rural counties in both Oregon and Washington were higher than in metropolitan counties in the late 1980s. In Oregon, the 1989 unemployment rate in metropolitan counties

was 5.3 percent, compared to 7.7 percent in rural counties. In Washington, the unemployment rate in metropolitan counties was 6.9 percent, compared to 8.6 percent in rural counties. (The Washington unemployment data were for 1988, to correspond with the 1988 telecommunications data.)

Figure 6-2 shows that the average rural resident in Oregon had an income of $14,179 in 1989. The average metropolitan area resident in Oregon, by contrast, had an annual income 19 percent higher—$16,886. In Washington, the average rural resident had an income of $14,069 in 1988. The average Washington metro area resident had an income 21 percent higher—$17,021. These results, taken together with the unemployment data shown in Figure 6-1, confirm that in Oregon and Washington, like the rest of the nation, urban economic performance is better than rural economic performance.

For those who wish a more detailed look at these data, Appendix C lists all counties in both Oregon and Washington in order of population density (defined as the number of people per square mile of county land area). Appendix C also presents the unemployment rate, average income and the key telecommunications measures for each county.

The statistical tests of the four hypotheses require using counties, rather than people, as the basic unit of analysis. Such aggregated county data often do not show as clear a picture of rural-urban differences as averages across all rural people, compared to all urban people.* Because the county level data show less variation, it is more difficult to show a significant relationship with aggregated county data.

Rather than merely comparing metropolitan with rural counties, a more accurate picture can be obtained by looking at the same data along a continuum from most urban to most rural, based on the population density of the counties. In Oregon, the most densely populated county, in the Portland metropolitan area, has 1,208 people per square mile. The least densely populated counties in rural eastern Oregon have less than one

* For example, per capita income was calculated separately for each county, and then an average of those averages was calculated for rural and for metro counties. In Oregon in 1989, the average urban county had per capita income of $15,914, only 5 percent higher than the average rural county per capita income of $15,095. This 5 percent difference contrasts sharply with the 19 percent difference seen in Figure 6-2, which compares the average income of all rural residents with that of all urban residents. Similarly, Washington 1988 county income data showed urban counties ahead of rural counties by about 6 percent, $15,102 to $14,296. These differences in the county averages are not large enough to be significant, despite the very real differences between the incomes of urban and rural people, as shown in Figure 6-2. This anomaly is the result of a few rural counties with very low population having higher per capita incomes than those in the richest metropolitan counties in their state. These counties were places where large farms or ranches dominated the local economy.

Figure 6-1 Percent of Unemployment

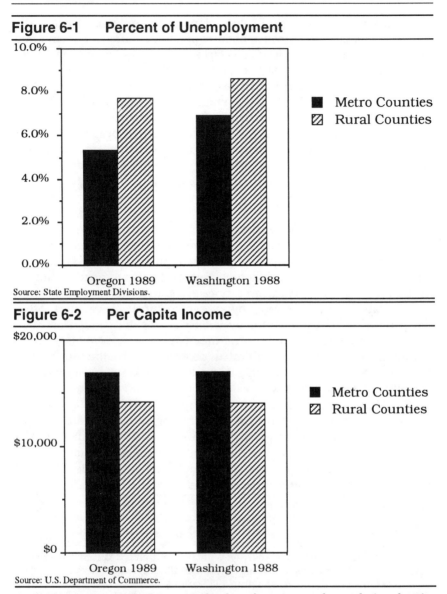

Source: State Employment Divisions.

Figure 6-2 Per Capita Income

Source: U.S. Department of Commerce.

person per square mile. In our study, therefore, we used population density as a measure of rurality.

To examine quantitatively the relationship between two measures, the standard statistical procedure is to calculate the extent to which knowledge of one measure (for example, population density) predicts the other (for example, unemployment rate). Statisticians call the measure of the relation-

Table 6-1   Population Density Related to Economic Measures

Population Density	Unemployment Rate	Per Capita Income
Oregon	r = -.32*	r = .26
Washington	r = -.45*	r = .36*

* significant (5% level)

ship, which they label with the symbol "r," a "correlation coefficient." The "r" value measures the size of the relationship, which may range from zero (indicating no relationship) to one (indicating a perfect correlation of one variable with the other) or to minus one (indicating a perfect inverse relationship between one variable and the other). When the value of the correlation coefficient "r" is large enough that the probability of getting from random data a correlation as large or larger than the one observed is less than 5 percent, statisticians typically judge the correlation to be significant.

Table 6-1 shows the results of testing for statistical significance the relationship between population density and the two economic variables, unemployment rate and per capita income, in the two states. The correlation between population density and unemployment rate showed a significant inverse relationship in both states. (The negative correlation results from counties with lower population densities having higher unemployment rates.) In Washington, counties with higher population densities also had higher per capita income, as shown by the significantly positive correlation coefficient.

Thus, three of the four measures (unemployment rate and per capita income in the two states) confirm Hypothesis 1: the economic performance of rural areas is worse than urban areas. (The fourth measure, Oregon income, was flawed because of insufficient variation in county aggregate data, as discussed above.)

Taken together, the data presented in Table 6-1 and Figures 6-1 and 6-2 confirm Hypothesis 1, which predicted that more densely populated counties have better economic performance than less densely populated counties.

Population Density and Telecommunications

Figure 6-3 shows the percentage of households in Oregon and Washington without telephones, compared to the national average, for the years 1984 through 1990. Oregon telephone penetration comes close to the national average, while Washington's is significantly better. By 1990, only 2.8 percent of Washington households were without telephones, compared to 7.2 percent in Oregon. Nationwide, 6.7 percent of households did not have telephones.

Figure 6-3   Percent of Households Without Telephones

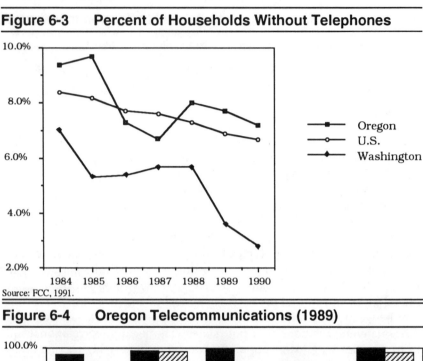

Source: FCC, 1991.

Figure 6-4   Oregon Telecommunications (1989)

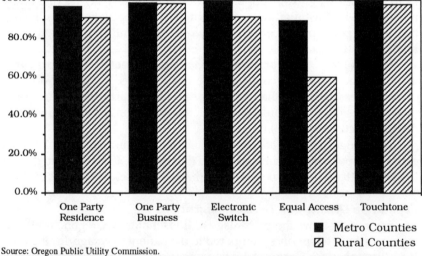

Source: Oregon Public Utility Commission.

Figure 6-4 shows the availability of modern telephone facilities in rural and urban counties in Oregon at the end of 1989. In rural counties, 91 percent of the residences with telephones had single-party service, compared to 96 percent in metropolitan counties. More than 98 percent of business lines had single-party service in both rural and metro counties. Electronic (or digital) switches served more than 91 percent of rural telephone lines, compared to more than 99 percent in metro counties. Nearly all telephones in the state had touchtone service available, although sometimes only as an option costing more than basic rotary-dial telephone service.

The biggest difference between rural and urban counties is in the number of phone lines with equal access to competitive long-distance carriers (achieved by dialing 1 plus the wanted phone number). While 89 percent of telephone lines in metro counties had equal access in 1989, only 60 percent of telephones in rural counties had equal access.

Figure 6-5 shows similar rural and urban data for Washington State in mid-1988. The gap between metro and rural counties in number of households served with single-party phone service was even greater: 14 percent of residence telephones in rural counties were still on multiparty service, compared to four percent in urban counties. Even three percent of the business lines in rural counties still had multiparty service, compared to less than one percent in urban counties. While digital or electronic switches served 90 percent of the metro county telephone lines, such switches served only 69 percent of rural county telephone lines.

Table 6-2 shows the relationships between population density and availability of modern telephone facilities in Oregon and Washington. As expected, more densely populated counties in both states had a higher proportion of single-party residential and business telephones and a larger proportion of telephone lines served by an electronic telephone switch. In

Figure 6-5   Washington Telecommunications (1988)

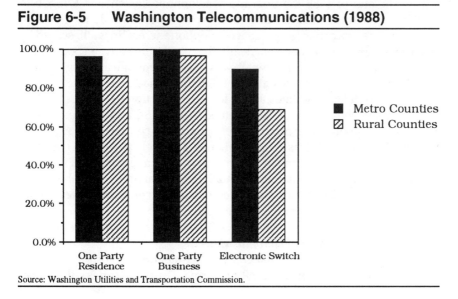

Source: Washington Utilities and Transportation Commission.

Table 6-2   Population Density Related to Telecommunications

	Oregon 1989	Washington 1988
Residence Single-party	r = .36*	r = .47*
Business Single-party	r = .21	r = .45*
Electronic Switch	r = .12	r = .33*

* Significant (5% level)

Washington, using 1988 data, all three telephone variables (residential single-party service, business single-party service and the availability of electronic switching) resulted in a statistically significant correlation with county population density.

In Oregon also, urban counties had a significantly higher percentage of residential single-party telephone lines than rural counties. The percentage of Oregon business telephones with single-party service was so large that the relationship with population density, although in the predicted direction, was not significant. By late 1989 only one rural county in Oregon had more than five percent of its business telephone lines still on multiparty service—compared to seven Washington counties that had more than five percent of business lines on multiparty service in mid-1988.

By the end of 1989 the upgrade of telephone switches in Oregon to digital or electronic analog was nearing completion. In only six of the 36 counties were more than ten percent of telephone access lines still served by electromechanical switches. As a result, the correlation between population density and type of telephone switch was not large enough to be significant.

On the average, in both states, rural counties had a higher proportion of multiparty telephone lines and a lower proportion of lines served by electronic switches. The results presented in Table 6-2 and Figures 6-4 and 6-5 confirm Hypothesis 2: more densely populated counties do have better telecommunications infrastructures than less densely populated counties. Despite aggressive modernization programs that have upgraded the rural telecommunications infrastructure much faster than in most of the rest of the country, rural telephone service in both Oregon and Washington remains poorer than urban telephone service.

Telecommunications and Economic Measures

Hypothesis 3 predicted that counties with better telecommunications infrastructure have better economic performance than counties with poorer

Table 6-3   Unemployment Related to Telecommunications

	Oregon 1989	Washington 1988
Residence Single-party	r = -.45*	r = -.03
Business Single-party	r = -.31*	r = -.07
Electronic Switch	r = .10	r = -.35*

* Significant (5% level)

telecommunications infrastructure. The unemployment rate is one important measure of economic performance. A correlation between telecommunications and unemployment rate could have several explanations. Counties with higher unemployment could be less able to afford modern telecommunications, or counties that could afford better telecommunications might be stimulating more local business, thus contributing to lower unemployment rates. The national data discussed in section 3, above, suggest that both effects are likely to be present.

Table 6-3 shows that, in Oregon, a higher percentage of single-party residential or business telephone lines was significantly correlated with lower unemployment rates. The percentage of telephone lines served by electronic switches did *not* correlate with the unemployment rate—because most rural telephone switches had been upgraded to electronic switches by the end of 1989. In Washington, the higher the percentage of telephone lines served by electronic switching, the lower the unemployment rate. The percentage of single-party phone lines in Washington counties did not correlate with county unemployment.

Table 6-3 provides partial support for Hypothesis 3, which said that counties with better telecommunications infrastructure have better economic performance than counties with poorer telecommunications infrastructure. Several of the correlations are significant, although different variables serve as significant predictors in Washington compared to Oregon. The only surprising result was the lack of correlation between unemployment and single-party service in Washington. We do not know why this prediction failed in one state.

The relative lack of county variation in income levels, particularly in Oregon, make the unemployment data a better indicator of economic performance for the present analysis. Nevertheless, the correlation in Washington counties between per capita income and the percentage of county telephones served by an electronic switch was .35—a significant correlation.

Controlling for Population Density

The tests of Hypothesis 3, presented in Table 6.3, do not provide a complete picture of the relationship between telecommunications and rural economic performance. A third variable, population density (or other factors correlated with population density), may have influenced the levels of both telecommunications and economic performance. In counties with lower population density, the costs of telecommunications are usually higher; telephone lines stretching out over longer distances to reach fewer customers cost more per customer. Also, economic performance tends to be less robust in counties with lower population density because the market size is smaller and costs are usually higher (largely because of the greater transportation costs involved).

Telecommunications may be a way to reduce these economic penalties of rural life, but the quality of the telecommunications network itself may be affected by identical penalties. Sparse population and geographic isolation not only impede economic development, they make it more difficult to upgrade the rural telecommunications networks. To get a clearer picture of a complex situation, we must look at the relationship between telecommunications and population density, *and* how they individually and together affect economic performance. After all, many other factors besides telecommunications contribute to the inferior economic performance of rural counties. These other factors usually correlate with population density (which we used as a surrogate for the other factors influencing rural economic performance). Therefore, it is important to show that the relationship between telecommunications and economic performance remains significant, after controlling for the relationship between population density and economic performance.

The Pacific Northwest data discussed to this point thus serve as a preamble to the testing of Hypothesis 4. That proposition, it will be recalled, states that the quality of telecommunications infrastructure continues to be a significant predictor of county economic performance after controlling for differences attributable to population density.

We used a technique called "multiple correlation analysis" to test this hypothesis. This technique tests the extent to which a combination of predictor variables can be used to predict another variable, for example, county unemployment rates. This statistical method finds the extent to which each predictor variable is a significant independent predictor, after accounting for the predictive capability of the other variables.

Table 6-4 shows the extent to which population density, percentage of residential phone lines with single-party service and percentage of phone lines served by electronic switching—each individually and all three together—predict Oregon county unemployment rates. The multiple correla-

Table 6-4 Predicting Oregon Unemployment from Population Density and Telecommunications Measures

	Amount of Correlation	Variance Explained
Population Density	-.32*	10%*
Residential Single-party	-.45*	20%*
Electronic Switching	.10	1%
All Three Combined	-.53*	28%*

* Significant (5% level)

tion analysis showed that population density and residential single-party service were both significant independent predictors of Oregon county unemployment rates, after controlling for variation that could be accounted for by the other variables.

The combination of all three variables accounted for 28 percent of the variation in Oregon county unemployment rates. (This percentage was slightly less than the sum of the individual predictions, presumably because population density predicted part of the variance in unemployment rate that was also predicted by the telecommunications measures.) Electronic switching was not a significant predictor, presumably because by the end of 1989 there were so few electromechanical switches remaining in Oregon. Similar analyses attempting to predict Oregon county variations in income were not meaningful because of insufficient variation in county averages of per capita income.

Table 6-5 is the Washington State analog of Table 6-4, which uses Oregon county data. Table 6-5 shows the extent to which population density, percentage of residential telephone lines with single-party service and percentage of phone lines served by electronic switching—each individually and all three combined—predict Washington county unemployment rates. The multiple correlation analysis showed that population density and electronic switching were both significant independent predictors of Washington county unemployment rates, after controlling for variation in unemployment rates that could be accounted for by the other variables. The combination of all three variables accounted for 35 percent of the variation in Washington county unemployment rates. This percentage was slightly but not significantly more than the sum of the individual predictors.

Table 6-6 shows how the three predictor variables correlate with per capita income in Washington counties. The multiple correlation analysis

Table 6-5 Predicting Washington Unemployment from Population Density and Telecommunications Measures

	Amount of Correlation	Variance Explained
Population Density	-.45*	20%*
Residential Single-party	-.03	0%
Electronic Switching	-.35*	12%*
All Three Combined	-.59*	35%*

* Significant (5% level)

Table 6-6 Predicting Washington Income from Population Density and Telecommunications Measures

	Amount of Correlation	Variance Explained
Population Density	.36*	13%*
Residential Single-party	.01	0%
Electronic Switching	.35*	12%*
All Three Combined	.53*	28%*

* Significant (5% level)

shows that population density and electronic switching were both significant independent predictors, after controlling for variation in county average income that could be accounted for by the other variables. The combination of all three variables accounted for 28 percent of the variation in per capita income levels in Washington counties.

Taken together, the data presented in Tables 6-4 through 6-6 confirm Hypothesis 4. These data confirm that the level of development of telecommunications infrastructure is a significant predictor of the level of economic development. This was confirmed after controlling for population density, the measure of rurality used in this analysis. These results do not, by themselves, definitively prove a causal connection between telecommunications infrastructure and rural economic development. They do provide statistical evidence of a significant relationship between telecommunications infrastructure and economic development.

That relationship is not merely a coincidence that results from more rural (less densely populated) counties having poorer economic performance and poorer telecommunications infrastructures. After controlling for the level of economic performance predicted by population density, a strong independent relationship between telecommunications infrastructure and economic performance remains.

When taken together with the causal evidence provided by the national time series data discussed in section 3, above, these results provide persuasive quantitative statistical evidence that rural telecommunications infrastructure investment, when combined with development strategies making effective use of that investment, does lead to economic development. In other words, in a modern economy, improved telecommunications can reduce the economic penalties of being rural.

5. THE TELECOMMUNICATIONS CONNECTION

The national data provide the evidence of a causal connection between telecommunications infrastructure investment and economic growth in the country as a whole. These national results show clearly that when past telecommunications investments were made, the other factors necessary for economic growth usually were present also, or soon followed.

The county data from two states provide a more detailed picture of the interrelationship of population density, telecommunications infrastructure and rural economic performance. This more detailed picture confirms that counties that have upgraded rural multiparty phone service to single-party service and replaced electromechanical telephone switches with modern digital switching capability, perform better economically than counties that have not done so. This remains true after controlling for the effect of population density on economic performance.

Of course, the correlations found in Oregon and Washington remain a *description* of relationships found in those two states. For an *explanation* of why those relationships occur we must depend on the national data, which also show correlations between telecommunications infrastructure and economic performance. The national time series data did confirm the hypothesis that investment in telecommunications infrastructure led to economic growth.

The process of achieving the economic benefits is complex. Upgrading the telephone technology improves the quality and variety of telecommunications services available. It is the use of those services by rural residents, businesses, government and other institutions that causes the resulting economic gains. Those gains may result from a better informed workforce, productivity gains in local businesses, or from better information about markets and business opportunities. Modern telecommunications infrastructure is the enabler that makes such gains possible.

Research findings alone will not decide policy. Nevertheless, the better the research evidence, the more informed the policy debate can be. The evidence reported here provides further support for a policy goal of using modern telecommunications as one element of an integrated rural development strategy. Taken together with the many case studies showing how telecommunications has helped specific communities, these data provide compelling evidence for reforms in state telecommunications policy.

The vision of using telecommunications to improve the rural economy is not a conjectural theory or idealistic dream. It is a vision supported by an impressive body of both anecdotal and statistical evidence. Unlike many legislative issues that may turn on intuition, emotion or isolated anecdotes, the case for improved rural telecommunications is supported by rigorous quantitative analysis and many specific examples. Together, they show that telecommunications policy can serve as a powerful instrument to spur rural development.

As always, the major challenge is how to get there from here. The answers will vary from community to community and state to state, of course, but there are many specific policy goals and actions that can help translate the vision into reality. We now turn to the problems of implementation, with a detailed menu of state policy goals and recommended actions.

CHAPTER 7

Building Electronic Byways: Goals and Recommendations

1. THE VISION

There is an old saying, "If you don't know where you are going, any road will take you there." The opposite is equally true: people and institutions with clearly stated goals are more likely to find the right road to reach their destination. This chapter offers some specific goals and policy recommendations that, taken together, form a coherent vision for using telecommunications to help improve the economy and the quality of life in rural America.

This vision does not equate development with urbanization or homogeneity. Rather, it recognizes that rural communities vary immensely and are likely to have quite different needs and ambitions. Yet whether they are in farming districts or mill towns, fishing villages or retirement communities, people in most rural communities share a yearning to improve the quality of their lives. They do not seek special treatment or handouts. They do seek *enabling tools* that give them an opportunity to develop their potential, keep pace with urban businesses, improve their schools, and minimize the penalties of being rural.

In the United States, we are proud of our heritage as a land of opportunity where those people who want to better themselves can do so. One challenge facing rural America in the 1990s is preserving this tradition of equal opportunity. This task is both a moral necessity and an economic necessity. In the decades to come, the U.S. competitive advantage in the global economy will depend primarily upon the skills and education of our workforce. With shortages of well-educated labor looming ahead, improving rural education will yield social benefits and enhance our global competitiveness.

As earlier chapters make clear, telecommunications can play a vital role in providing equal opportunities for rural communities. A modern telecommunications infrastructure by itself cannot guarantee development, of course. But the absence of such infrastructure can act as a major barrier to development. Much as the interstate highway system opened up development possibilities for parts of rural America, so telecommunications can open up new linkages to a wider world, helping rural communities participate in the information-based economy of the 1990s.

The process for achieving such a future is complicated, however. Planning and building rural telecommunications is quite different from the planning and building of traditional infrastructure and from other development investments. A competitive, private-sector marketplace cannot by itself provide adequate rural telecommunications. Nor can communities or counties, by themselves, build a telecommunications infrastructure in the same way they might build water mains, sewer lines and local roads. Federal and state budget allocations—the chief means of building major highways—do not offer an appropriate model for telecommunications investment.

Building a telecommunications infrastructure is more complex for many reasons. Its technical aspects are often not well-understood by policy makers and its economic value may not be fully appreciated. Perhaps most critically, coordinating state telecommunications policies with the concerns of the private sector and rural communities can be difficult and confusing. Local governments do not have meaningful authority over telephone carriers, which state governments regulate. State governments also have limited ability to influence the deployment of privately owned companies' resources. Finally, local carriers are regulated monopolies and are not subject to direct competitive pressures (except for services that bypass the public switched telephone network). In sum, the planning and installation of advanced telecommunications are quite different from the simpler process governing construction of public roads.

As a way to interact with the "outside world," telecommunications has some distinct advantages. Not every community can have a major highway. But it is economically feasible for every community in the country, including the most remote hamlets and homesteads, to connect with the information resources available via "electronic byways." Although standard telephone technology using cables and copper wire may be too expensive in some locations, new radio and satellite telephony techniques make it possible to serve any rural location economically.

Given the modest costs and potentially large benefits, we believe that it is time for rural America to enjoy a standard of telecommunications taken for granted in urban areas: *universal opportunity of access to modern telecommunications services.* This is a policy goal that can be afforded and achieved, without additional taxpayer funds, through adjustments in state regulatory and procurement policies. This new standard should not require new regulatory burdens or subsidies, but rather the elimination of some regulatory barriers and the creation of incentives for private sector investment.

The general goal for both urban and rural policy should be "universal information access," defined as the opportunity for every business and home in the United States to have affordable access to publicly available information services in all media, whether voice, data or images. Most services (especially voice and data services) should be available through the public switched telephone network, although video and some audio services may be provided by cable television, communication satellites or wireless over-the-air transmission. Mobile communications also should be available, to both rural residents and urban residents, through cellular telephones or comparable technologies.

As rural America contemplates its telecommunications future, it must do more than try to catch up with the previous generation of technology and services now used in urban areas. It must *anticipate* the ways in which the urban infrastructure will be changing. Otherwise, scarce resources may be wasted on "old" equipment, as urban facilities and services leap ahead into the next generation of technology. Rural communities seeking adequate narrowband voice and data services, for example, should anticipate that broadband data and video services will likely follow, as they have in urban areas. If such future needs are not anticipated, rural areas may complete upgrades of their facilities to meet prior standards, only to find themselves again locked into an inferior position.

Although planning telecommunications infrastructure necessarily involves a diverse collection of players, state government is the primary actor. With two notable exceptions, state leadership will be decisive in achieving significant progress. First, the future of cellular (mobile) telephone services will be largely determined by the FCC, which granted licenses for rural service areas in 1990. Over the next five years, cellular telephone services should expand throughout much of rural America as the new licensees begin service. The availability of video information services also will be decided by the federal government. Federal law currently prohibits telephone carriers from offering video information services except in rural communities of fewer than 2,500 people.

Since state leadership for change should come from several key parties, we propose below a specific set of goals and recommendations for each of them:

- the governor and legislature (section 2);

- state and local economic development agencies (section 3);

- state regulatory commissions (section 4); and

- providers of telecommunications equipment and services (section 5).

There are two important reasons why the proposals outlined below are achievable. First, the financing for new telecommunications infrastructure can be secured almost entirely through the private sector, given the proper economic incentives and policy changes; hardly any new costs will be borne by residential consumers or state treasuries. Second, all of the goals and recommendations of this chapter can be achieved by states without federal legislative, judicial or regulatory changes. The environment is ripe for change. What is most needed is concerted leadership.

2. RECOMMENDATIONS FOR STATE GOVERNORS AND LEGISLATORS

For governors and state legislators, using telecommunications to help spur economic development offers a rare political opportunity: the chance to secure major benefits for business, education and other constituencies without imposing noticeable costs on consumers or state government. As the preceding chapters suggest, the potential benefits are significant. Because they can be achieved through regulatory and administrative changes—without major commitments of tax funds—controversy is unlikely.

Four general steps are necessary:

1. Make telecommunications and development policy reform more visible and comprehensible so that it can be given priority in the state government's agenda.

2. Build a consensus for a set of state telecommunications goals that are tailored to specific state needs and development possibilities.

3. Establish incentives for state government agencies and the private sector to cooperate to achieve those goals.

4. Provide an ongoing process through which progress toward those goals can be measured, and, if necessary, policies can be adjusted.

There are two primary vehicles by which state governments can affect telecommunications: the state regulatory commission and the state government procurement process. In many states, the regulatory commission functions under a legislative mandate narrowly crafted to provide consumers protection from potential abuses by monopoly utilities. That function should be broadened, so that the commissions also can focus on long-term development objectives as they formulate regulatory policy.

The state government's process for buying telephone and other telecommunications network services also holds great promise for stimulating change. Typically, the procurement function is coordinated at a relatively low bureaucratic level, in a general services department or in separate offices in different agencies. If consolidated and raised to a higher level in the state government's administration, the state's combined purchasing power for telecommunications networks can elicit new products and services from vendors. Procurement policy can be a potent strategic tool for promoting advanced telecommunications statewide through the public switched telephone network. The new telecommunications services also can bring new efficiencies and responsiveness to state government.

Based on examples from many states, we offer the following specific recommendations to help executive and legislative branches of state governments exploit the rich promise of telecommunications.

Recommendation 1:

State governors and legislatures should develop a comprehensive telecommunications plan with specific goals appropriate to the conditions of their states.

In states that have begun this process, there have been two primary entities for developing telecommunications plans: a task force appointed by the governor (see chapter 2) and a joint committee created by the legislature (see chapter 5). However organized, the planning process must be conducted by top policy makers and must solicit the views of a wide diversity of business and civic leaders, academics, citizens, government employees, and others. As the process in Washington State showed, no one group had all the answers; the best insights and practical solutions emerged from a broad-based cooperative process. This open collaboration not only helped generate the best information, analyses and proposals, it helped build a consensus for change. The goals and proposals were seen as politically legitimate, which made their achievement easier.

Recommendation 2:

Each state should establish a full set of performance measures to monitor progress toward meeting state goals for its telecommunications infrastructure.

Setting goals is not enough. Telecommunications planners also must prepare periodic "report cards" on the progress made in achieving stated goals, using specific performance measures. The starting point for such a monitoring process is an inventory of the existing telecommunications infrastructure. The state regulatory commission should be able to supply or obtain much of the data, and development agencies should help set telecommunications goals and monitor progress toward achieving those goals.

The infrastructure inventory should include the major fiber optic routes in and through the state; the long distance carrier points of presence (the "on-ramps" to electronic highways); the location of telephone switches from which specialized services are available (such as dial-up videoconferencing); and the location of gateways for access to value-added networks and other information services. Legislative authority may be required to obtain and publish the necessary data. For each indicator, data should be compiled for both urban and rural areas (by comparing data for metropolitan and non-metropolitan counties, for example). The survey conducted by Washington State in 1988 is a good model (see chapter 5).

If telecommunications planners hope to identify failures to meet their goals and make necessary policy adjustments, they must articulate a clear set of performance measures. One important measure, for example, is the percentage of households served by single-party touchtone service. Other measurements should evaluate improvements in quality of service, such as the percentage of telephone lines that can reliably transmit fax and data. Some measures are discussed in section 4, below. The report of an Oregon task force on telecommunications policy appointed by Oregon Governor Barbara Roberts in 1991 provides a useful list of other performance measures (see Appendix D).

Recommendation 3:

State legislatures should authorize their regulatory commissions to consider economic development potential as they regulate telecommunications.

Regulatory commissions perform a quasi-judicial function as they balance competing interests, particularly those of consumers and the regulated carriers. Regulatory commissions cannot be the sole, or even the primary, body responsible for exploiting the development potential of the telecommunications infrastructure. Nevertheless, as they make policy judgments, they should have explicit authority to take economic development into account as one interest to be balanced against others. (Most state regulatory commissions do not currently have this explicit authority.) By making a clear grant of this authority, legislatures would both sensitize regulatory commissions about the development potential of telecommunications and give them an unequivocal and sensible mandate.

Recommendation 4 :

State legislatures should authorize their regulatory commissions to use incentive regulation as an alternative to traditional rate-of-return regulation.

Since most of the telecommunications infrastructure for economic development will be built by regulated telecommunications carriers, appropriate regulatory incentives will be needed. Unfortunately, traditional rate-of-return regulation, designed to prevent monopoly abuses, is not likely to spur the necessary investments and innovation. As explained in chapter 2, incentive regulation holds much greater promise for eliciting new investment in advanced telecommunications.

Recommendation 5:

State economic development agencies should be authorized to become advocates for telecommunications policies that serve economic development goals.

As the importance of telecommunications to the economy increases, state agencies charged with stimulating economic development should champion the building of the necessary infrastructure. They should work closely with local or county economic development councils to find out infrastructure needs, and they should promote the needed policy changes. Within limits, development agencies may take their own initiatives in this area, but their success will depend critically on the guidance and support of governors and legislatures. (More specific recommendations for state development agencies are included in section 3, below.)

Recommendation 6:

State governments should establish a high level, centralized telecommunications authority within the state government. This body would coordinate, evaluate and set priorities for the state's own telecommunications and information technology efforts, including voice, data and image processing and transmission.

State telecommunications network planning requires much more than buying voice telephone service and dedicated lines linking government offices. As the various electronic media (voice, data, image-processing) convert to digital formats for transmission purposes, technologies are converging. This presents an opportunity to use telecommunications networks strategically. Integrating voice, data and video technologies into the same digital network can improve both the quality and efficiency of state government's delivery of services.

A central telecommunications authority within state government also can help state agencies work more effectively and efficiently. As information sources proliferate within a state, common standards are increasingly necessary for state agencies to interconnect with each other on their various voice, data and image networks. In many states, tax dollars could be saved by avoiding duplicative state government networks. Dealing successfully with these issues requires a coordinated focus of attention at a high level within state government administration.

Most states could benefit from a state authority that focuses on telecommunications, information technology and information services—just as many large corporations have combined these functions under the leadership of a Chief Information Officer. Combining the strategic planning responsibility for these functions at a senior level in the executive branch of government can yield valuable benefits. Telecommunications and information technologies can be deployed more effectively and efficiently, and state government information and services can be made available more widely to the state's citizens.

Recommendation 7:

Planners of state government telecommunications services should design them to increase citizens' access to public information and services without regard to geographic location or income.

A variety of government services and information sources could be made more widely available to citizens, at less expense, through creative uses of telecommunications. The benefits would be particularly valuable for rural residents, whose remoteness often limits their access to state government information and services.

All citizens, rural and urban, could interact more effectively with state government if state agencies had voice mail systems, toll-free 800 numbers, and audio information access services (which provide recorded explanations of frequently used services). All state residents also could benefit from computer access to non-confidential state government data networks and to recorded voice information systems activated by touchtone phones. Both systems would allow information about government services to be provided more efficiently and made more widely accessible. State government video image networks, including those designed for distance education applications, could allow citizens living in rural locations to gain teleconferencing access to government hearings.

Recommendation 8:

> *The state government process for procurement of telecommunications should be used to help develop a modernized public switched network throughout the state.*

State governments have two compelling reasons to establish dedicated networks separate from the public switched network offered by the telephone companies. The first is price; a dedicated network, which may use lines leased from the telephone company, costs a lot less. The second is technical features; the capabilities needed for most government data and image networks are not universally available on public switched telephone networks.

In urban areas, the resulting bypass of the public switched network has not created serious problems for other users. There are competitive alternatives for specialized services and a large enough volume of general business to stimulate telephone carrier investment in the public network. In rural areas, however, a dedicated government network may hinder development. If the major state government applications bypass the public switched network, the remaining rural business may not be sufficient for carriers to make the investments needed to offer advanced telecommunications services.

Government data networks for lottery terminals and other government applications are often the first data networks in rural areas. If those networks operate on dedicated lines, spin-off benefits for rural communities may be lost. Rural small businesses may not enjoy electronic data access to outlying branches, government agencies, suppliers and customers. Distance education may be the most promising application to bring video information access to rural areas. But a dedicated education network may block any rural development of telemedicine and business teleconferencing applications.

There is an alternative, but it requires close cooperation among the state agency responsible for telecommunications procurement, telecommunications carriers, and the state regulatory commission. The challenge is to obtain the advanced features needed by state government through the public switched network at a reasonable cost—and in so doing, make similar features available to other users. For such a scenario to make economic sense to government agencies trying to be frugal with taxpayer funds, telecommunications carriers would have to offer special high-volume government discount rates to match the prices that could be achieved with a dedicated network. Carriers also would have to add to the public switched network the kinds of features needed for government applications.

Before such volume discount prices could go into effect, the state regulatory commission would have to approve the special prices and, perhaps, the necessary network investments. Although this sort of co-operation among state government procurement agencies, regulatory commissions and telephone carriers may be difficult, it could speed the public availability of a sophisticated rural telecommunications infrastructure. This, in turn, could yield many benefits for rural development.

Recommendation 9:

State governments should support pilot projects involving telecommunications applications that could benefit rural development.

Mindful of their distinct needs, states could learn more about the actual promise of telecommunications applications through pilot projects. The most common pilot projects, as described in chapter 3, involve distance education. Others are exploring the uses of advanced telecommunications networks to improve rural health care and other services.

A novel pilot project, now being considered by the State of Washington, would explore the value of a comprehensive statewide electronic mail capability linking state agencies, counties and Educational Service Districts. The network also would connect with public access electronic mail services to enable communication with any citizen in the state. Some states may wish to go beyond electronic mail and establish an electronic data interchange network linking the state government with its suppliers. In the process, such a network could stimulate the electronic interconnection of state businesses. Another project could be provision of electronic citizen access to the non-confidential information in state government databases. Yet another type of project could be a pilot telecommuting project, to find out what changes in personnel practices may be necessary to take advantage of new telecommunications technologies.

In evaluating potential pilot projects, state governments would do well to choose applications that promise the greatest long term benefits for their state. Each pilot project should include an evaluation component so that the cost effectiveness of later projects and programs can be assessed.

3. GOALS AND RECOMMENDATIONS
FOR DEVELOPMENT AGENCIES

Rural development planners are likely to think of telecommunications as an arcane specialty that they would rather leave to the experts than learn about themselves. This is shortsighted. The telecommunications infrastructure and services needed to support rural development in the Information Age are too important to be left to telecommunications specialists. Despite the versatility and potential of telecommunications to leverage development, telecommunications is not easily or widely understood by development planners as a development tool.

This barrier will not be overcome unless development planners learn more about telecommunications and advocate its deployment for a range of rural development purposes. Development planners also must become a powerful force for educating state agencies, rural businesses, educators and young people about telecommunications: their varied applications, effective utilization and economic benefits.

This section presents five specific telecommunications policy goals for development agencies, and offers specific recommendations for achieving those goals.

Development Goal 1:

Increased statewide awareness of the linkages between telecommunications and development

As noted in chapter 1, the U.S. economy is in the midst of an historic structural transformation, from an economy based on mass production of standardized goods to one based on information and specialized goods and services. If rural communities are to survive this transition and prosper in the new economy, they will need help. Communities that fail to interconnect with the emerging electronic superhighways may find themselves ghost towns in the 21st century. To help these at-risk communities, development agencies need to increase their own awareness and understanding of telecommunications problems and opportunities.

Development Recommendation 1.1: Development agencies should sponsor regional workshops to share information about innovative uses of telecommunications and identify rural telecommunications needs.

Regional workshops or conferences can be a highly effective vehicle for educating rural communities about telecommunications and development. They help development agencies learn about rural needs and allow innovative users to share stories about their telecommunications projects. Workshops also educate participants about potential telecommunications applications and, in so doing, help participants identify their own telecommunications needs. (See chapter 3 for examples of workshops jointly sponsored by telephone companies and development agencies.)

Development Recommendation 1.2: Development agencies should convene task forces to set goals for the modernization of the state's telecommunications infrastructure and plans for its use to stimulate development.

The first recommendation to state governors and legislatures is to develop a statewide plan. A task force may be a key part of this process. It can help gather the most diverse information about existing needs and help forge a consensus among influential constituencies in the state. As chapter 2 describes, several states have appointed telecommunications policy task forces.

To ensure that each task force integrates telecommunications goals with the state's economic development plans, the state development agency should help organize and staff the undertaking. It is also important that influential providers and users of telecommunications services and major players in state development programs participate in the task force. The resulting report should set specific, measurable goals for the state. If rigorously researched and widely circulated, a task force report can help change public understanding of telecommunications and build momentum for policy changes.

The task forces should be reminded that the availability of telecommunications technology is not enough. They also should make plans for use of improved infrastructure to achieve development objectives. Those utilization plans should influence the goals for infrastructure development to ensure that the necessary facilities and services are available for the planned applications.

Development Goal 2:

More sophisticated advocacy for telecommunications policies that serve development goals

The fate of small businesses in rural communities will increasingly depend upon the telecommunications services available through the public switched telephone network. This issue is especially important to rural communities because small businesses will generate much of the growth in new jobs, both rural and urban, over the next decade.

Unfortunately, small businesses and rural communities, acting individually, do not have the market power to assure that their telecommunications needs will be met by their monopoly provider. Nor do they have the time, expertise or financial resources to press their case with the regulatory commission. If they are to be effective at all, they need a collective advocate at the regulatory commission.

Economic development agencies may be the best hope small businesses and rural communities have for collective advocacy at the regulatory commission. In most states, development agencies would have to learn about the issues and hire or train the appropriate staff to take on this function. Yet because the issues are fundamental to rural economic development, such sophisticated advocacy is needed.

Development Recommendation 2.1: State development agencies should become credible advocates for rural development interests at the state regulatory commission.

Few development agencies have anyone on their staff with specific training or experience in telecommunications advocacy. Nevertheless, these views are important in the regulatory process. State development agencies may be better equipped than any other public or private body to argue the case for an advanced telecommunications infrastructure and for regulatory policies that promote development goals. If no one articulates this perspective, regulatory commissions are likely to hear only from telephone carriers and possibly consumer advocates, who may argue against infrastructure investment because they fear it would lead to higher residential telephone rates. Even if the regulatory commissions have clear legislative authority to consider economic development goals, they will be hard pressed to act on them if no one offers evidence or advocacy for those goals.

Development Goal 3:

Better understanding among small businesses and rural communities of the many valuable uses of telecommunications services

Small businesses may be the best hope for sustained job creation and economic development, especially in rural areas. Yet this potential is reduced because small businesses may not know how to take advantage of new telecommunications services. Small businesses are discouraged easily by the technical barriers, the pace of technological change, the confusing array of vendors, and the complexity of regulations. Many small businesses could benefit from programs designed to help them navigate past these problems, so that they could exploit telecommunications profitably in their enterprises.

Development Recommendation 3.1: State development agencies should build a telecommunications component into small business assistance and rural community development programs.

States have small business assistance programs, including cooperative extension and small business development centers. Telecommunications assistance should be included in these programs, or made available through a separate telecommunications assistance office. One example is the Telecommunications Education Trust (TET), created by the California Public Utilities Commission, to educate Californians about telecommunications. These programs may not only help small businesses, they also may help state agencies themselves improve their productivity and public outreach.

One TET-funded project is a series of *TeleFacts Guides* for small and minority businesses and nonprofit organizations, produced by the Telecommunications Management and Policy Program at the University of San Francisco. The guides cover such topics as choosing a long distance carrier, local telephone services and discounts, facsimile and computer communications, voice mail, cellular telephones, pay phones, the effective use of telecommunications in small businesses, and other topics. Similar guides could be developed for other states, with information on carriers and regulations specific to each state. Such materials would be useful in any small business development program.

Development Recommendation 3.2: Development agencies should sponsor training courses on telecommunications for community and economic development professionals.

The key to providing adequate small business and rural development assistance is having knowledgeable trained staff. Few economic development professionals know enough about telecommunications to provide detailed assistance on the topic to their constituency. Offering appropriate courses and training seminars for development professionals would help to fill that gap.

Development Goal 4:

A rural workforce trained to meet the telecommunications needs of rural business

The complexity and proliferation of new telecommunications technology and services will increase at an accelerating rate in the next decade. Both urban and rural workers will need the knowledge and skills to use these new tools effectively, just as they have to become increasingly computer literate. Community colleges may be the appropriate institutions to develop and offer such courses.

Development Recommendation 4.1: Development agencies should work with community colleges to establish telecommunications training courses.

Community colleges may be the best place to offer practical telecommunications courses to prepare a workforce to use effectively voice, data, video and multimedia telecommunications. Many community colleges already have small business development or small business assistance centers. By adding expertise in telecommunications, community colleges can become key nodes in a statewide network for telecommunications information, training and technical assistance.

Development Recommendation 4.2: State development agencies should encourage the establishment and expansion of distance learning programs for both student and adult education.

As described in chapter 3, telecommunications-based distance learning programs can deliver courses on virtually any subject to all high schools and community colleges, however small or distant. Students not only learn about new subjects, they experience firsthand the benefits of telecommunications. This familiarity with distance learning may make them more receptive to "lifelong learning," which workers in the coming decades will increasingly need for updating their skills or retraining for new jobs. Training courses and expert advice can be delivered by telecommunications not only to community colleges and schools, but also to workplaces and homes.

Development Goal 5:

Aggregation of rural and small business demand for modern telecommunications services

In pursuit of the largest markets, telecommunications carriers tend to focus on the needs of large companies and urban markets. Small businesses and rural communities that are captive to a single carrier, individually do not have the clout to obtain better telecommunications infrastructure—so their needs may go unfilled. To remedy this problem, new means should be found to bring together the demand of rural and small business users, so that collectively they will get the attention of the carriers.

Development Recommendation 5.1: Development agencies should work with rural communities and small businesses to help them to obtain collectively the telecommunications services they might not be able to obtain individually.

Some communities and small businesses may need outside help to aggregate enough demand to get the attention of their telephone carrier. Development agencies can fill the void by working with rural communities and small businesses to help them identify needs and pool their requirements. They can then serve as advocates with the telecommunications carriers and regulatory commissions to help meet the demand.

Some might object that development agencies should not take on a marketing function that sellers of services normally provide. However, this function may be necessary in some regions where monopoly telephone carriers have not learned yet how to market their services effectively to rural and small business users.

In some states, rural telephone carriers themselves have aggregated demand from their rural customers. A group of small Iowa rural telephone carriers organized Iowa Network Services to share a centralized advanced digital switch linked by optical fiber to each rural telephone carrier. This approach gave rural communities equal access to competitive long distance carriers and the advanced features available through the shared central switch. This model is now being replicated in Minnesota (see chapter 2).

4. GOALS AND RECOMMENDATIONS
FOR STATE REGULATORY COMMISSIONS

As discussed in chapter 1, investments in telecommunications are not governed by normal decentralized market forces but by monopoly carriers, whose decisions require state regulatory approval. Plans to modernize a state's telecommunications network, therefore, require close coordination of state telecommunications policies with state and regional development programs. Such coordination recognizes that a modern telecommunications infrastructure is at least as important to a state's economic development objectives as transportation, water and electrical power.

Coordination of telecommunications and development objectives is unusual. Telecommunications regulators may not understand how their decisions can affect economic development. Development planners, for their part, may not recognize how telecommunications can aid regional and community development. To bridge this "knowledge gap" and foster new connections between these "two cultures," state governments should establish a formal ongoing mechanism—such as an inter-agency committee—to foster regular communication between regulatory commissions and development agencies.

Besides working together to achieve general goals, regulatory commissions and development agencies should collaborate to tackle more immediate, specific problems and opportunities. Coordination can ensure that newly recruited or growing businesses will have adequate telecommunications; that small businesses can obtain modern telecommunications services through the public switched network; and that adequate telecommunications is available to support regional development programs.

Regulatory commissions cannot pursue these and other goals in a vacuum. If new telecommunications policies are going to work, commissions must expand their base of empirical knowledge. Through public hearings, regulatory commissions should solicit the testimony of development agencies, telecommunications carriers, local businesses, consumer advocates and individual citizens. Some hearings should be held in rural areas so that rural residents can participate and commissioners can experience rural conditions firsthand. To reach even further into rural areas while dramatizing the uses of telecommunications, commissioners could use audio teleconferencing or videoconferencing networks (where available) to solicit the views of rural residents.

Regulatory commissions not only need to get more facts and firsthand testimony, however; they also need to see beyond the traditional analytic framework that historically has governed the regulation of electricity, water and gas utilities. For such utilities, the marginal cost—that is, the cost for each additional unit of consumption—is higher than the average cost. Therefore, increasing supply generally costs more than reducing demand (through such means as energy efficiency and other conservation measures). In telecommunications, the opposite is true. The marginal cost—that is, the cost for each increase in the use of telecommunications—is *less* than the average cost of services. Increased usage reduces the average cost of telecommunications services. This direct cost reduction comes on top of the already substantial economic benefits that telecommunications can yield by making businesses and markets more efficient.

This section presents six interrelated goals for state regulatory commissions and specific recommendations for achieving those goals.

Regulatory Goal 1:

Universal Single-party Touchtone Service

The primary goal of state regulatory commissions should be a new "universal service" standard: affordable universal access to single-party touchtone telephone service. This new standard does not require universal broadband fiber optics at this time; it could be met through the narrowband capacity of copper wires or radio technologies.

There are three key elements to this new definition of universal service:

1. Bring telephone service to those currently without service;

2. Upgrade multiparty telephone service to single-party service; and

3. Upgrade rotary dial service to permit touchtone telephones to operate on all telephone lines.

Universal telephone service has been a longstanding policy goal of most states, and of the federal government. Telephone service is necessary for economic development; for the delivery of various public services, including emergency responses; and for routine community and personal communication.

Even though the initial goals of universal service are close to being met—more than 93 percent of all American households now have telephone service—providing affordable access to some form of telephone service to the remaining seven percent should continue to be a major policy goal. This is especially important for rural America, where access to telephone service is significantly lower than the national average.

In today's world, however, traditional notions of universal service are far too modest. Given the realities of our national economic life, we need a broader definition of universal service—namely, affordable access to both single-party service and touchtone service.

Although multiparty lines are an anachronism in urban areas, they are still common in some rural areas (see Appendix A). Multiparty lines not only limit privacy, but are unsuitable for communications requiring reliable operation of computer modems, facsimile and answering machines, and other specialized equipment such as terminals for the hearing impaired. In many states, tariffs prohibit the use of such equipment on multiparty lines because of problems they may create for other users of the same line. Multiparty lines are less reliable as well; they have more down time for repairs and have higher maintenance and repair costs than single-party lines. Paradoxically, multiparty service is more costly than single-party service in modern telephone networks because of additional "bridging" costs required at the central office switch to create a multiparty line.

Touchtone service is another important feature that should be universally available today. As we have seen in the preceding chapters, access to information is becoming more critical for both businesses and individuals in rural and urban locations. More frequently, touchtone service is being used to provide access to information. When we call a business, we frequently hear computer-generated responses like: "Press 1 for the sales department; press 2 for customer service; press 3 for accounting." When we call for information on road conditions, the state highway department tells us to enter the number of the highway to get recorded information. Calls to the IRS or the state tax department start with a request to enter numbers that automatically direct the call to the person most likely to have the answer. Even our answering machines often require a touchtone phone to retrieve messages when we are away.

Touchtone service also is indispensable to access a variety of on-demand information services generically known as "audiotex." By 1988 more than 4,000 audiotex services were being sold through 900 and 976 telephone numbers. A leading industry analyst projects that the national 900 number services will grow by more than 800 percent over the next five years (Digital Information Group, 1990a, 1990b).

Fortunately, rural customers need not scrap rotary telephones until they are ready to upgrade. Touchtone lines can be installed so that rotary telephone instruments can still operate, enabling customers to upgrade terminal equipment at their convenience.

How Can We Measure Progress?

The indicator of progress toward the traditional definition of universal service is the percentage of households with telephone service. Progress toward the goals of single-party service and touchtone service can be measured by the percentage of total subscribers served by these respective improvements.

Instead of using three separate measures, regulatory commissions may wish to adopt a single, revised universal service goal of single-party touchtone service. Progress toward that goal would be measured by the percentage of households that have such service.

Barriers to Universal Single-party Touchtone Service

There are three primary barriers to universal telephone service in the United States: poverty, physical disability (including speech or hearing impairment), and geographic distance from the nearest point of service availability. Approximately 200,000 U.S. households are without telephone service for this third reason (Parker and others, 1989).

The major barrier to single-party service is the pricing policy known as "suburban mileage charges." Under this policy, a rural customer living outside a town can obtain single-party telephone service only by paying a mileage-based monthly fee in addition to regular monthly service charges. Typically, this special fee is significantly higher than the flat rate charges for multiparty service. As a result, single-party service is often too expensive for rural residents even though, ironically, single-party service may be cheaper for the telephone carrier to provide than multiparty service.

Sometimes, regulators justify the price differential as a way to keep costs low for poor rural subscribers. However, if those subscribers require subsidies, it would be preferable to provide specific, targeted subsidies rather than distort the rates for all. In some locations, single-party service is delayed by the lack of financing needed for new construction to upgrade from multiparty lines. REA loans are generally available to independent rural telephone carriers for this purpose.

The primary barrier to touchtone service is the lack of modern switching equipment (which would provide other benefits as well, such as improved line quality and such services as call forwarding, call waiting and conference calls). Modernizing the rural telephone network is largely a matter of regulatory incentives. For example, state regulators could allow faster recovery of the capital costs of older equipment still in service. Or they could authorize current telephone rates to include previously unrecovered costs for older equipment taken out of service.

Another barrier to universal touchtone service is the practice of many carriers (with the blessing of state regulators) to charge higher prices for touchtone service than for rotary dial service. This pricing policy is hard to justify because carriers incur no additional costs when touchtone service is provided through a digital or electronic analog switch. Rotary dial service may be *more* expensive than touchtone service because of greater maintenance costs and the slower rate at which it processes calls through the switch. Eliminating this arbitrary pricing differential (as recently done in California) would help make touchtone service more affordable and accessible.

Other network modernization incentives could be integrated into the various incentive regulation plans under consideration in many states. For example, authorization of higher profit margins for telephone companies could be conditioned on achievement of single-party touchtone service goals.

Regulatory Recommendation 1.1: All state regulatory commissions should participate to the maximum extent allowed in the FCC's "lifeline" program, which reduces the monthly basic telephone service fee for eligible households by as much as $7.00 below the normal charges.

The FCC has ordered that the federally imposed $3.50 monthly fixed charge for access to the interstate long distance telephone network (the "access charge") be waived for poor households either partially or entirely. The actual waiver would depend upon the amount of subsidy authorized by states—up to $3.50—which would then be matched by the federal government. The program encourages states to use a fraction of intrastate telephone charges to help reduce basic network access charges for poor households. State regulatory commissions decide eligibility for lifeline telephone service; some states simply adopted the eligibility standards for food stamps or other assistance programs.

The source of the federal lifeline funds is a tiny percentage of all U.S. interstate long distance phone charges. Telephone subscribers in states that do not participate fully are paying into the federal lifeline fund without needy residents in their states getting their share of the benefits. At present, some states do not participate at all, while others participate at amounts less than the $7.00 per month maximum discount.

Regulatory Recommendation 1.2: All state regulatory commissions should participate in the FCC's "Link-up America" program, which reduces the installation and deposit charges for telephone service for eligible poor households by $30.00.

Poor people change residences more often than other people, to obtain affordable housing or relocate closer to perceived economic opportunities. For these Americans, telephone service is frequently unaffordable. An FCC survey found that for poor people, installation and deposit charges often are more of a barrier to obtaining telephone service than the monthly service charges.

To deal with this problem, the FCC established the "Link-up America" program for those households eligible for lifeline service. Funds are collected from the same source—a tiny fraction of the revenues from interstate long distance calls. State regulatory commissions administer the program but do not provide any matching funds.

Regulatory Recommendation 1.3: State regulatory commissions should encourage "local service only" options for subscribers who would otherwise be denied access to both local and long distance service.

Many low income households are denied access to basic telephone service because they have a poor history of payment for long distance charges. The typical way to deny access is to require a large deposit, before providing service to people with poor credit records. The recommended policy would allow carriers to block access to long distance services for people with a poor record of paying for such services and who are unable to provide a suitable deposit. It also would maintain basic local service for such subscribers, provided they pay their local phone bill on time. Since they pay for local service monthly in advance, no deposit would be required. Service could be discontinued, of course, if they do not pay the monthly bill.

Regulatory Recommendation 1.4: All state regulatory commissions should establish "relay services" that enable persons using teletype or other terminals for the speech- or hearing-impaired (or those with other disabilities) to communicate through the telephone network with people using ordinary telephones.

The Americans with Disabilities Act, enacted by Congress in July 1990, authorizes the FCC and the states to provide relay systems so that speech- or hearing-impaired people using teletype or equivalent keyboard terminals can communicate with people using regular voice telephones. The Act also provides guidelines for these systems (see chapter 3).

States may choose to finance such relay services through a small surcharge on all telephone bills. Some states may choose to apply a means test before providing terminal equipment at subsidized rates. Small or thinly populated states may want to organize a consortium of nearby states to share the costs of a multistate relay system.

Regulatory Recommendation 1.5: State regulatory commissions should encourage competition for service to all locations where telephone carriers charge extraordinary installation fees.

In many states, telephone carriers have an exclusive franchise to serve a particular territory. The primary rationale for exclusive telephone franchises is to achieve universal service by allowing telephone carriers to offer averaged rates throughout a service area. An exclusive franchise may be needed to prevent competitors from "cream-skimming" the more profitable locations, leaving the less densely populated areas unserved.

Despite this rationale, some telephone companies charge as much as $5,000 per mile from the nearest point with existing telephone service, for new installations at rural locations. These "line extension" charges often are sufficient to recover all of the capital costs of providing service, using underground buried cable, plus profit on the investment. Some telephone companies have been accused of also including these costs in the rate base, to be recovered a second time from monthly phone charges.

State commissions may be reluctant or unable to require service provision to such locations without a special construction charge. Regulatory commissions understandably may worry that courts would overrule commission orders to make such investments. Ordering an uneconomic investment could be ruled unconstitutional confiscation of private property. In other cases, regulators may be reluctant to add costs to the telephone rate base that could result in increased rates for all users.

Instead of requiring carriers to make investments that they consider uneconomic, the regulatory commission should remove their exclusive right to the territory they chose not to serve at standard rates. Line extension charges could still apply to locations outside exclusive franchise territory, but other carriers could compete for that business.

A rural pro-competition policy is particularly important as a way to encourage new technologies, which are showing that telephone services for remote rural Americans need not be expensive. Some carriers may be able to use the FCC-approved BETRS (Basic Exchange Telephone Radio Service) or satellite technology at lower cost than buried telephone cable. Others may be willing to accept a lower profit margin, using normal investment financing and recovering costs over time from monthly telephone rates. Whatever the cost-effectiveness of these alternatives, other carriers currently are prevented from providing service in a territory for which another carrier has an exclusive franchise.

The alternate carrier may be eligible to obtain a subsidy for local telephone rates from the FCC-controlled "universal service fund," sometimes called the high cost fund. A small fraction of all interstate long distance phone rates is used to reimburse local telephone carriers that have particularly high costs of connecting their subscribers to the public switched telephone network. State regulatory agencies that do not reallocate unserved territory—that is, who do not reassign it to a carrier who will serve it—are in effect letting their state's interstate long distance calls contribute to the universal service fund, without allowing their residents to receive the full benefit of the federally mandated subsidy.

Even without taking advantage of the universal service fund, the alternate carrier most likely will be eligible to recover some of its service costs from the interstate long distance rate "pool." Carriers receive funds from the pool in proportion to their costs of providing access for long distance service. Bell operating companies have chosen to withdraw from the pool, and therefore do not receive any benefits from it. However, the

FCC requires them to make some payments into the pool to help maintain the geographic rate-averaging policy.

From the perspective of the carrier that previously had an exclusive franchise for unserved territory, such a competitive policy could be described as a "serve-it-or-lose-it" policy. The proposed competitive policy—essentially, a "sunsetting" of exclusive territorial rights in unserved areas—is a necessary first step for introducing service to many locations. Given the choice of serving or losing to competition part of their territory, some carriers may choose to serve at their standard installation fees, without extraordinary construction charges. Others may choose to give up territory, rather than make investments they consider uneconomic. This forfeited territory can then be reallocated to another carrier that is willing to serve, usually with lower cost technology, with REA support, or with access to federal subsidies. In a rare state move to authorize adjustments to carrier franchise boundaries, the Oregon legislature in 1991 authorized the Oregon Public Utility Commission to adopt such a pro-competitive rural service policy, while maintaining exclusive franchises for territories served at standard rates.

Another form of rural competitive policy would allow remote residents to provide their own transmission equipment to connect with carrier facilities. In the earlier history of rural telephony, such connections, called "farmer lines," were commonly used to extend service to rural locations. The principle still should apply to currently unserved locations. Regulatory commissions should order carriers to connect with customer-provided transmission equipment whenever the carrier is unwilling to provide the necessary facilities itself, at standard installation rates.

Regulatory Recommendation 1.6: State regulatory commissions should solicit competitive bids for telephone service to locations outside telephone franchise boundaries. The commissions should then grant franchise authority (and corresponding service obligations) to qualified low bidders.

This recommendation is applicable to states with territory currently unallocated to any local exchange carrier and to states adopting regulatory recommendation 1.5 above, which would create newly unallocated territory from prior exclusive franchises. The problem occurs mostly in western states. Oregon, for example, has substantial unserved territory.

State commissions could ask residents living outside exclusive franchise territories to apply to the commission for telephone service. A bona fide request for service would trigger a process of soliciting bids from qualified carriers. The commission could then grant exclusive franchises to bidders who offer installation without line extension charges or other extraordinary construction charges. A non-exclusive franchise could be awarded if the low bidder proposes an extraordinary construction fee. When there is a tie for lowest installation bids, the carrier offering the lowest monthly recurring charges could be awarded the franchise.

Putting unserved territory "up for bids" in this fashion may stimulate the use of innovative technical solutions such as BETRS and satellites as ways to reach remote, hard-to-serve locations. Another result might be the formation of new carriers specializing in serving widely distributed remote locations with innovative technology.

Regulatory Recommendation 1.7: All state regulatory commissions should eliminate "suburban mileage charges" from basic single-party telephone service rates.

This policy change will help make basic telephone service more affordable and accessible in rural locations. Replacing mileage-based monthly charges with flat rate charges may require a slight increase in the basic flat rate for all subscribers; carriers still need to recover their total costs, after all. A requirement for a compensating rate increase to all users is likely to be rare, however. Given the recent cost-reducing productivity gains in the telephone industry, it is more likely that the regulatory choice will be between removing suburban mileage charges and giving all users a minor rate reduction. Washington State found that, by using a high cost fund and lifeline service, suburban mileage charges could be eliminated statewide without undue burden for any subscribers.

Regulatory Recommendation 1.8: State regulatory commissions should redefine basic telephone service to include touchtone service.

A formal redefinition of this sort would mean that carriers could not charge more for touchtone service than for rotary dial service. It also would make single-party touchtone service available under lifeline programs. It no longer makes sense for single-party touchtone service to be considered a "luxury" feature that should be denied to lifeline subscribers, especially when so many government and business information services are accessible only via touchtone service.

Regulatory Recommendation 1.9: State regulatory commissions adopting incentive regulation plans should include an incentive to encourage universal access to single-party touchtone service.

Regulators could adopt a "management by objectives" approach, instead of making detailed procedural and pricing decisions that might be made better by telephone carrier management. Under such an approach, regulators would set the policy goals, such as universal access to single-party touchtone service. Telephone carriers then could be given incentives to achieve those goals. For example, regulatory commissions could grant carriers additional pricing flexibility, if progress toward universal single-party touchtone service reaches or exceeds specific measured goals. Alternately, they could allow carriers to retain a higher profit percentage when the policy goals are achieved.

Traditional regulation is a blunt instrument to prod companies into doing anything that is not necessarily in the best financial interests of their shareholders. By contrast, regulatory incentives that reward carriers for achieving policy goals are likely to elicit the wholehearted, creative support of carriers. Incentive regulation recognizes that shareholders and subscribers share many common goals and need not be adversaries; there are "win-win" situations that can benefit everybody. This stems largely from the recent revolutions in telecommunications and information technologies, which enable carriers to reduce costs while also improving the variety and quality of services.

A recurring criticism of rate-of-return regulation is that it is a form of cost-plus contracting in which the telephone carrier recovers from telephone ratepayers all of its costs, plus a percentage profit. In such regulation, there is little incentive (and sometimes a disincentive) to reduce or control costs, because companies using lower cost technology would have a lower base on which to calculate their percentage profit. Some critics have argued that this approach has led to too much "gold-plating," or unnecessary investment, in telephone networks. Price caps and other incentive regulation schemes are intended to solve this problem by giving telephone carriers an incentive to lower costs—namely allowing them a higher percentage profit when costs are lower.

With this rationale, the FCC recently changed the method of regulation of large local telephone carriers from traditional "rate-of-return" regulation to "price cap" regulation—a form of incentive regulation that regulates prices instead of profits. Smaller carriers have the option of changing to price caps. This federal change is likely to put more pressure on state regulators also to move from "rate-of-return" to incentive regulation.

Some state incentive regulation proposals require that carriers spend a specified dollar amount on upgrading rural telephone switches or other network facilities (for example, "the Michigan plan" for Michigan Bell). Such investment may be a politically expedient price for a carrier to pay to obtain incentive regulation, but it is not necessarily an economically efficient way to provide modern network services to rural customers.

The brute force approach to meeting this objective would be to replace old rural telephone switches with modern full-featured digital switches.

Yet the same goal might be achieved more economically by using a full-featured centralized host switch somewhere in each LATA. Basic services could be provided through small remote switches with limited local features, while a full range of features would be available via fiber optic trunk lines connecting remote switches with the central host switch. This approach could provide the same service as full-featured switch upgrades yet be more economical.

Measuring dollars spent as a way to assess compliance with incentive regulation programs is a perverse and inefficient way of providing incentives for efficiency in network investment. It would be preferable to specify measurable service goals and then allow carriers to retain a higher profit percentage if they meet those goals. For example, it would be easy to measure the percentage of total households in the franchise territory with single-party touchtone service. By linking the reward to a measurable objective, carriers have ample incentive to find efficient ways to meet the objective. Local carriers could provide reports on their service performance themselves, subject to independent audit, just as their financial performance is subject to audit.

Regulatory Goal 2:

Service Quality Sufficient for Voice, Fax and Data

Now that fax and data transmission have become routine business needs, areas with poorer quality service are disadvantaged. High quality telephone lines allow data transmissions that are more reliable, faster and cheaper. Because lines are sometimes poorer in rural areas, rural customers more often have to retransmit garbled fax pages and transmit data more slowly. They pay more not only in terms of their own wasted time but also in long distance charges for slower (and therefore more costly) data transmission.

One risk of incentive regulation is that telephone carriers, in their quest for higher efficiency and profits, will choose to defer maintenance, and delay the upgrading of older, less reliable equipment, especially in rural areas. The U.S. experience with price cap regulation is still too limited to assess whether deterioration of service will occur. AT&T, which is now subject to price cap regulation, is rapidly replacing older equipment and improving network quality. AT&T's behavior may be a response to competition from other long distance carriers, which is increasingly based on quality of service as well as on price. Price caps for U.S. local exchange carriers are too new to judge their effects on service quality, particularly in rural areas. The experience in the United Kingdom, which pioneered price caps, gives some cause for caution, however. There, British Telecom's quality of service declined in some areas after price cap regulation was introduced (Rudd, 1988).

U.S. concerns about service quality in the new regulatory environment are reflected in proposed federal legislation introduced by Congressman John Bryant of Texas (Bryant, 1991) that would require the FCC to "improve and enforce network quality standards on the local exchange carriers." The bill calls for joint federal-state consultation to develop a consensus on network quality standards and procedures for auditing compliance.

How Can We Measure Progress?

Typical quality of service indicators include the number of network outages, average time to restore service, and the number of customer complaints. Such measures are insufficient, however, to measure the quality of substandard lines. Regulators should establish specific technical performance standards appropriate for reliable facsimile and data transmission. Periodic technical testing of random samples of telephone lines (for example, 200 per month) would be required to measure compliance.

Most regulatory commissions do not have sufficient resources to conduct such technical compliance testing. Nevertheless, they can require an audit by an independent technical firm that would provide certified reports to the commission, just as independent financial auditors provide certified independent audits of the financial performance of the telephone carriers.

Barriers to High Quality Service

Many barriers to improved service quality are embedded in the social and organizational structure of the workplace, as U.S. manufacturers have found in their attempts to compete against higher quality Japanese products. Many local telephone carriers still have a monopoly utility culture. They generally do not have the aggressive, flexible corporate culture needed in today's more competitive telecommunications environment. They do not seize new opportunities quickly, do not always welcome change, and do not give first priority to customer-responsive service and marketing. If real and enduring change is to occur, policy makers may have to devise new and creative forms of incentive regulation. Regulators should revise specific regulations, such as long depreciation schedules, that impede improved service quality. More importantly, they should use the incentive of higher profits to speed the transition of telephone carrier culture to one of continuing improvement in service quality and customer responsiveness.

In the telephone industry, quality is improved by modernizing the physical plant: for example, by replacing older, less-reliable, electromechanical switches with modern digital switches; by replacing weather-prone overhead telephone wires with underground cable; and by replacing older air-filled cables (which develop moisture leaks) with gel-filled cable or optical fiber. Often the replacement of older equipment, even if it is not yet fully paid for out of depreciation charges, saves extensive recurring maintenance expenses.

Under rate-of-return regulation, carriers passed on maintenance costs to telephone subscribers. Shareholders could be penalized when equipment was taken out of service before being fully depreciated. Therefore, to achieve significant quality improvements, regulators should reassess the network modernization incentives (or disincentives) implicit in current modes of regulation.

Executives of publicly traded telephone companies, who have a duty to shareholders as well as subscribers, may not approve the capital budgets for rural equipment modernization. They may conclude that modernization of equipment in rural communities will generate less internal return on investment (profit) than other investments, such as the purchase of foreign telephone companies or cable television systems. This practice amounts to "redlining," a refusal by a vital business to invest in a certain region. It becomes a self-fulfilling prophecy, because by assuming that insufficient profits could be generated, carriers are hindering the very economic development that could spawn more business (and profits) for the telephone company—as well as benefits for the community.

Regulators can do much to dispel the perception (fostered by rate-of-return regulation) that regulation is a "zero-sum game," in which any gains by subscribers necessarily come at the expense of telephone companies, and vice versa. Incentive regulation can help convert the situation into a "win-win" situation, in which telephone companies can serve both their shareholders and their subscribers by offering better service at a reasonable price—the normal scenario in non-monopoly, competitive markets.

Regulatory Recommendation 2.1: State regulatory commissions should establish mandatory, audited telephone service quality standards and should include a service quality component in any incentive regulation program they adopt.

Explicit, measurable standards of service quality can help ensure that incentive regulation will not result in worse service. Two sets of proposals are worth exploring. The Bryant bill specifies: ". . . standards shall, at a minimum, include measurement of local exchange carrier service installation, operator-handled calls, network call completion, transmission and noise requirements, and customer trouble reports" (Bryant, 1991). A 1989 proposal by former New York State Commissioner Eli M. Noam recommended taking a set of quality measures that the Commission had already devised, assigning weights to each measure, and then using the weighted average to yield a single factor that could be used in an incentive regulation formula (Noam, 1989). This approach would give a telephone carrier an economic incentive to maintain and improve quality.

Service quality standards should apply to all telephone exchanges, not just to area-wide averages. Noam suggests a factor to take account of telephone exchanges with poorer service than the average. Whatever the mechanism, regulators must ensure that carriers provide the data by location (such as by exchange) so that problems in rural areas can be identified. Otherwise, rural trends will be lost in statewide or franchise-wide averages.

The conventional wisdom in telephone regulation is that lower costs will result in lower quality (or that companies may choose to lower quality as a way to cut costs). Yet the experience of U.S. manufacturing companies struggling to compete with higher quality Japanese products—often by introducing Japanese production methods—has been the exact opposite. While it may seem counter-intuitive at first, U.S. companies have been learning that improving quality has the effect of lowering costs. This is because the earlier a problem is caught and fixed, the less it costs to correct. The Japanese have learned that "do it right the first time" results in cheaper and higher-quality products than a quality control system based upon "inspect and rework."

Among telephone carriers, this principle is well illustrated by field maintenance. Compared to investments in improved design, installation, and preventive maintenance, field maintenance is the most expensive operational procedure. One telephone company that recently adopted a "do it right the first time" program found it was able to reduce new access line installation costs by nearly 20 percent, while responding more rapidly to new service requests (Bohlin and others, 1991).

By insisting on ever-improving standards of service quality, regulators will be doing both ratepayers and telephone carriers a great service. If the telephone industry learns the quality control lessons learned by other industries, a system of quality incentive bonuses may help it quickly reduce costs and boost profits. If, on the other hand, the telephone industry has to learn the lesson the hard way—by experience—then state quality incentive requirements will start it down the right path.

Regulatory Recommendation 2.2: State regulatory commissions should change regulatory policies that inhibit network modernization, including depreciation schedules and rules for amortization of costs of older equipment taken out of service.

State regulators have traditionally used lengthy depreciation schedules to minimize the annual depreciation charges included in telephone rates. For example, depreciating equipment over 20 years means that one-twentieth of the capital cost is charged to users each year, whereas a ten-year depreciation schedule for the same equipment results in one-tenth of the capital cost (or twice as much) being charged each year. In the first ten years of a 20-year depreciation schedule the charges are correspondingly lower. In the later years, however, the charges are higher than they would otherwise be, both because of the deferred capital costs and because of the higher interest and other return-on-investment charges associated with the longer depreciation schedules. Over the life of the equipment, longer depreciation schedules result in higher total costs to subscribers. The principle is no different from consumer financing of an automobile purchase. Consumers will pay less in total payments for an automobile when they finance it over three years than when they finance it over five years.

One effect of long depreciation schedules may be to keep prices unnecessarily high by delaying the introduction of cost-saving modern technology. They also may work against network quality by delaying the replacement of older, more problem-prone equipment, because telephone companies often are not allowed to continue collecting depreciation charges from subscribers once the equipment is taken out of service. Therefore, they keep old equipment in service until it is fully paid for, even though it may be technically obsolete.

The traditional approach toward depreciation schedules may have had merit when technology changed slowly. In the current climate of rapid technological change in computer, switching and transmission technologies, it has a perverse long-run effect on both network quality and the availability of new services. In general, shorter depreciation schedules advance the policy goals of improving network quality and making modern services universally available. Rural users in particular would benefit from policies that encourage the availability of reliable, modern services. A recent report of the National Regulatory Research Institute (Lawton, 1988) discusses in great detail regulatory approaches that encourage network modernization.

Some regulators and consumer advocates may object that most network modernization is intended to serve business users, but residential users have to pay most of the costs. However, the costs to residential users are likely to be even higher if the network is not upgraded. There are two reasons: First, telecommunications, like computers, is a declining-cost industry; network additions that stimulate increased usage result in lower, not higher, average costs. Second, if the public switched telephone network is not upgraded to meet the needs of business users, they are more likely to build private networks that bypass the public switched network, leaving more network costs to be recovered from residential users.

Economic development is better served by upgrading the public switched network because it makes efficient communications available to all businesses, not just large companies who can afford to build a bypass network. And smaller businesses contribute to much of the growth in the economy.

Regulatory Goal 3:

Extended Area Service (EAS) and Reduced Intrastate Long Distance Rates

City dwellers can conduct most of their personal and business affairs —such as calls to local schools, merchants, doctors, and local government offices—with local calls. For rural residents, by contrast, a higher percentage of such calls are long distance. This penalty disadvantages rural businesses whose customers and suppliers can reach them only by long distance calls. It is no exaggeration to say that the expense of long distance calling can seriously affect the economic viability of entire rural communities. They have come to rely more on long distance calling as their economies have become more specialized and interdependent, and as our society has become more mobile. As rural communities have developed broader horizons, their need for long distance calling has increased.

In most states, intrastate long distance calling is priced substantially above costs in order to subsidize local rates. Although rural residents may enjoy lower local rates because of that subsidy, they usually pay more for intrastate long distance calls because of their different calling patterns. On balance, the net effect of the present rate structure may be that (usually poorer) rural residents are subsidizing (usually richer) urban residents. One solution is to offer rural Extended Area Service—that is, a flat monthly rate for all calls made within an extended area.

Recent technological advances in the telephone network have lowered dramatically the costs of long distance calling. FCC policies have encouraged some, but not all, of this cost reduction to be passed on to consumers in the form of lower prices for interstate calls. State regulators have been slower to pass these cost reductions along to users of intrastate long distance services. Consequently, consumers often pay more for intrastate long distance calls than for interstate calls.

Rather than reduce intrastate long distance rates as costs have declined, state regulators have used the profits from long distance service to subsidize basic local monthly charges. The resulting distortion of the underlying economic reality may be doing a disservice not only to rural residents but to everyone in the state, because it discourages the broadening of business and social horizons beyond the local community.

Rural residents typically make more long distance calls than urban residents of the same income. The subsidy of local service by artificially high intrastate long distance charges thus falls disproportionately on rural customers. It would be fairer to reduce the subsidy, with a corresponding increase in basic local rates.

How Can We Measure Progress?

There are several ways to define the boundaries of a "community of interest" appropriate for local service rates. A good indicator is telephone calling patterns, as revealed by the average numbers or percentages of calls to adjacent areas. Also, subscribers can be surveyed to find out the areas they might want for EAS.

Some EAS proposals suggest that the local calling area for rural residents should correlate with the local percentage of total intrastate calls made by urban residents. Using this model, rural and urban residents would be treated roughly alike; the "local service" boundaries for rural residents would be extended until their percentage of local calls matched those of urban residents.

This is the approach used by the Washington Utilities and Transportation Commission, which decided in December 1990 that, in exchanges where less than 80 percent of intraLATA calls are local, local calling areas should be extended until 80 percent of their intraLATA calls are also local calls. Colorado, Georgia and Louisiana have decided that local calling areas should be extended to enable all residents to reach their county government offices with a local call (see chapter 2). One index for assessing progress is the number of telephone exchanges meeting revised EAS rules, expressed as a percentage of total telephone exchanges.

The best way to measure progress in reducing intrastate long distance rates is to measure the extent to which prices for long distance calls are based on costs plus a reasonable profit. This is quite different from the current situation, in which long distance rates are set above costs in order to generate subsidies for basic telephone rates. A legitimate exception should be made for subscribers served by specific, targeted subsidies, such as an intrastate lifeline service fund or an intrastate universal service (high cost) fund. In this manner, a policy of economically distorted rates for everyone, designed to keep local calling cheaper, would be replaced with specific subsidies targeted to those in particular need.

Barriers to Extended Area Service

A major barrier to EAS service is the subsidy that flows from intrastate long distance toll service to local service—a policy that both stimulates EAS demand and thwarts its implementation. If long distance toll charges were reduced, some of the demand for EAS might diminish. EAS converts former long distance calls into local calls.

EAS implementation usually requires larger increases in local rates in rural areas than in urban areas because of the loss of the subsidy from toll revenue. This can be a problem for rural areas desiring EAS with an adjacent urban area. One solution, recently ordered by the Oklahoma Public Utility Commission (1991), established equal price increases for EAS in different exchanges. Since the costs were higher in the rural exchange than in the urban exchange, because of the greater loss of subsidies from long distance calls, the Commission used the previous intrastate toll revenue-sharing mechanism to let the two different telephone companies recover the costs of EAS implementation. The result was that rates for EAS in the rural community were less than they would otherwise have been.

Regulators with an understandable concern for keeping basic local rates affordable for poor subscribers may be reluctant to reduce the subsidy that flows from long distance calls to local rates. On the other hand, long distance rates that are priced significantly above cost—the typical circumstance today—encourage large users to leave the public switched network in favor of cost-based private networks. The consequence of bypass is to reduce the revenue that could otherwise help keep basic rates low. To keep the public network viable for all users, therefore, it is preferable to price long distance prices closer to cost.

Costs per call drop when the number of calls increases. Lower long distance prices would lead to higher calling volumes and therefore more calls over which to spread the fixed costs. When a monopoly carrier provides most intrastate long distance service, there is no competitive pressure to shift away from older pricing structures. Consequently, monopoly carriers may not know how much additional demand would emerge with lower prices. Rather than take a risk, they may prefer to stay with their familiar rate structure.

Regulatory Recommendation 3.1: State regulatory commissions should establish Extended Area Service policies that enable residents to reach their major communities of interest with "local" calls.

EAS is not a way to give telephone subscribers free services that they previously had to pay for, but a way to reallocate costs so that the basic local rate is increased to cover the cost of calls within a newly enlarged local calling area. Most (but not all) communities select EAS when given a choice. This policy recommendation is not intended to force a change on communities that do not want EAS. Rather, it is intended to ensure, at minimum, that communities wishing to enlarge the local calling area will have that option. If telecommunications were offered in a competitive marketplace, most communities would already have EAS in response to strong customer demand. Because of the monopoly structure of most local telephone service, regulatory assistance is necessary to give telephone customers that choice.

Regulatory commissions may need to arbitrate to help telephone companies reach a satisfactory renegotiation of separations and settlements. A pooled "high cost" fund may be required to prevent inequities for some users and carriers. The process of getting to EAS services may not be pleasant for either the regulators or the telephone companies, but on balance, the payoff for telephone users and for community and economic development generally should be worth the painful behind-the-scenes process of getting there.

One argument against EAS is that it increases local telephone rates and therefore works against the policy goal of keeping local rates affordable to low-income subscribers. This problem can be addressed by making measured service rates available as an option for low-volume users. With measured service, customers who use the phone very little, pay only for the local calls they make instead of paying for unlimited local calling. In general, lifeline rates or other subsidy programs targeted to those needing assistance should be preferred to a structure that distorts the rates for everybody.

Regulatory Recommendation 3.2: State regulatory commissions should maintain geographic rate averaging for intrastate long distance calls.

Traditionally, long distance rates were based on distance, independently of whether the call was on a major intercity trunk route or a higher cost rural route. Consequently, calls between a rural location and a city or between two rural locations are often the same price as calls between two major cities that are the same distance apart. This tradition has been maintained by the FCC for interstate calls and by most states for intrastate calls. Some states have moved to deregulate or otherwise deaverage intrastate rates. The result will be higher rates per mile for rural routes.

Customers in rural areas who do not have equal access to competitive long distance carriers (see recommendation 3.3, below) would be the primary victims, if regulators allow geographic rate deaveraging. Customers in rural locations would suffer from rising monopoly prices, unchecked by competitive alternatives.

Telephone carriers may argue correctly that they need some form of deaveraging to compete with bypass providers. Regulators should therefore allow volume deaveraging (that is, volume discount pricing) rather than geographic deaveraging. Rural telephone carriers may need to offer volume discount prices to their major business and government customers to keep them on the public switched network.

Regulatory Recommendation 3.3: State regulatory commissions should allow intrastate long distance competition within each LATA established by the Modified Final Judgment (MFJ) of the AT&T Consent Decree.

Most states with more than one LATA permit interLATA competition, a policy that brought lower prices and improved quality to interLATA long distance calling. However, strong intraLATA competition is rare, resulting in unnecessarily higher prices for many intrastate calls. State regulatory commissions should follow the example of the FCC—which brought competition to interLATA calling through a policy of "equal access" or "1+ dialing"—and bring similar competition to intraLATA calling.

Under the FCC's "equal access" policy, telephone subscribers choose a long distance carrier for interstate service and use that carrier by dialing a "1" before each long distance call. If subscribers wish to use a different carrier for a particular call, they dial five digits before the number. While urban subscribers generally have equal access, many rural subscribers still do not have any choice of long distance carriers, let alone equal access. Unlike most urban subscribers, they are served by only one long distance carrier.

The addition of intraLATA competition to interLATA competition may be necessary to create rural traffic volumes sufficient to attract competitive interexchange carriers to enter the rural market. In Iowa, rural equal access for both interstate and intrastate calling was introduced through Iowa Network Services, a cooperative effort of the state's small rural telephone carriers that pooled all of their long distance traffic to connect with competing long distance carriers at a shared central switch (see chapter 2).

Many other states have introduced intraLATA competition, but they still require subscribers to dial five digits to reach an alternate carrier. This is an improvement over a monopoly long distance carrier, but effective intrastate competition probably will require intrastate equal access.

Equal access competition, or the threat of competition, may be necessary to keep long distance prices low on rural as well as intercity routes. Competition also may help to improve the quality of service on rural long distance routes. (Some rural telephone carriers that have modernized their local switches and lines complain that their customers have poor long distance service because the monopoly intraLATA long distance carrier has not modernized the long distance lines connecting their community to the rest of the national network.) Introducing competitive intraLATA service would not only give rural subscribers a choice of long distance carriers for intrastate calling, it would advance the federal goal of giving greater subscriber access to competitive interstate long distance carriers.

Regulatory Recommendation 3.4: State regulatory commissions should encourage lower intrastate long distance rates.

In many states, it currently costs more to make an intrastate long distance call than it does to make a cross-country interstate call. State economic development goals would be better served if it were less expensive to make intrastate calls.

Higher intrastate long distance charges result from local telephone carriers charging long distance carriers "access charges" for the use of the local exchange switches and local lines from the switch to the subscribers' telephones. (These carrier access charges are different from the subscriber access charges discussed in regulatory recommendation 1.1, above.) The carrier access charges pay for a portion of the "fixed" costs, such as the local switch and local lines that need to be there anyway for local service, even if subscribers made no long distance calls. When the same carrier provides local and intraLATA long distance services, the subsidy mechanism is an internal, "hidden" cost. When two separate carriers are involved, however, regulators set up a system for allocating the costs; the carrier access charge is a commonly used technique.

Keeping carrier access charges high has been a way of keeping local rates low. In essence, local carriers extract a subsidy from long distance telephone rates to help pay for local service. Eliminating all non-traffic sensitive costs from the access charge mechanism, except for targeted lifeline and high cost subsidies, would remove most of the subsidy from long distance calls. Subscribers would benefit from the lower long distance rates that result when long distance carriers are required to pass on the savings from reduced access charges to their long distance customers. If the additional usage and the discouragement of bypass resulting from lower long distance rates are insufficient to compensate for the lost revenues, then an increase in subscriber charges for basic local service may be required.

The traditional rationale for this subsidy has been the policy goal of "universal service," which has been interpreted as keeping basic local rates affordable to all. Now that 93 percent of U.S. households have telephone service, the goal of reaching the remaining 7 percent will be served better by directly targeted policies, as discussed in connection with regulatory goal 1 above. The current mechanism of distorting economic rates for the 93 percent who are served has reached the limits of its effectiveness. Of course, any transition should be made gradually to avoid "rate shock" for subscribers.

Some users will be worse off and some will fare better as a result of these changes; people who never make long distance calls could have higher total phone bills, while those who make many intraLATA long distance calls would have lower total phone bills. Nevertheless, on balance, the economy as a whole and rural economies in particular are likely to benefit from these changes.

Regulatory Goal 4:

Universal Enhanced 911 (E911) Service

Emergency 911 service has saved lives throughout the country. Nonetheless, some rural areas are still without 911 service. In the version of 911 service most commonly available, a central dispatch center takes emergency calls and routes them to the appropriate emergency service jurisdiction. One problem with standard 911 service is that the dispatcher must learn the location of the emergency from the caller. If the caller cannot provide the address quickly, valuable time and possibly lives may be lost. The solution to this problem is enhanced 911 (E911) service. With E911, an automatic number identification feature in the telephone system shows the dispatcher the calling phone number, and a computerized database links each phone number to the location of the telephone. The dispatcher can then send help even if the caller cannot speak or describe the location.

How Can We Measure Progress?
Progress toward this goal can be measured by the percentage of telephone exchanges (or percentage of subscriber telephone lines) with access to E911 service.

Barriers to E911 Service
Funding for both the incremental telephone carrier costs for the service and the centralized dispatch function often comes from small surcharges on telephone bills. Further telephone network modernization may be needed to provide E911 service in some locations. The incremental costs for converting 911 to E911 could be handled with a small increase in the 911 telephone bill surcharge, if necessary.

In some rural locations, the failure of local governments to decide whether a new or existing agency will operate the central dispatching service has delayed 911 service. A barrier to E911 in rural areas is the need for unique, unambiguous addresses. Unincorporated rural areas often have duplicate street or place names or lack uniform numbering and address schemes. County governments must solve these problems to construct useful E911 databases.

> *Regulatory Recommendation 4.1: State regulatory commissions should work with local government agencies to make E911 services available from all telephones throughout the state.*

The advantages of E911 service may be particularly significant in rural areas where there are many different emergency service providers and distances are greater than in urban areas. In a rural county the 911 dispatcher may be many miles away from the caller and unfamiliar with the local place names and not know which of several agencies provides emergency service to the caller's location. The database can help the dispatcher locate the caller and quickly contact the appropriate emergency service. The benefits to rural telephone subscribers will outweigh the costs of resolving the organizational and technical issues associated with E911 implementation.

Regulators may need to decide which E911 costs can be paid from telephone funds. Some jurisdictions choose a telephone "tax" to pay for staffing and dispatching costs as well as the telephone costs.

Regulatory Goal 5:

Widespread Access to Optional Information Services

Optional services available by or through telephone carriers are commonplace in urban America, but may not be available to rural subscribers. Call waiting, call forwarding and three-way (conference) calling can be useful productivity tools for small businesses anywhere. Centrex business services (which provide some of the features of a private business telephone exchange through the public switched network), voice messaging, and other carrier services can be as valuable to rural subscribers as urban ones. Some carriers are offering urban "gateway" services for computer access to information providers. These should be made accessible also to rural subscribers.

How Can We Measure Progress?

For optional services that the regulatory commission decides are sufficiently useful for large numbers of subscribers, availability can be measured by the percentage of telephone exchanges offering the services.

Barriers to Accessibility of Information Services

The market for optional services in rural areas may be small, offering little incentive for carriers to provide statewide availability. However, once the basic network has been upgraded to universal single-party touchtone service at suitable quality levels, the incremental costs of offering additional services may be quite low, provided they can be offered remotely from a central switch. Because they are prevented by the Modified Final Judgment from offering interLATA services, Bell operating companies would be required to equip an appropriate host switch within each LATA.

Not all new services will prove successful. It would be questionable public policy to require universal availability of all new services before trials and initial service offerings show their utility and sufficient customer demand. Nevertheless, once a service has been proven useful, it should be made available generally.

Value-added networks (VANs) such as SprintNet (formerly Telenet) and BT Tymnet provide computerized access to several electronic information providers, including CompuServe, Dialog and Dow Jones News/Retrieval. These services can be accessed with a local call in most large cities, but usually require a long distance toll call from rural locations. Tymnet and Telenet do offer a toll-free 800 number for network access, but they charge the information providers a significantly higher hourly rate than for standard access. The higher charge usually is billed back to the user, so that 800 number service is more expensive than local call access.

Regulatory Recommendation 5.1: State regulatory commissions should encourage statewide local access to information services that are generally available in urban areas.

Once the goals of network modernization, quality and access are achieved, the incremental costs of offering additional services, particularly from a centralized shared telephone switch, are likely to be quite low. In some situations, it may be appropriate to encourage small independent carriers to share a centralized host switch to make advanced services more widely available.

EAS services may make it more attractive for value-added networks to add local access nodes in each EAS area. Policies that encourage small independent carriers to share a common interface point, such as the rural Iowa carriers' shared central switch, also may attract value-added networks to provide access at that same location. Sometimes, it may be appropriate for regulatory commissions to order access to services throughout an entire franchise area as a condition for approval of the service offering.

It should be noted that this state recommendation does not address the federal issue of whether telephone carriers should be permitted to provide services including information content. Rather, the intent is to encourage widespread availability of the infrastructure necessary to access information services, regardless of who provides them.

Regulatory Goal 6:

Public Network Utilization for Distance Education

Investment in human capital, particularly through quality public education, may be the most important single contribution to economic development, rural or urban. Unfortunately, many rural schools do not have enough students or a sufficient tax base to support a full range of quality course offerings, particularly in science and foreign languages. Some rural schools have addressed this problem by obtaining courses from distant sources such as the Texas-based TI-IN network, which provides courses by satellite. Other rural schools (in Kansas, Maine, Minnesota and Oklahoma, for example), have begun cooperative projects to share teachers and courses among several schools (see chapter 3). Fiber optic technology now being installed in telephone networks can be used for video networks linking rural schools.

How Can We Measure Progress?

In states where distance learning is planned to improve rural education, regulatory commissions can measure success by answering two questions: Have any regulatory barriers to educational use of public networks been removed? And, has the commission given prompt approval to carrier requests for tariffs designed for distance learning applications?

Barriers to Public Network Utilization for Distance Education

Rural distance education projects were discussed above in chapter 3. If these early projects are to lead to general improvements in rural education, rural schools will need affordable opportunities to try out telecommunications technologies for distance education. They may find that sharing teachers over a video network is the most cost-effective means of offering courses they cannot afford to offer in each school. Therefore, approaches to pricing and access to technology need to be worked out among school districts, carriers, and regulators.

One approach to distance education is to construct a dedicated network, using, for example, satellites, microwave, coaxial cable, or optical fiber. An alternate strategy is to use a multi-purpose public network. When educational interactive video services are provided through a shared public network rather than a dedicated private network, other applications may be added, such as medical consultations and business videoconferencing. Without the core educational application to share the costs of the basic infrastructure, the other applications may never be viable in rural areas.

Regulatory Recommendation 6.1: State regulatory commissions should encourage flexible tariff structures for distance learning networks.

As discussed in chapter 3, it may be appropriate for regulatory commissions to adopt long-run incremental cost pricing to enable public services such as education to use fiber capacity that would otherwise go unused. Deep volume discounts for video channels, which require much more capacity, may be more appropriate than rates designed for multiple voice channels. Volume discount pricing is consistent with legislative and regulatory goals for universal service; incremental revenue from increased usage helps reduce the average costs and therefore can benefit everyone.

Special educational or public service discounts and occasional use tariffs (leasing capacity by the hour) may be appropriate in the early stages before course offerings are developed fully. Educators may want to use compressed digital video technology that requires less bandwidth than broadcast quality video. Carriers should be prepared to offer data transmission rates for fractional T1 services (that is, a portion of a T1 carrier, which transmits approximately 1.5 million bits of data per second.) Some rural educators and businesses also may want to take advantage of new dial-up videoconferencing services offered over telephone lines by some carriers (known in the industry as "switched 56 kilobit service"). To help ensure availability of capacity in the appropriate quantities, regulatory commissions may need to require that any broadband tariffs include a provision permitting resale and shared use.

5. RECOMMENDATIONS
FOR TELECOMMUNICATIONS PROVIDERS

If the goals of the three preceding sections are to be achieved, the telecommunications industry must become actively involved in the process. This section is directed to the telecommunications industry, including the rural carriers, equipment suppliers, and providers of new specialized services, such as cellular and satellite communications networks. Investing time and money in rural development is not only good citizenship for the telecommunications industry, it is good business. Stimulating the growth of businesses and information-related business activities will spur greater demand for telecommunications services.

The telecommunications industry should be a natural supporter of the preceding goals and recommendations, which are intended to remove regulatory barriers, encourage the telecommunications industry to upgrade the rural infrastructure, and encourage the industry to offer rural services comparable to those generally available in urban areas. Without these improvements, rural areas could fall farther behind, resulting in a further decline in rural businesses and lower telecommunications revenues. Telecommunications providers therefore have a strong self interest in supporting rural development.

Provider Recommendation 1: Telephone carriers should upgrade their facilities to provide universal single-party touchtone service with quality levels suitable for reliable data and facsimile transmission. They also should upgrade facilities to meet demands for access to distance learning, other video and data applications, and a variety of enhanced services as they become available.

As argued above, providing the infrastructure is a basic, necessary condition for economic development. Carriers should upgrade their facilities as rapidly as the regulatory and economic environments allow. Yet even this step will not guarantee economic development. To ensure a reasonable return on their infrastructure investment, carriers also will need to take further actions, as discussed below.

Provider Recommendation 2: Telecommunications equipment and service providers should design and promote equipment and services to meet the needs of rural users.

In the increasingly competitive telecommunications arena, providers other than telephone carriers will play a growing role in rural areas. Over the next five years, cellular (mobile) telephone services will become increasingly available to rural service areas. Cable television and satellite systems already play a key role in bringing information and entertainment to rural America. Data broadcasting, mobile satellite and radio paging services also may expand in rural markets.

Suppliers of radio telephone equipment, such as the FCC-approved BETRS, should find a good rural market. In the satellite industry, very small aperture terminals (VSATs) are used for data, voice and video applications in rural private networks, such as the Wal-Mart network. This technology also could be used to bring basic telephone services to presently unserved remote rural locations. In an increasingly competitive marketplace, the telecommunications equipment industry will need to keep pace with the needs of rural telephone companies and their customers.

Provider Recommendation 3: Telecommunications providers should market their products and services effectively.

In other fields, this recommendation would hardly be necessary because it is so central to the success or failure of most businesses. Telephone carriers, however, come from a monopoly environment where, in the past, they could afford to be order-takers for one service, voice telephony. Now they have many services to offer and are subject to competition from customer premises equipment suppliers, cellular services, paging services and a host of private network bypass arrangements.

It is in the providers' own self-interest to learn to market their services effectively. The most important lesson, and perhaps the most difficult one to learn, is that market success comes from understanding what problems people are trying to solve—and then offering effective solutions at affordable prices.

Although modernized switching and transmission technology has enabled large telephone companies to reduce their rural staff and save money while improving quality, it has also diminished their local presence. This may prove to be a serious marketing liability, because a local presence helps a company learn about and better understand rural needs. To help cultivate personal contacts and market their services, providers should consider establishing a marketing group based in a rural location. Telecommunications carriers, in their own self-interest, could develop rural telemarketing strategies for themselves and as role models for other industries to follow.

Telecommunications equipment suppliers need to learn a key marketing lesson that the computer industry learned long ago: marketing to an intermediary in the distribution channel is no substitute for end user marketing. Selling a switch with advanced features to a telephone company will not result in much repeat business if the switch manufacturer does not understand what features the users need and why. Equipment manufacturers should become more involved with carriers in joint marketing to end users.

Provider Recommendation 4: The telecommunications industry should offer telecommunications training for the present and future workforce.

There was a time when using telecommunications meant dialing a number on the telephone, or dialing 0 if you needed help. Now we live in a world of data networks, fax machines, custom calling options, cellular telephones, competitive long distance carriers and a sometimes bewildering proliferation of customer premises equipment choices. The public switched network is about to add out-of-band signaling (Signaling System 7), which will reduce call set-up times and introduce new services such as ISDN, switched broadband data services and broadband ISDN (BISDN). Proposed personal communication networks (PCNs) may bring us pocket telephones, if not Dick Tracy wristwatch telephones. As computers and communications continue to converge, users will need to know more about these new technologies and how to use them effectively.

The telecommunications industry needs to help prepare the workforce to cope with the new telecommunications environment. Who better to take the initiative than the industry that stands to gain the most from greater public understanding of the tools it has to offer?

Telecommunications companies should offer short courses, demonstrations and training programs, including "open houses" and hands-on familiarization programs, on their own premises or at convenient locations. Longer courses should be offered through community colleges and other educational institutions, as discussed above. Providers should contribute staff members as instructors and provide instructional materials and demonstration equipment. They should cooperate with economic development agencies to achieve development goals 3 and 4 (better small business and community understanding of telecommunications services, and a rural work-force trained in telecommunications), discussed above in section 3.

Provider Recommendation 5: Telephone carriers should provide local leadership for economic development programs in the communities they serve.

The common themes that characterize successful community development programs are leadership and cooperation. Telephone company managers may be able to provide that key leadership ingredient for successful community development.

It takes someone committed to working with local community leaders to achieve consensus and to follow-up with implementation of community development programs. Part of the process is finding social and economic support for entrepreneurial businesses in the community through a local economic development council, chamber of commerce, or other community organization. Whatever the direction chosen, telephone company managers often have better contacts with state and federal government agencies, and could help the community to obtain external assistance. Outside funding is often available only to communities that have gone through a process of assessing their strengths and weaknesses and drawing up a community plan. Telephone company managers can help prepare such plans.

Provider Recommendation 6: Telephone carriers should contribute trained staff to economic development programs in their service areas.

Large telephone carriers should commit dedicated, full-time staff to help promote economic development. While this may not be possible for smaller rural carriers, they can sponsor development training programs and educate their management about the carrier's self-interest in economic development activities. Committing staff to economic development projects is more than corporate good citizenship. It is a solid investment for future business.

Provider Recommendation 7: Telephone carriers should help local entrepreneurs and economic development projects obtain financing.

REA loans for business and economic development are available for non-utility businesses, when an REA-supported utility is a sponsor and guarantor of the loan. The Organization for the Protection and Advancement of Small Telephone Companies (OPASTCO) has a Fund for Rural Education and Development (FRED) that may provide some funds for rural economic development. Larger telephone companies have more extensive contacts with investment bankers and government agencies. They should be able to help worthy entrepreneurs and development projects obtain third-party financing.

Provider Recommendation 8: Telephone carriers should make direct investments in rural economic development.

There are several ways that telephone carriers can invest in economic development in their service areas. One example is through discounted telephone rates. In Georgia, BellSouth has received approval from the state Public Service Commission to help businesses locating or expanding in the state's forty poorest rural counties. BellSouth will waive all normal deposits, service connection fees and installation charges, and offer a 50 percent discount on monthly fees (other than long distance charges) for a year (Telecom Publishing Group, 1990). For other states considering special development rates, regulatory approval will be required. In many states, legislative changes may be required to give regulators the authority to approve such rates. As another development initiative, telephone companies could establish a pool of funds for loans and equity investments in businesses that are starting up, relocating or expanding in the telephone service area.

6. HOW CAN THESE RECOMMENDATIONS BE PAID FOR?

The electronic highway analogy may lead people unfamiliar with the telecommunications industry to conclude that it will be too costly to provide access to modern electronic superhighways from every community. However, the assumption that universal access is unaffordable, is false. It is economically feasible to provide broadband service connecting every telephone exchange in the country, including those in small rural communities, and to provide high quality narrowband access (for voice and data) for every household in the country. Broadband links for video and high-speed data can be provided wherever the business, educational or other applications require it. This level of universal access can be achieved without tax increases or significant increases in consumer telephone bills.

Both switching and transmission costs are declining because of continuing technology improvements, just as the costs of computers have declined while quality and capacity increased. For remote rural areas, a variety of innovative technologies, including radio telephony, satellite transmission using very small earth stations, and remote host switching arrangements, can be used to provide services economically. We need not assume that the same technology must be used in rural and urban areas to deliver comparable services.

The infrastructure recommendations of this chapter are cast in terms of services that should be available to users, not particular technologies. The current conventional wisdom is that digital switching will be introduced everywhere and that fiber optic transmission will be required for connections between telephone switches and for high-volume subscriber distribution links. Nevertheless, conditions throughout the country vary so much that any universal technology prescription will be wrong for some locations. Rapid changes in technology assure that many of today's technology prescriptions will be wrong tomorrow. For example, in November 1990, a Texas company announced a new product that adapts analog telephone switches to handle digital information, thereby providing services normally available only via a digital switch (*Wall Street Journal*, 1990).

It is not necessary for regulators to micro-manage the carriers' technology choices to achieve service and quality goals. Rather, it is preferable to give carriers economic incentives to provide the desired variety and quality of services in the most economical way.

Because local telephone carriers have been regulated monopolies without major incentives for cost reductions, there are ample opportunities for productivity gains in the industry. Universal access to high quality telecommunications networks is not only affordable, it can be provided without any increase or reallocation of tax dollars. Almost all of the needed capital funds can be raised through private sector investment and borrowing. Of course, some rural telephone carriers will continue to need access to REA loan funds.

Although large investments will be required, the anticipated profits to be gained in return for that investment should be sufficient to raise the necessary capital. Telephone subscribers, on the average, are unlikely to see higher total telephone bills, except for increased usage. Some individual prices may go up as greater total efficiency is achieved from making prices more closely correspond to costs. But for each increase resulting from that adjustment, there will be corresponding decreases elsewhere.

As the modernized network is used more heavily—a result of lower prices, a wider range of services, and special development measures—the higher demand will generate new revenues to repay, over time, the costs of the investment. All users should benefit because the increased usage should lead to lower average costs. The regulatory incentives proposed above should be sufficient to generate within the telecommunications industry self-sustaining growth, which is the purpose of most development initiatives in other sectors of the economy.

In trying to harvest the many benefits of telecommunications technologies, the challenge is to craft incentives that will extend electronic highways and byways throughout rural America. Telecommunications providers and rural development advocates should both remember, however, that telecommunications alone is not enough. Putting a modern infrastructure in place is a necessary starting point. The continuing challenge is to develop the uses and applications of modern electronic byways that will contribute to economic development and improved quality of life for all rural Americans.

Trends in Upgrading the Rural Telecommunications Infrastructure

1. INDICATORS OF MODERNIZATION

The preceding chapters highlighted the importance of upgrading rural telecommunications facilities. We have selected two indicators of modernization to illustrate the status and future trends of upgrading the rural infrastructure: percentage of multiparty lines and percentage of digital switches. Elimination of multiparty lines is important to ensure immediate access to telephone service and ability to transmit data and facsimile (fax). Local carriers need digital switches to offer a variety of features and services such as call forwarding, call waiting and voice messaging.

REA borrowers provided the data presented here. This group of carriers provides an interesting subset of independent companies for examining rural trends because they are generally smaller and operate in more rural areas than other independent LECs. Of course, larger independent companies and the RBOCs also provide services in rural areas. However, data on their facilities is available only by company. Since they generally serve a much higher percentage of urban than rural customers, it is not possible to learn the status of their rural facilities using aggregate company data. Therefore we have relied on data from REA borrowers, all of which serve rural areas.

2. MULTIPARTY SERVICE

Table A-1 shows the decline in multiparty service lines among REA borrowers, from 554,000 multiparty lines in 1984 to 256,000 in 1989. The number of multiparty access lines for REA borrowers has declined by 12 to 17 percent per year. In 1989, approximately five percent of access lines were

Data for this appendix were compiled and analyzed by Robert Wysor of Economic and Management Consultants International, Inc.

Table A-1   Number of Multiparty Lines for REA Borrowers

Year	Number of Borrowers	Exch in Operation	Access Lines (000s)	Multiparty Lines (000s)	Percent Change	% Multi Access
Total U.S.						
1984	946	5,843	4,961	554		11.2
1985	942	5,828	4,913	474	-14.4%	9.6
1986	935	5,716	4,964	395	-16.6%	8.0
1987	920	5,662	5,171	341	-13.7%	6.6
1988	913	5,653	5,275	300	-12.0%	5.7
1989	903	5,623	5,486	256	-14.8%	4.7
South East						
1984	135	823	1,298	101		7.8
1985	135	811	1,329	81	-19.5%	6.1
1986	136	824	1,394	70	-14.1%	5.0
1987	135	829	1,470	59	-15.6%	4.0
1988	131	805	1,416	48	-18.6%	3.4
1989	129	793	1,460	30	-37.4%	2.1
West						
1984	134	809	433	49		11.2
1985	135	825	435	39	-19.6%	9.0
1986	132	821	451	32	-16.9%	7.2
1987	130	834	452	27	-16.4%	6.0
1988	128	844	505	21	-22.2%	4.2
1989	125	840	529	18	-17.0%	3.4
South Central						
1984	171	1,751	1,109	210		19.0
1985	164	1,717	1,130	183	-13.0%	16.2
1986	161	1,535	988	137	-25.1%	13.9
1987	158	1,507	985	126	-7.8%	12.8
1988	157	1,489	1,001	116	-7.9%	11.6
1989	153	1,480	1,063	108	-6.7%	10.2
North East						
1984	155	765	1,029	158		15.3
1985	158	775	915	142	-9.8%	15.6
1986	158	835	1,027	132	-6.9%	12.9
1987	153	803	1,150	110	-17.3%	9.5
1988	154	810	1,216	99	-10.0%	8.2
1989	156	815	1,276	85	-14.4%	6.7
North Central						
1984	351	1,695	1,092	36		3.3
1985	353	1,700	883	28	-21.7%	3.2
1986	348	1,701	1,105	24	-17.3%	2.1
1987	344	1,689	1,115	19	-19.0%	1.7
1988	343	1,705	1,137	15	-21.1%	1.3
1989	340	1,695	1,158	14	-4.0%	1.3

Source: REA; Calculations by EMCI, Inc.

multiparty. Projections of current trends show that the percentage of multiparty access lines should decline to under one percent by 1993 (see Figure A-1). This projection assumes that improvements in technology (such as BETRS) will reduce the costs of the most expensive multiparty upgrades in later years. The projection also assumes that REA loan programs continue to be available at current rates.

Figure A-2 shows the regions defined by the FCC for rural cellular telephone license lotteries. Several studies of rural telecommunications use this regional classification. Figure A-3 shows considerable variation among the regions in the percentage of multiparty lines in operation. The north central region had the lowest percentage of multiparty lines in 1989, 1.4 percent. The south central and northeast regions had the highest percentage of REA borrower multiparty access lines in service in 1989: 10.2 and 6.7 percent, respectively. These two regions accounted for 75 percent of all multiparty lines. The timing of multiparty line upgrades will vary by region. The south east region REA borrowers may eliminate multiparty lines by the end of 1991, while the south central region will have multiparty lines in service beyond 1994.

3. SWITCHING EQUIPMENT

The REA does not directly track the number of analog or digital switches, but it does collect data on the number of digital host switches (a host switch contains the subscriber database and switch logic). This figure

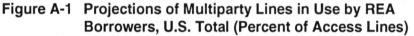

Figure A-1   Projections of Multiparty Lines in Use by REA Borrowers, U.S. Total (Percent of Access Lines)

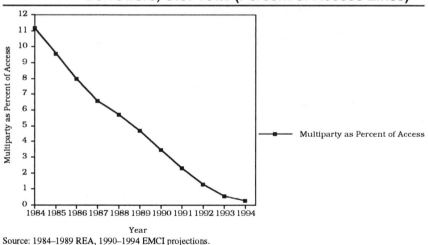

Source: 1984–1989 REA, 1990–1994 EMCI projections.

234

Figure A-2 Telecommunications Regions

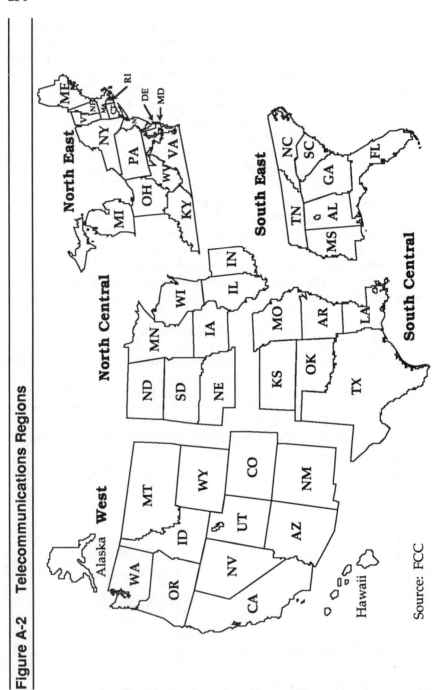

Source: FCC

Figure A-3   Regional Projections of Multiparty Lines in Use by REA Borrowers

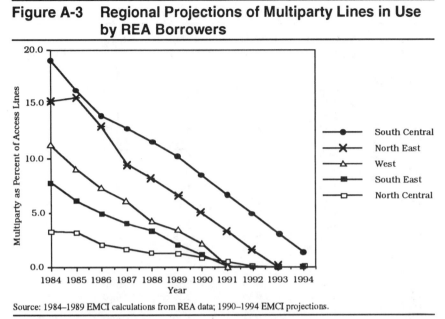

Source: 1984–1989 EMCI calculations from REA data; 1990–1994 EMCI projections.

can be compared to the number of exchanges to estimate the number of digital and analog exchanges. (The number of digital host switches approximates the number of digital exchanges in operation.)

Table A-2 shows that 59 percent of REA borrower exchanges used analog switches in 1989 compared to 81 percent in 1984. This corresponds to an increasing number of digital switches in service (41 percent of exchanges in 1989). However, digital switches serve more than 41 percent of all access lines, because the exchanges with the most access lines are usually upgraded to digital before other exchanges. The percentage of REA borrowers exchanges with digital host switches will increase to over 90 percent in the early 2000s, assuming current regional rates of upgrade (see Figure A-4).

As with multiparty lines, the south central and northeast regions lag behind the other regions in digital switch upgrades. At current upgrade rates, the western region will be almost entirely digital for REA borrowers by 1997, while the south central region will still have analog exchanges well into the next century.

The western region has the highest percentage of digital exchanges (61 percent). As with other regions, the south central and northeast regions lag the other regions in digital switch upgrades. At current upgrade rates, the western region of REA borrowers will be almost entirely digital by 1997, while the south central region will still have analog switches well into the next century (see Figure A-5).

236

Table A-2   Switching Equipment Used by REA Borrowers

Year	Number of Borrowers	Exch in Operation	Digital Exchange	Analog Exchange	Digital % of Exchange
Total U.S.					
1984	946	5,843	1,134	4,709	19
1985	942	5,828	1,381	4,447	24
1986	935	5,716	1,560	4,156	27
1987	920	5,662	1,834	3,828	32
1988	913	5,653	2,093	3,560	37
1989	903	5,623	2,277	3,346	41
South East					
1984	135	823	162	661	20
1985	135	811	189	622	23
1986	136	824	240	584	29
1987	135	829	294	535	35
1988	131	805	358	447	44
1989	129	793	382	411	48
West					
1984	134	809	289	520	36
1985	135	825	335	490	41
1986	132	821	377	444	46
1987	130	834	432	402	52
1988	128	844	470	374	56
1989	125	840	510	330	61
South Central					
1984	171	1,751	245	1,506	14
1985	164	1,717	310	1,407	18
1986	161	1,535	304	1,231	20
1987	158	1,507	348	1,159	23
1988	157	1,489	415	1,074	28
1989	153	1,480	450	1,030	30
North East					
1984	155	765	149	616	19
1985	158	775	164	611	21
1986	158	835	194	641	23
1987	153	803	218	585	27
1988	154	810	268	542	33
1989	156	815	298	517	37
North Central					
1984	351	1,695	289	1,406	17
1985	353	1,700	393	1,307	23
1986	348	1,701	445	1,256	26
1987	344	1,689	542	1,147	32
1988	343	1,705	582	1,123	34
1989	340	1,695	637	1,058	38

Source: REA; Calculations by EMCI, Inc.

Figure A-4   Projections of Analog Switches in Use by REA Borrowers, U.S. Total (Percent of Exchanges)

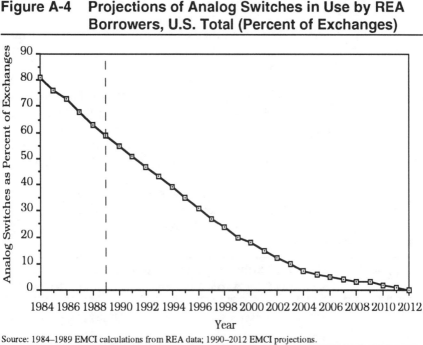

Year

Source: 1984–1989 EMCI calculations from REA data; 1990–2012 EMCI projections.

Figure A-5   Regional Projections of Analog Switches in Use by REA Borrowers (Percent of Exchanges)

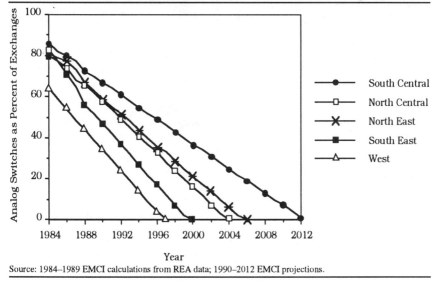

Year

Source: 1984–1989 EMCI calculations from REA data; 1990–2012 EMCI projections.

4. COMPARING REA BORROWERS WITH THE BOCS

We may compare these projections with data on digital switching upgrades provided by the RBOCs, keeping in mind that these company-wide data include both urban and rural facilities (see Table A-3). The highest percentage of access lines served by digital switches is projected to be installed by Nynex (70.2 percent), serving New York and New England, followed by BellSouth (66.4 percent), serving the southeast, and Bell Atlantic (65.5 percent), serving the mid-Atlantic states. The lowest percentage of lines served by digital switches will be offered by RBOCs serving the western states, namely Pacific Telesis (43.1 percent) and US West (44.0 percent).

Since the RBOCs are likely to upgrade services to urban customers before rural customers, it appears that in many rural parts of the country, customers of REA borrowers will be served by digital switches before RBOC rural customers.

Table A-3   Advanced Technology Deployment by Regional Bell Operating Companies by Year-end 1990 and 1994

	Digital Deployment			Digital Deployment	
	Percent of Central Offices	*Percent of Access Lines*		*Percent of Central Offices*	*Percent of Access Lines*
Ameritech			*Pacific Telesis*		
1990	64.5	40.4	1990	59.4	35.6
1994	77.7	54.5	1994	66.9	43.1
Bell Atlantic			*Southwestern Bell*		
1990	72.9	48.3	1990	31.9	25.8
1994	86.8	65.5	1994	74.4	44.9
BellSouth			*US West*		
1990	78.2	51.1	1990	38.4	35.3
1994	82.9	66.4	1994	55.5	44.0
NYNEX					
1990	57.9	56.7			
1994	85.0	70.2			

Source: Statement on behalf of the International Communications Association before the Subcommittee on Telecommunications and Finance of the Committee on Energy and Commerce of the U.S. House of Representatives, May 10, 1990.

U.S. Rural Telecommunications: Organizations and Agencies

1. NATIONAL TELECOMMUNICATIONS ASSOCIATIONS

Several national associations represent the telecommunications carriers. They include the following:

NECA

The National Exchange Carriers Association is the financial clearinghouse distributing the revenues collected from long distance telephone charges that are allocated to cover the local switching and access line costs associated with long distance calls.

National Exchange Carriers Association (NECA)
100 South Jefferson Road
Whippany, NJ 07981
Telephone (201) 884-8000

NRTA

The National Rural Telecom Association has represented the interests of commercial REA telephone borrowers in Washington for almost 30 years. The association concentrates its activities on preserving the telephone lending programs of the Rural Electrification Administration as viable sources of financing for rural telephone companies at reasonable rates of interest.

National Rural Telecom Association (NRTA)
1455 Pennsylvania Ave., NW, Suite 1200
Washington, DC 20004
Telephone (202) 628-0210

NRTC

The National Rural Telecommunications Cooperative was organized in 1986 through the combined efforts of the National Rural Electric Cooperative Association (NRECA) and the National Rural Utilities Cooperative Finance Corporation, an organization that had previously been concerned primarily with rural electric cooperatives. NRTC is also supported by the NTCA. NRTC is owned by approximately 425 rural utility cooperatives. The primary focus of NRTC is satellite communication for rural video and data applications.

National Rural Telecommunications Cooperative (NRTC)
P.O. Box 9994
Washington, DC 20016
Telephone (202) 944-2539

NTCA

The National Telephone Cooperative Association is the voice of 450 small and rural telephone carriers, about half of them cooperative and half commercial companies. NTCA has been actively defending rural telephone interests at the FCC, in recent court proceedings and before Congress. NTCA has been particularly concerned with issues of financing for rural telephone carriers and has been a strong defender of the telephone loan programs of the REA in the Department of Agriculture. In addition to its work on Capitol Hill and at the FCC, NTCA provides a full range of services to its members, including seminars, a variety of publications, and a comprehensive package of insurance and benefits plans. NTCA, with 55 employees, has the largest staff dedicated to serving the rural telephone industry.

National Telephone Cooperative Association (NTCA)
2626 Pennsylvania Avenue NW
Washington DC 20037
Telephone (202) 298-2300

OPASTCO

The Organization for the Protection and Advancement of Small Telephone Companies, founded in 1963, has approximately 375 members, all local exchange carriers with fewer than 50,000 access lines. In addition to representing its members' interests in matters before the FCC, Congress, the REA, and other government and industry forums, OPASTCO has strong education and publications programs which provide its members with timely industry information with a specific small company focus.

Organization for the Protection and Advancement
  of Small Telephone Companies (OPASTCO)
2000 K Street NW, Suite 205
Washington DC 20006
Telephone (202) 659-5990

USTA

The major telephone carrier industry association is the United States
Telephone Association, founded in 1897 as the "independent" (that is, non-
Bell) telephone company association. Since the local Bell companies were
spun off from AT&T in 1984, they too have been members of the enlarged
USTA, which now has more than 1,100 members representing more than 99
per cent of the telephone access lines in the country. USTA has a "Small
Company Committee" and a small company affairs department with
supporting staff to assist its smaller members.

United States Telephone Association (USTA)
900 19th Street, NW, Suite 800
Washington, DC 20006
Telephone (202) 835-3100

2. STATE TELEPHONE ASSOCIATIONS

In addition to the national associations listed above, there are also state
associations of local exchange carriers. These state associations are primarily concerned with issues arising from their members' common interests
before state regulatory bodies.

The following associations generally represent all of the telephone
companies in their state. Some states and regions also have associations of
small telephone companies or cooperatives, which can be contacted
through NRTA, NTCA, and OPASTCO.

Alabama-Mississippi Independent Telephone Association
660 Adams Avenue
Montgomery, AL 36104

Alaska Telephone Association
201 East 56th Avenue, Suite 230
Anchorage, AK 99518

Arizona-New Mexico Telephone Association
P.O. Box 1450
Clovis, NM 88101

Arkansas Telephone Association
1218 West 6th Street
Little Rock, AR 72201

California Telephone Association
1900 Point West Way, Suite 215
Sacramento, CA 95815

Telecommunications Association of Colorado
3810 Pierce Street
Wheat Ridge, CO 89933

Florida Telephone Association
P.O. Box 1776
Tallahassee, FL 32302

Georgia Telephone Association
1900 Century Boulevard, Suite 8
Atlanta, GA 30345

Illinois Telephone Association Inc.
P.O. Box 730
Springfield, IL 62705

Indiana Telephone Association
54 Monument Circle, Suite 200
Indianapolis, IN 46204

Iowa Telephone Association
1601 22nd Street, Suite 209
West Des Moines, IA 50265

Kansas Telecommunications Association
700 Jackson SW
704 Jayhawk Tower
Topeka, KS 66603

Kentucky Telephone Association
861 Corporate Drive, Suite 200
Lexington, KY 40503

Louisiana Telephone Association
P.O. Box 2548
Sulphur, LA 70663

Telephone Association of Maine
c/o Lincolnville Telephone Company
R.F.D. 1, Box 263
Lincolnville, ME 04849

Maryland/District of Columbia Telephone Association Inc.
4710 41st Street NW
Washington, DC 20016

Telephone Association of Michigan
122 South Grand, Suite 205
Lansing, MI 48933

Minnesota Telephone Association
386 North Wabasha Street, Suite 770
St. Paul, MN 55102

Mississippi Valley Telecommunications Association
8753 Windom Avenue
St. Louis, MO 63133

Missouri Telephone Association
P.O. Box 785
Jefferson City, MO 65102

Montana Telephone Association
P.O. Box 2166
Great Falls, MT 59403

Nebraska Telephone Association
200 Executive Building
Lincoln, NE 65808

Nevada Telephone Association
P.O. Box 70670
Reno, NV 89570

New Hampshire Telephone Association
13 Central Street
P.O. Box 577
Farmington, NH 03835

New Mexico Telecommunications Association
c/o Communications Diversified Inc.
2832 Girard Boulevard NE
Albuquerque, NM 87107

New York State Telephone Association
111 Washington Avenue, Suite 207
Albany, NY 12210

North Carolina Telephone Association
3717 National Drive, Suite 105
Raleigh, NC 27612

North Dakota Telephone Association
P.O. Box 588
Fargo, ND 58107

Ohio Telephone Association
150 East Broad Street, Room 220
Columbus, OH 43215

Oklahoma Telephone Association
2200 Classen Boulevard, Suite 850
Oklahoma City, OK 73106

Oregon Independent Telephone Association
555 Union Street, NE
Salem, OR 97301

Pennsylvania Independent Telephone Association
P.O. Box 1169
Harrisburg, PA 17108

South Carolina Telephone Association
P.O. Box 470
Charleston, SC 29730

South Dakota Association of Telephone Cooperatives
1515 N. Sanborn Boulevard
Mitchell, SD 57301

Tennessee Telephone Association
Parkway Towers, Suite 2018
James Robertson Parkway
Nashville, TN 37219

Texas Telephone Association
3701 Executive Center Drive, Suite 200
Austin, TX 78731-1689

Utah Independent Telephone Association
P.O. Box C
Orangeville, UT 84537

Virginia Telephone Association
700 East Main Street, Suite 1420
Richmond, VA 23219-2662

Washington Independent Telephone Association
504 14th Street SE, Suite 250
P.O. Box 2473
Olympia, WA 98507

West Virginia Telephone Association
P.O. Box 30
St. Marys, WV 26170

Wisconsin State Telephone Association
6602 Normandy Lane
Madison, WI 53719

Wyoming Telephone Association
110 Franklin
Pinedale, WY 82941

3. REGULATORS

FCC

The Federal Communications Commission has jurisdiction over interstate communications. FCC policies encouraging competition, especially in long distance telephony and business telecommunications, are requiring rural carriers to adapt to a new environment. The Common Carrier Bureau is the branch of the FCC responsible for telecommunications. The FCC's current chairman is Alfred C. Sikes.

Federal Communications Commission (FCC)
1919 M Street NW
Washington, DC 20554
Telephone: (202) 632-7000.

NARUC

The National Association of Regulated Utility Commissioners provides a forum for exchange of information among state utilities regulators, monitors federal and state policies, and carries out research through its National Regulatory Research Institute (NRRI).

National Association of Regulated Utility Commissioners (NARUC)
1102 ICC Building
12th and Constitution, NW
P.O. Box 684
Washington, DC 20044-0684
Telephone (202) 898-2200

National Regulatory Research Institute (NRRI)
Ohio State University
1080 Carmack Road
Columbus, Ohio 43210

State Regulatory Commissions

Each state has a regulatory body responsible for intrastate telecommunications. These are generally known as public utilities commissions. Most have responsibilities for other utilities such as water, electricity, and gas; some also have responsibility for transportation.

The following are the state regulatory commissions responsible for telecommunications:

Alabama Public Service Commission
Box 991
Montgomery, AL 36101-0991

Alaska Public Utilities Commission
1016 W. 6th Avenue, Suite 400
Anchorage, AK 99501

Arizona Corporation Commission
1200 West Washington Street
Phoenix, AZ 85007

Arkansas Public Service Commission
1000 Center Street
Box C-400
Little Rock, AR 72203

California Public Utilities Commission
505 Van Ness Avenue
California State Building
San Francisco, CA 94102

Colorado Public Utilities Commission
1580 Logan Street, Logan Tower
Office Level 2, Room 140
Denver, CO 80203

Connecticut Public Utility Control Department
One Central Park Plaza
New Britain, CT 06051

Delaware Public Service Commission
P.O. Box 457
Dover, DE 19901-0457

District of Columbia Public Service Commission
450 Fifth Street NW
Washington, DC 20001

Florida Public Service Commission
101 East Gaines Street, Fletcher Building
Tallahassee, FL 32399-0850

Georgia Public Service Commission
244 Washington Street NW
Atlanta, GA 30334

Hawaii Public Utilities Commission
465 South King Street
Kekuanao Building, First Floor
Honolulu, HI 96813

Idaho Public Utilities Commission
Statehouse
Boise, ID 83720

Illinois Commerce Commission
527 East Capitol Avenue
Box 4950
Leland Building
Springfield, IL 62794-9280

Indiana Utility Regulatory Commission
913 State Office Building
Indianapolis, IN 46204-2284

Iowa Department of Commerce - Utilities Division
Lucas State Office Building
Des Moines, IA 50311

Kansas State Corporation Commission
1500 Arrowhead Road
Topeka, KS 66604

Kentucky Public Service Commission
730 Schenkel Lane
Box 615
Frankfort, KY 40602

Louisiana Public Service Commission
One American Place, Suite 1630
Baton Rouge, LA 70825

Maine Public Utilities Commission
242 State Street
State House, Station 18
Augusta, ME 04333

Maryland Public Service Commission
231 East Baltimore Street
American Building
Baltimore, MD 21202-3486

Massachusetts Department Of Public Utilities
100 Cambridge Street , 12th Floor
Boston, MA 02202

Michigan Public Service Commission
6545 Mercantile Way, Box 30221
Mercantile Building
Lansing, MI 48910

Minnesota Department of Public Service
790 American Center Building
150 E. Kellogg Boulevard
St. Paul, MN 55101

Mississippi Public Service Commission
Box 1174
Walter Sillers State Office Building, 19th Floor
Jackson, MS 39215-1174

Missouri Public Service Commission
Truman State Office Building
Box 360
Jefferson City, MO 65102

Montana Public Service Commission
2701 Prospect Avenue
Helena, MT 59620-2601

Nebraska Public Service Commission
300 The Atrium
1200 N Street
Lincoln, NE 68509

Nevada Public Service Commission
727 Fairview Drive
Carson City, NV 89710

New Hampshire Public Utilities Commission
8 Old Suncook Road, Building 1
Concord, NH 03301-5185

New Jersey Board of Public Utilities
Two Gateway Center
Newark, NJ 07102

New Mexico Public Service Commission
224 East Palace Avenue
Marian Hall
Santa Fe, NM 87501

New York Department Of Public Service
Three Empire State Plaza
Albany, NY 12223

North Carolina Utilities Commission
430 North Salisbury Street
Box 29510
Raleigh, NC 27626-0510

North Dakota Public Service Commission
State Capital
Bismark, ND 58505

Public Utilities Commission of Ohio
180 East Broad Street
Borden Building
Columbus, OH 43266-0573

Oklahoma Corporation Commission
500 Jim Thorpe Office Building
Oklahoma City, OK 73105

Public Utility Commission of Oregon
Room 330, Labor & Industries Building
Salem, OR 97310

Pennsylvania Public Utility Commission
Box 3265
Harrisburg, PA 17120

Rhode Island Public Utilities Commission
100 Orange Street
Providence, RI 02903

South Carolina Public Service Commission
111 Doctors Circle
Drawer 11649
Columbia, SC 29211

South Dakota Public Utilities Commission
500 East Capitol Avenue
Pierre, SD 57501

Tennessee Public Service Commission
460 James Robertson Parkway
Nashville, TN 37243-0505

Public Utility Commission of Texas
7800 Shoal Creek Boulevard
Suite 400N
Austin, TX 78757

Public Service Commission of Utah
160 East 300 South
Box 5850
Heber M. Wells Building, 4th Floor
Salt Lake City, UT 84110

Vermont Public Service Board
89 Main Street
Montpelier, VT 05602

Virginia State Corporation Commission
1220 Bank Street
Box 1197
Jefferson Building, Suite 1220
Richmond, VA 23209

Washington Utilities & Transportation Commission
1300 South Evergreen Park Drive S.W.
Chandler Plaza Building
Olympia, WA 98504-8002

Public Service Commission of West Virginia
201 Brooks Street
Box 812
Charleston, WV 25323

Wisconsin Public Service Commission
4802 Sheboygan Avenue
Box 7854
Madison, WI 53707

Wyoming Public Service Commission
700 West 21st Street
Cheyenne, WY 82002

4. FEDERAL POLICY MAKERS

Executive Branch

Two federal government departments have substantial policy responsibility for rural telecommunications. One is the Department of Agriculture, whose Rural Electrification Administration is a major source of financial assistance for rural telephone carriers as well as a source of technical advice to rural carriers on standards and equipment. The Department of Agriculture's Economic Research Service conducts studies on infrastructure and economic development.

Rural Electrification Administration (REA)
U.S. Department of Agriculture
Washington, DC 20250
Telephone (202) 720-9540

Economic Research Service
U.S. Department of Agriculture
1301 New York Avenue NW
Washington, DC 20005-4788
Telephone (202) 344-2264

The National Telecommunications and Information Administration (NTIA) in the Department of Commerce has overall federal telecommunications policy responsibility. NTIA is currently completing a study of the national telecommunications infrastructure. Janice Obuchowski is Assistant Secretary for Commerce and Information.

National Telecommunications and Information Administration (NTIA)
Department of Commerce
14th Street and Constitution Avenue NW
Washington, DC 20230
Telephone (202) 377-1800

Legislative Branch

In both the Senate and the House of Representatives, the key committee concerned with rural development in general and the REA in particular is the Agriculture Committee. The House Agriculture Committee is chaired by Representative E. de la Garza (Texas). The subcommittee with oversight over REA is the Conservation, Credit and Rural Development Subcommittee, chaired by Representative Glenn English of Oklahoma. The Senate Agriculture Committee is chaired by Senator Patrick Leahy of Vermont. The subcommittee with oversight over the REA is the Rural Development and Rural Electrification Subcommittee, chaired by Senator Howell Heflin of Alabama.

In both the House and the Senate, the appropriations committees, and in particular the agriculture subcommittees, which together set the REA loan level appropriations for each fiscal year, are critical players. The Senate

Rural Development and Related Agencies Subcommittee is chaired by Senator Quentin N. Burdick (North Dakota). The House Appropriations Subcommittee is chaired by Representative Jamie L. Whitten (Mississippi). In both houses the Commerce, Justice and State subcommittee of the Appropriations Committee sets the FCC funding levels for operation for each fiscal year. The Senate Subcommittee is chaired by Senator Ernest F. Hollings (South Carolina) and the House Subcommittee is chaired by Representative Neal Smith (Iowa).

In both Houses, the Budget Committees set the policy and ceiling spending levels allocated to individual appropriations subcommittees. The Senate Budget Committee is chaired by Senator James Sasser (Tennessee) and the House Budget Committee is chaired by Representative Leon E. Panetta (California).

The Senate Commerce Committee, chaired by Hollings, its Communications Subcommittee, chaired by Senator Daniel K. Inouye (Hawaii), and the Telecommunications and Finance Subcommittee of the House Energy and Commerce Committee, chaired by Representative Edward Markey (Massachusetts), are the authorizing and overview committees for telecommunications policy.

The Senate Finance Committee, chaired by Senator Lloyd Bentsen (Texas), and House Ways and Means Committee, chaired by Representative Daniel Rostenkowski (Illinois), handle revenue matters that impact the tax exempt status of cooperatives, telephone excise taxes and other small business concerns.

The Judiciary Committees, chaired by Senator Joseph R. Biden (Delaware) in the Senate and Representative Jack Brooks (Texas) in the House, have oversight of the Justice Department and are involved in MFJ (Modified Final Judgment) legislative proceedings concerned with the oversight of the AT&T consent decree.

In the House of Representatives, the Information, Justice and Agriculture subcommittee of the Government Operations Committee (chaired by Representative E. Robert Wise, Jr. of West Virginia) has investigative oversight of REA telephone programs.

OTA

The Office of Technology Assessment carries out studies for the Congress on potential effects of technological applications. OTA has recently published a study on rural telecommunications: *Rural America at the Crossroads: Networking for the Future* (1991). Two other recent OTA studies relevant to rural telecommunications are *Critical Connections: Communication for the Future* (1990) and *Linking for Learning: A New Course for Education* (1989).

Office of Technology Assessment (OTA)
U.S. Congress
Washington, DC 20510-8025
Telephone (202) 224-8996

5. FINANCING SOURCES

REA

A major source of capital funds for rural telephone carriers is the Rural Electrification Administration, established as part of the U.S. Department of Agriculture in the 1940s to provide loans and technical assistance to rural utilities, both electric and telephone.

Funds are available through the REA's revolving loan fund, through the Rural Telephone Bank (RTB) for which REA provides staffing, and through the Federal Financing Bank (FFB), based on REA recommendations.

REA also administers a Rural Development Fund through which REA borrowers may apply for loans for rural economic development activities. Telephone companies may get from REA interest free loans up to $100,000 to invest in rural development projects.

Rural Electrification Administration (REA)
U.S. Department of Agriculture
Washington, DC 20250
Telephone (202) 720-9540

RTFC

The Rural Telephone Finance Cooperative (RTFC) is an affiliate of the National Rural Utilities Cooperative Financing Corporation (usually abbreviated as CFC). CFC was formed in 1969 by a group of rural electric cooperatives to provide private financing for rural electric cooperatives. The telephone affiliate, RTFC, is a supplemental lender to carriers whose primary source of capital funds is REA.

The Rural Telephone Finance Cooperative (RTFC)
1115 30th St. NW
Washington, DC 20007
Telephone (202) 337-6700

CoBank

CoBank, the National Bank for Cooperatives, was established on January 1, 1989, when the Central Bank for Cooperatives merged with ten district Banks for Cooperatives in various parts of the country. CoBank is part of the Farm Credit System established by the U.S. Department of Agriculture. All of the rural telephone systems that have been certified as eligible for REA financing may also borrow from the National Bank for Cooperatives.

National Bank for Cooperatives
P.O. Box 5110
Denver, CO 80217
Telephone (303) 740-4000

Public Telecommunications Facilities Program
The Public Telecommunications Facilities Program (PTFP) is operated by the NTIA in the Department of Commerce. PTFP has funded equipment used in interactive distance education. In general, PTFP provides funds for equipment purchases and some planning grants for public and educational broadcast facilities (radio and television) and nonbroadcast facilities such as cable television, instructional television fixed service (ITFS) systems, satellite transmission and reception equipment.

Public Telecommunications Facilities Program (PTFP)
National Telecommunications and Information Administration
Department of Commerce
14th Street and Constitution Avenue NW
Washington, DC 20230
Telephone (202) 377-5802

Star Schools Program
The Star Schools Program, created by Congress in 1988, provides grants for partnerships set up to develop systems and programs for distance learning. Eligible partnerships must include a state or local education agency, or a public agency or corporation already established to operate or develop telecommunications networks for education. All partnerships must be statewide or multistate.

Star Schools Program
Educational Networks Division
Office of Educational Research and Improvement
U.S. Office of Education
555 New Jersey Avenue NW
Washington, DC 20208
Telephone (202) 219-2116

The Telecommunications Industry

Telephone companies themselves may provide support for rural telecommunications projects. The Bell operating companies, independent companies such as GTE and Rochester Telephone, and the major interexchange carriers such as AT&T, MCI and US Sprint may offer grants, access to their facilities at no charge, or reduced rates for some educational projects. Major vendors of telecommunications equipment may also offer grants or in-kind donations for rural projects.

Oregon and Washington County Data

The following tables report, for each county in the two states, the following variables: population density, unemployment rate, per capita annual income, percent of residential telephones with single party service, percent of business telephones with single party service, and percent of telephone access lines served by electronic or digital switches.

Table C-1   Economy by County (Oregon, 1989)

County	Density	Percent Unemployment	Per Capita Income
Multnomah*	1208.2	5.6	$18,308
Washington*	368.6	3.0	$18,596
Marion*	175.2	5.8	$14,957
Clackamas*	139.5	3.6	$18,191
Benton	101.8	3.5	$16,687
Yamhill*	79.5	5.6	$14,585
Polk*	63.5	6.2	$13,582
Lane*	59.2	5.6	$15,049
Columbia	52.7	7.2	$13,891
Jackson*	50.6	6.7	$14,046
Linn	39.1	7.8	$13,059
Lincoln	39.1	6.0	$14,722
Josephine	39.0	7.8	$11,438
Clatsop	37.9	6.4	$16,484
Coos	37.5	9.8	$13,608
Hood River	30.8	8.2	$15,438
Deschutes	21.4	6.7	$15,836
Tillamook	19.0	6.8	$13,360
Umatilla	18.6	9.7	$13,805
Douglas	18.2	7.8	$13,353
Union	12.2	7.4	$14,026
Curry	10.4	6.4	$13,799
Klamath	9.6	7.8	$13,540
Wasco	8.6	8.4	$16,672
Jefferson	6.8	6.0	$13,880
Baker	5.1	8.1	$14,056
Crook	4.4	7.2	$14,120
Morrow	3.9	12.5	$17,015
Malheur	2.7	7.3	$12,969
Sherman	2.7	6.7	$24,474
Wallowa	2.4	7.5	$16,362
Grant	1.8	8.8	$13,589
Gilliam	1.5	4.1	$18,965
Lake	0.9	9.5	$14,443
Wheeler	0.8	9.8	$19,560
Harney	0.7	11.0	$13,510

* Metro County

Table C-2 Economy by County (Washington, 1988)

County	Density	Percent Unemployment	Per Capita Income
King*	679.5	4.7	$20,624
Kitsap*	461.8	5.4	$15,067
Clark*	351.5	5.7	$14,391
Pierce*	334.9	6.3	$14,661
Island	260.8	4.7	$14,276
Thurston*	213.3	6.2	$14,710
Snohomish*	205.1	5.3	$16,568
Spokane*	202.9	6.2	$14,373
Cowlitz	72.1	7.4	$14,192
Benton*	60.7	7.7	$14,810
Whatcom*	57.5	7.2	$13,950
SanJuan	54.2	4.4	$17,482
Yakima*	43.8	10.8	$13,063
Skagit	41.7	8.7	$14,783
Mason	39.0	7.1	$12,427
WallaWalla	38.7	7.2	$15,108
GraysHarbor	33.2	9.5	$13,852
Clallam	31.5	8.2	$14,142
Asotin	27.7	5.7	$13,732
Franklin	27.5	10.5	$13,901
Lewis	24.1	8.9	$12,782
Grant	19.5	10.2	$13,615
Pacific	19.5	8.7	$14,120
Whitman	17.5	2.8	$15,027
Chelan	16.7	10.0	$15,680
Douglas	14.0	7.2	$14,289
Wahkiakum	13.4	8.2	$13,567
Stevens	12.3	8.7	$11,573
Kittitas	11.0	9.8	$13,008
Jefferson	10.6	5.9	$14,330
Klickitat	8.9	12.6	$13,393
Adams	7.0	11.1	$15,413
PendOreille	6.4	11.0	$10,656
Okanogan	6.0	12.0	$13,240
Skamania	4.8	17.0	$12,687
Columbia	4.7	13.6	$15,927
Lincoln	3.8	4.9	$21,324
Garfield	3.2	4.8	$19,555
Ferry	2.8	11.5	$10,117

* Metro County

260

Table C-3   Telecommunications by County (Oregon, 1989)

County	Percent Residential Singleparty	Percent Business Singleparty	Percent Electronic Switch
Multnomah*	98.6	99.9	100.0
Washington*	96.7	99.6	100.0
Marion*	97.6	94.5	100.0
Clackamas*	98.5	99.9	95.7
Benton	97.4	99.9	100.0
Yamhill*	92.7	96.3	100.0
Polk*	93.9	98.5	100.0
Lane*	96.9	99.5	100.0
Columbia	91.1	99.1	90.4
Jackson*	96.5	99.7	100.0
Linn	91.7	97.7	100.0
Lincoln	95.8	99.1	100.0
Josephine	93.3	96.7	99.4
Clatsop	92.7	99.5	100.0
Coos	84.8	97.7	67.9
Hood River	95.4	99.3	99.8
Deschutes	93.1	99.5	100.0
Tillamook	91.7	99.1	100.0
Umatilla	95.3	98.5	100.0
Douglas	92.2	98.8	84.4
Union	87.3	97.8	83.3
Curry	81.8	96.8	58.9
Klamath	95.8	99.0	100.0
Wasco	94.8	98.8	100.0
Jefferson	91.3	98.8	100.0
Baker	91.5	97.9	95.4
Crook	91.6	99.0	100.0
Morrow	86.1	97.3	100.0
Malheur	90.4	99.7	95.6
Sherman	85.5	95.6	100.0
Wallowa	79.2	95.4	4.0
Grant	92.1	98.3	72.6
Gilliam	91.3	96.6	100.0
Lake	95.0	98.2	100.0
Wheeler	91.8	99.3	100.0
Harney	81.9	91.1	100.0

* Metro County

Table C-4 Telecommunications by County (Washington, 1988)

County	Percent Residential Singleparty	Percent Business Singleparty	Percent Electronic Switch
King*	98.7	99.9	91.9
Kitsap*	97.3	99.7	99.9
Clark*	96.9	99.6	99.1
Pierce*	97.7	99.8	97.3
Island	93.6	99.5	100.0
Thurston*	96.7	99.5	96.3
Snohomish*	93.1	99.7	79.2
Spokane*	96.6	99.8	99.5
Cowlitz	94.2	99.1	99.5
Benton*	96.2	99.8	47.8
Whatcom*	91.1	98.8	90.9
San Juan	68.8	93.9	82.5
Yakima*	95.4	98.9	86.8
Skagit	87.4	98.7	43.3
Mason	87.9	97.4	100.0
Walla Walla	95.7	98.0	94.8
Grays Harbor	92.0	99.1	95.3
Clallam	93.0	98.3	49.3
Asotin	96.6	98.8	100.0
Franklin	94.1	99.5	95.8
Lewis	85.6	96.9	13.2
Grant	91.5	98.8	74.1
Pacific	87.6	97.0	68.9
Whitman	87.6	97.3	37.6
Chelan	85.8	98.4	69.2
Douglas	74.7	92.6	47.3
Wahkiakum	86.1	96.1	79.5
Stevens	73.1	95.2	39.7
Kittitas	92.4	98.6	100.0
Jefferson	88.0	98.8	98.1
Klickitat	85.9	95.9	41.5
Adams	88.8	94.9	96.8
Pend Oreille	64.4	93.4	9.2
Okanogan	84.6	98.0	87.7
Skamania	98.8	98.5	92.7
Columbia	87.1	93.3	0.0
Lincoln	75.0	89.6	100.0
Garfield	77.9	94.0	100.0
Ferry	81.0	98.0	0.0

* Metro County

State Telecommunications Infrastructure Measures

(Reprinted from Appendix 1 and Appendix 2 of *Oregon's Next Trail*, a report to Governor Barbara Roberts from the Governor's Task Force on Telecommunications, Salem OR, April, 1991.)

1. List of Possible Performance Measures for Determining the State of State Government's Network

. . . [A state government organization] should provide a status report every two years. That report shall include, but need not be limited to the following:

1. A map and description of the telecommunications networks operated by the state government on government owned or leased facilities, such description to include the type of facilities and transmission capacities.

2. A description of the current use of those networks for public access to public information and a statement of plans and ideas for possible changes in those networks that could improve public access to public information.

3. A summary of what the state government is doing and plans to do, in connection with the procurement and operation of state networks, that may change the general availability of public telecommunications infrastructure for information access for all Oregonians. In particular, the report should describe how government network procurement could stimulate the general availability on the public switched network of the services and features being purchased for state government networks.

4. For each of the three objectives listed below, the report should provide quantitative measurements of the current status, proposals for specific quantitative goals for future time periods, and discussion of what needs to be done to achieve the goals. Measurements and goals should be specified for the state as a whole and for each county.

   a. Public access to state government information and public services by voice telephone

      (i) The report should specify the percent of Oregon households with toll free voice telephone access to state government information and services.

      (ii) If user fees or telephone toll charges are required for any Oregon resident to have access to state government voice information networks, the report should specify for such networks the percent of Oregon households that would be required to pay in combined user fees and telephone toll charges 25 percent more than the lowest combination of telephone charges and user fees required for similar access.

      (iii) If voice telephone access to a central state government telephone number for state government information directory and referral service is provided, the report should specify the percent of Oregon households with toll free access to such service.

   b. Public access to public information available on state government computer networks

      (i) The report should specify the number of state government databases containing public (not private, proprietary or confidential) information accessible through state government data networks. The report should specify the percent of those databases to which all Oregon residents are permitted at least read-only access to the public information in those databases.

      (ii) The Executive Department should establish a common standard protocol for access to and interface with government databases and data networks. Of the publicly accessible databases reported under 5(b)(i) above, the report should specify the percent that are accessible via that common standard.

c. Public access to government video networks

(i) The report should specify the percent of Oregon communities with a video information access node on a government network (for example, via Ed-Net).

(ii) The report should specify the percent of communities with such a video information access node, for which the video network node can be used for video access to state government, either for legislative hearings, for video teleconferencing with a state government office, or other state government video information access.

2. List of Possible Performance Measures for Gauging the Health and Capability of Oregon's Public Telecommunications Infrastructure

The Oregon Public Utility Commission has regulatory oversight of the public switched telecommunications network in Oregon. The Public Utility Commission should provide a report each biennium. That report should: (1) describe the current state of Oregon's publicly accessible telecommunications infrastructure, (2) provide a summary of what the commission is doing and plans to do to further improve the availability of telecommunications infrastructure for information access for Oregonians, and (3) provide recommendations for changes needed, if any, to achieve the goal.

The commission report should include, but need not be limited to: (1) results of measurement of the current status of each of the 13 specific objectives listed below, (2) proposals for specific quantitative goals for each objective to be achieved in later time period, and (3) discussion of what needs to be done to achieve those goals. Measurements and goals should be specified for the state as a whole, for each county and for each local exchange telecommunications utility's franchised territory, if applicable.

1. **Universal telephone service:**

    percent of households with a telephone

2. **Single party service:**

    a) percent of residential telephone lines with single party service

    b) percent of business telephone lines with single party service

3. **Touchtone service**

   a)   percent of residential telephone lines on which a touchtone phone would operate without any changes by the local exchange carrier (not optional availability for an additional fee, but "works now" status)

   b)   percent of business telephone lines on which a touchtone phone would operate without any changes by the local exchange carrier ("works now")

4. **Service quality standards**

   The commission should specify technical service quality standards suitable both for reliable voice communication and for facsimile and data transmission at speeds up to 9600 bits per second without special line conditioning.

   a)   percent of residential lines meeting this quality standard

   b)   percent of business lines meeting this quality standard

5. **Extended area service**

   a)   percent of telephone exchanges in which 80 percent or more of intra-LATA calls are local or extended area service calls

   b)   percent of telephone exchanges from which a call to the seat of county government is a local call

6. **Enhanced emergency service (E911)**

   a)   percent of telephone exchanges with all lines served by 911 service

   b)   percent of telephone exchanges with all lines served by E911 (enhanced 911, with automatic number identification)

7. **Equal access**

   percent of telephone exchanges with equal access to competitive long distance carriers on all exchange access lines

8. **Intrastate toll**

   annual percent changes since 1984 in typical intrastate toll charges compared to typical interstate toll charges for both switched and dedicated access

9. **Optional vertical services**

   percent of telephone exchanges for which optional custom calling services such as call waiting, call forwarding and three-way calling are optionally available to all exchange subscribers

10. **Mobile (cellular) telephone service**

    percent of geographic territory (in square miles) in which mobile (cellular) telephone service is available

11. **Voice messaging and other audio information services**

    a) percent of exchanges with voice messaging optionally available with no long distance toll charges required to reach the information provider

    b) percent of exchanges with other audio information services available with no long distance toll charges required to reach the information provider

12. **Information gateway and other data information services**

    a) percent of exchanges with access to a data information gateway, such as CompuServe, Prodigy, Tymnet or SprintData (formerly Telenet), with no long distance toll charges required to reach the gateway or information provider (excluding 800 number access)

    b) percent of exchanges with switched broadband data services with a data rate of at least 56 kilobits per second available

13. **Distance learning and other video information services**

    a) percent of schools with access to video distance learning service

    b) percent of telephone exchanges with video telemedicine or business teleconferencing services available using either analog or compressed digital video technology

In addition to the above, the commission should include in its report a map showing the major fiber optic, microwave, cable and other telecommunications facilities for public switches interexchange telecommunications service in Oregon, and indicating the placement of the points of presence of the major interexchange carriers.

The report should also include a listing, by local exchange carrier within each county, of the percent of their local exchanges served by (a) digital switches, (b) electronic analog switches with stored program control, and (c) electromechanical switches.

The report should also include a statement by the commission concerning the procedures used, if any, to coordinate with the Oregon Economic Development Department to assure that telecommunications infrastructure is in place to meet the needs of specific economic development goals and projects.

access charges
Telephone subscribers pay subscriber access charges, typically $3.50 per month for residential subscribers, to local telephone carriers for access to the interstate public switched long distance network. Long distance carriers also pay carrier access charges to local telephone carriers for the use of local lines to complete long distance calls.

ACS
Appalachian Communication Services (London, Kentucky).

Ameritech
The regional Bell holding company serving the Great Lakes region.

analog
A signal that varies in a continuous manner (as contrasted with a digital signal).

AT&T
American Telephone and Telegraph.

ATI
AgriTechnics International (Washington State); also Aurora Telemarketing Inc. (Nebraska).

audiotex
An interactive audio information service available for a fee to users of touchtone telephones.

bandwidth
The capacity of a communications channel, expressed in hertz (cycles per second).

Bell Atlantic
The regional Bell holding company serving the mid-Atlantic States.

BellSouth

The regional Bell holding company serving the southeast United States.

BETRS

Basic Exchange Telephone Radio Service; a radio-based telephone system for serving isolated areas.

BiCEP

Business/Industry Community Education Partnership (Wisconsin).

BISDN

Broadband ISDN. (See ISDN.)

BOC

Bell Operating Company; the BOCs are grouped under seven regional holding companies (RHCs or RBOCs).

broadband channel

A communication channel, such as microwave, coaxial cable, satellite, or fiber optics, that transmits data at rates of megabits (million bits) per second or higher. (See narrowband channel.)

bypass

Telecommunications transmissions that avoid part or all of the public switched network.

CCA

Countryside Computer Alliance (New York).

CCITT

International Consultative Committee for Telegraphy and Telephony; a committee established by the International Telecommunication Union that recommends worldwide transmission standards.

cellular telephone service

Mobile telephone service using a series of transmitters in local areas or cells. The transmission changes frequency as the driver moves between cells. The system allows frequencies to be re-used, thus providing much greater capacity than older mobile systems. Cellular telephone calls are connected into the public switched network.

Centrex

A service that uses the telephone company's switch to provide internal switching and other features for businesses and organizations; may be used instead of a customer premises PBX.

codec
Coder/decoder; equipment used to digitize and sample a video signal, and to regenerate an analog video signal at the receiving end.

compressed video
Digitized video that requires less bandwidth than standard motion video through use of codecs.

CPE
Customer premises equipment.

CPUC
California Public Utilities Commission.

digital
A discrete or discontinuous signal which transmits audio, data, and video as bits (binary digits) of information.

E911
Enhanced 911 emergency service; the caller's telephone number, location and other important information are stored in a computer and automatically displayed for the dispatcher when a 911 call is received.

EAS
Extended area service; the ability to call an extended area for a flat monthly rate instead of paying a toll charge for each call.

EDC
Economic Development Council.

EDI
Electronic data interchange; the use of computers and telecommunications technologies to process common transactions, such as invoices, shipping notices, and bills, that traditionally have entailed the transfer and processing of paper documents.

EDS
Electronic Data Systems.

electronic mail ("E-mail")
The use of telecommunications for sending textual messages. Messages are stored in users' "mailboxes" for retrieval on demand.

EMCI
Economic and Management Consultants International, Inc., Washington, DC.

EMRG
Electronic Marketing Resource Group (Demopolis, Alabama).

equal access
The ability to make a long distance call using a preselected long distance carrier by dialing 1 plus 10 digits (1+ dialing).

externalities
An economist's term for consequences external to an economic transaction. Negative externalities include environmental pollution that creates costs or disadvantages for people not party to the economic transaction. Positive externalities include general economic benefits resulting from telecommunications services beyond those reflected in the carriers' revenues.

facsimile (fax)
Equipment that transmits and receives documents over telephone lines.

FCC
Federal Communications Commission.

FFB
Federal Financing Bank.

fiber optics
Strands of hair-thin glass through which light transmits telecommunications signals.

FRED
Fund for Rural Education and Development, established by OPASTCO.

GAO
General Accounting Office.

gateway
Connection between networks using different protocols. Also the connection between a telecommunications carrier and an information provider.

GATSS
Global Agricultural Technology Sales and Services Center.

GNP
Gross National Product.

GTE
General Telephone and Electronics.

INS
Iowa Network Services.

IRS
Internal Revenue Service.

ISDN
Integrated Services Digital Network; an evolving set of international standards for a digital public telecommunications network.

ITFS
Instructional Television Fixed Service; a microwave frequency allocated by the FCC for educational use.

IXC
Interexchange carrier.

Just-in-Time
A production system in which parts are delivered from suppliers to the manufacturer as needed, rather than being stored on site.

KCC
Kansas Corporation Commission.

Kilobits
Thousands of bits of data (Kbits).

KINI
Kansas Independent Network, Inc.

LAN
Local area network; network linking computers at a single location.

LATA

Local Access and Transport Area; the geographical area within which Bell operating companies may carry traffic without violating the terms of the MFJ barring them from long distance services.

LEC

Local exchange carrier.

Lifeline

Fund to help low income telephone subscribers maintain access to basic local telephone service.

Link Up America

Program to provide federal assistance for half the cost of installation and deposit charges for residential telephone service, up to $30.

LTN

Legislative Teleconferencing Network (Alaska).

MAN

Metropolitan area network: a network linking computers at several sites in an urban area.

MCI

A major long distance carrier (formerly Microwave Communications Inc.).

MEANS

Minnesota Equal Access Network Services.

Megabits

Millions of bits of data (Mbits).

MFJ

Modified Final Judgment; the Consent Decree that broke up AT&T.

microwave

Radio communication using particular high frequencies (and therefore particularly short wave lengths), for example, 4 gigahertz (4 billion cycles per second).

modem

Modulator/demodulator; a device for converting digital data into analog signals for transmission over ordinary telephone lines and converting received analog signals to digital data for computer processing.

MSA
Metropolitan Statistical Area.

narrowband channel
A communication channel, such as copper wire or part of a coaxial cable channel, that transmits voice, facsimile or data at rates of kilobits per second, but not high speed data or video. (See broadband channel.)

NARUC
National Association of Regulatory Utility Commissioners.

NCS
National Consulting Systems Inc. (Omaha).

NCTS
North Central Telemarketing Services.

NECA
National Exchange Carriers Association.

NJBPU
New Jersey Board of Public Utilities.

NRTA
National Rural Telecom Association.

NRECA
National Rural Electric Cooperative Association.

NRTC
National Rural Telecommunications Cooperative.

NTCA
National Telephone Cooperative Association.

NTIA
National Telecommunications and Information Administration, U.S. Department of Commerce.

NYNEX
The Bell regional holding company serving New York and New England.

OPASTCO
Organization for the Protection and Advancement of Small Telephone Companies.

optical fiber
See fiber optics.

OTA
Office of Technology Assessment, U.S. Congress.

Pacific Telesis
The Bell regional holding company serving California and Nevada.

PBX
Private branch exchange; a private telephone switch located on the customer's premises, and used for internal communications.

PCN
Personal communications network; a proposed network composed of a variety of wireless services including cordless telephones, wireless private branch exchanges, and wireless local area networks.

POP
Point of presence; the point at which an interexchange carrier's circuits connect with local circuits for transmission and reception of long distance calls.

POTS
Plain old telephone service.

price cap
A regulation that sets the maximum price telephone companies can charge for a designated group of services. The set price changes over time, based on inflation and targets for improvements in productivity.

PSC
Public Service Commission; a state regulatory body.

PSVN
Panhandle Shar-Ed Video Network (Oklahoma).

PTFP
Public Telecommunications Facilities Program administered by the National Telecommunications and Information Administration.

PUC
Public Utilities Commission, a state regulatory body.

RAN
Rural Area Network.

Rate of return
A method of regulation that defines the total revenue a telephone company requires to provide services. The revenue requirement includes operating expenses, depreciation and taxes, and a "fair" return on its capital investment ("rate base").

RBOC
Regional Bell Operating Company or Regional Holding Company: One of the seven companies formed by the AT&T divestiture, including: Ameritech, Bell Atlantic, BellSouth, NYNEX, Pacific Telesis, Southwestern Bell, and US West.

RC&D
Resource Conservation and Development.

REA
Rural Electrification Administration, U.S. Department of Agriculture.

RHC
Regional Holding Company; more commonly called RBOC.

RHEC
Rural Health Education Center (Idaho).

RTB
Rural Telephone Bank.

RTFC
Rural Telephone Finance Cooperative.

satellite
A communications relay device orbiting the earth to permit communication among earth stations.

SCETV
South Carolina Educational Television.

SDN
South Dakota Network.

SERC
Satellite Educational Resources Consortium.

Southwestern Bell
The Bell regional holding company serving the mid-south and parts of the southwest.

SS7
Signaling System 7; a control system for the public telephone network that allows telephone company computers to communicate directly with each other for routing calls, using signaling circuits separate from the circuits used for the telephone calls themselves.

STARS
Statewide Telecommunications Access and Routing System (Minnesota).

T-carriers
A family of high speed, digital transmission systems. A T1 carrier has a capacity of 1.544 megabits per second.

TDS
Telephone and Data Systems, Inc.

Telemedicine
Use of telecommunications for medical diagnosis, patient care, and health education.

Telex
A public switched network connecting teletypewriters or other devices transmitting at 50 bits per second.

Telmex
Mexico's national telephone company.

TET
Telecommunications Education Trust (California).

TI-IN
A national educational satellite network based in Texas.

TPSC
Tennessee Public Service Commission.

universal service
Refers to the goal of providing basic telephone service to virtually every household.

USTA
United States Telephone Association.

US West
The Bell regional holding company serving the northwest, Rocky Mountain states, and parts of the midwest and southwest.

VAN
Value added network; a data communications system in which special features such as protocol conversion or database access are added to the underlying transmission capabilities.

VCR
Video cassette recorder.

Voice mail
A voice messaging system in which spoken messages are recorded for later play back or transfer to others.

VSAT
Very small aperture terminal, for satellite communications.

VTA
Vermont Telecommunications Agreement.

WAN
Wide area network; a computer network covering a large geographical area.

WUTC
Washington Utilities and Transportation Commission.

REFERENCES

Allen, John and Don A. Dillman. "Availability and Use of Information Technologies in Rural America." Unpublished paper presented at annual meeting of the Rural Sociological Society, Madison, WI, August 1987.

Arnheim, Louise. "Telecommunications Infrastructure and Economic Development in the Northeast-Midwest Region." Washington, DC: Northeast-Midwest Institute, April 1988.

Beamon, Clarice. "Telecommunications: A Vital Link for Rural Business." *OPASTCO Roundtable,* Spring 1990.

Beatty, Jim. "How Small Cities can 'Cash in' on 'Teleconomic Development.'" *Nation's Cities Weekly,* November 7, 1988, p. 3.

Beikmann, Gary G. "ITV: The Coax Connection." *OPASTCO Roundtable,* spring 1991, pp. 20–27.

Bohlin, Ron, Allan Roth and David C. Wenner. "Do LECs Need Magic to Cut Costs?" *Telephony,* June 24, 1991, pp. 28–34.

Bryant, John. *Local Network Quality Standards Act of 1991.* Bill HR 267. Congressional Record pp. E29–30, re-introduced January 3, 1991.

Burton, Lucy Greer. "Communication Technology for Rural Communities: A Qualitative Study of Rural Communities, Northeastern Washington State." Unpublished Masters thesis, Washington State University, Pullman, WA, 1989.

Citizens League. *Wiring Minnesota: State Goals for Telecommunications.* Minneapolis, MN, November 1989.

Cleveland, Harlan. "The Twilight of Hierarchy: Speculations on the Global Information Society." *Public Administration Review,* Vol. 45, 1985, p. 185.

Conway, Dick and Associates. *Rural Office Development in Washington State: Its Feasibility and the Role of Telecommunications.* Prepared for the Washington State Department of Community Development, Seattle, January 1988.

Corporation for Enterprise Development. *Playing by New Rules: Nine Economic Development Realities for the '90s.* Washington, DC, 1990.

Corporation for Enterprise Development. *The 1991 Development Report Card for the States.* Washington, DC, April 1991.

Coulter, Kristin. "The Telco in Rural Development." *OPASTCO Roundtable,* Spring 1990, pp. 11–12.

Cronin, Francis J., Edwin B. Parker, Elisabeth K. Colleran, and Mark A. Gold. "Telecommunications Infrastructure and Economic Growth: An Analysis of Causality." *Telecommunications Policy,* December, 1991 (in press).

Davidson, William H., Anne C. Dibble and Sandra H. Dom. "Telecommunications and Rural Economic Development." Redondo Beach, CA: MESA Inc., October 1990.

Deavers, Kenneth L., "The Reversal of the Rural Renaissance: A Recent Historical Perspective." *The Entrepreurial Economy Review,* Washington, D.C: Corporation for Economic Development, Vol. 8, No. 2, September/ October 1989.

Deloitte & Touche. *New Jersey Telecommunications Infrastructure Study,* Newark, NJ, January 1991.

Depo, Gerald E. *Telecommunications Concept for the Town of Bloomsburg.* Bloomsburg, PA, 1990.

Digital Information Group. *Information Industry Factbook, 1989–90.* Stamford, CT, 1990a.

Digital Information Group. *Information Industry Bulletin.* Stamford, CT, August 9, 1990b.

Dillman, Don A. *Rural Telephone Infrastructure and Economic Development in Washington State: A Case Study.* Technical Report 90-103, Social and Economic Sciences Research Center, Washington State University, Pullman, WA, 1990.

Dillman, Don A. "The Social Impacts of Information Technologies in Rural North America." *Rural Sociology*, Vol. 50, No. 1, 1985, pp. 1–26.

Dillman, Don A. and Donald M. Beck. "Information Technologies and Rural Development in the 1990s." *Journal of State Government*, Vol. 61, No. 1, January/February 1988. pp. 29–38.

Dillman, Don A., Leslie Peterson Scott, and John Allen. *Telecommunications in Washington: A Statewide Survey.* Technical Report, Social and Economic Sciences Research Center. Washington State University, Pullman, WA, 1987.

DRI/McGraw-Hill. *The Contributions of Telecommunications Infrastructure to Aggregate and Sectoral Efficiency.* Lexington, MA, November 1990.

Electronic Data Systems (EDS). *Use Assessment of Michigan's Telecommunication Systems.* Final Report, May 1990.

EMCI, Inc. Submission to Appalachian Regional Commission. Washington, DC, October 1991.

Ernst and Whinney Telecommunications Group (now Ernst and Young). *The Telecommunications Industry in Washington State: Market Competitiveness, Service Availability, and Cost-of-Service Methodologies.* Tacoma, WA, December 1985.

Estabrooks, Maurice F. and Rodolphe H. Lamarche, eds. *Telecommunications: A Strategic Perspective on Regional, Economic and Business Development.* Moncton, NB: Canadian Institute for Research on Regional Development, 1987.

Federal Communications Commission. *Telephone Subscribership in the U.S.* Washington, DC, June 1991.

Fowlkes, Roberta P. "Office of the Future." *State Journal.* Charleston, WV, August 1990, p. 11.

Fund for Rural Education and Development. *FRED Facts.* Washington, DC, OPASTCO, 1990.

Gallagher, Lynne and Dale Hatfield. *Distance Learning: Opportunities in Telecommunications Policy and Technology.* Washington, DC: Annenberg Washington Program of Northwestern University, May 1989.

Gallottini, Giovanna T. "Infrastructure: The Rural Difference." *Telecommunications Engineering and Management.* Vol. 95, No. 1, January 1, 1991, pp. 48–50.

Governor's Telecommunications Task Force. *Connections: A Strategy for Michigan's Future Through Telecommunications.* Lansing, MI, May 1990.

Guides for All Seasons, Quincy, CA. Personal communication, 1990.

Hardy, Andrew P. "The Role of the Telephone in Economic Development." *Telecommunications Policy,* Vol. 4, No. 4, December 1980, pp. 278–286.

Harris, Robert. "The Regional SS7 Network: An Intelligent Application for Rural Telcos." *Rural Telecommunications,* summer 1989, pp. 12–13.

Hartman, Paul M. and Schoonmaker, Robert C. *A Study of GTE Hawaiian Telephone Company Inter-Island Toll and Other Rates.* Prepared for the Public Utilities Commission, State of Hawaii, Honolulu, February 1991.

Hepworth, Mark. *Geography of the Information Economy.* New York: Guilford Press, 1990.

Herbers, John. "A Third Wave of Development." *Governing,* June 1990, pp. 43–50.

Hirata, Edward Y. and Edward K. Uchida. *Evaluation of the Hawaii Telework Center Demonstration Project.* Honolulu: Department of Transportation, State of Hawaii, September 1990.

Horowitz, Mitchell and Jonathan Dunn, "The 1989 Rural Economic Climate Report." *The Entrepreneurial Economy Review,* Washington, D.C: Corporation for Economic Development, Vol. 8, No. 2, September/October 1989, pp. 6–22.

Hudson, Heather E. *Communication Satellites: Their Development and Impact.* New York, NY: Free Press, 1990.

Hudson, Heather E. *When Telephones Reach the Village.* Norwood, NJ: Ablex, 1984.

Indiana Economic Development Council, Inc. *Lifelines to Rural Indiana: The Role of Telecommunications in Rural Economic Development.* Indianapolis, IN, May 1991.

International Communications Association. Statement before the Subcommittee on Telecommunications and Finance of the Committee on Energy and Commerce of the U.S. House of Representatives, May 10, 1990.

International Communications Association. *Incentive Regulation for the 1990s: Making the Business Case for Sound Reform.* International Communications Association (ICA) White Paper. Dallas, TX, 1991.

Irwin, Lois. *Telecommunications and Rural Development.* Community Colleges of Spokane and Washington State University, Spokane, WA, January 1990.

Joint Select Committee on Telecommunications of the Washington State Legislature. *1985 Final Report,* Olympia, WA, January 1985.

Joint Select Committee on Telecommunications of the Washington State Legislature. *1986 Final Report,* Olympia, WA, November 1986.

Kleinfield, N.R. "What is Chris Whittle Teaching our Children?" *New York Times Magazine,* May 19, 1991, pp. 32, 46–49, 79, 88.

Kottman, Karl and Jon Ochs. "The Palouse Project: Telecommunications." A preliminary report to the Joint Select Committee on Telecommunications, Olympia, WA: Washington State Council of Farmer Cooperatives, December 1986.

Lawton, Raymond W. *Telecommunications Modernization: Issues and Approaches for Regulators.* National Regulatory Research Institute, Columbus OH, 1988.

Lehner, J. Christopher. "Rural Development at a Crossroads: The Emergence of a National Consensus." *Rural Telecommunications,* fall 1989, pp. 36–41.

Lehner, J. Christopher. "Toward Rural Revival: The Telco-Community Partnership." *Rural Telecommunications,* summer 1990, pp. 10–15.

Lehner, J. Christopher and Ingrid K. Young. "Conspicuous Personalities: Ideas from Rural Telephony." *Rural Telecommunications,* winter 1989, pp. 8–26.

Lidman, Russell and Dorothy Lyons. "Personal Income Trends." Washington Institute for Public Policy, Olympia, WA, 1987.

Lloyd, Ann. "The Rural (Radio) Connection." *Rural Telecommunications*, fall 1988, pp. 20–22.

Local Extended Calling Advisory Committee. Final Report to the Washington Utilities and Transportation Commission, Olympia, WA, December 1988.

Lyons, Stephen. "Where Have All the Doctors Gone?" *Idaho The University*, Vol. 8, No. 2, spring 1991, pp. 7–11.

Manto, Charles. Personal Communication. Economic Development Corporation of the County of Marquette, MI, 1990.

Massachusetts Department of Public Utilities. "New England Telephone." Docket 89-300, Boston, MA, June 30, 1990.

Murr, Lawrence E., James B. Williams, and Ruth-Ellen Miller. *Information Highways: Mapping Information Delivery Networks in the Pacific Northwest*, Hypermap, Portland, OR, 1985.

National Consulting Systems. *The NCS Guide to Attracting Back Office Industries*. Omaha, NE, 1991.

National Telecommunications and Information Administration, *Telecom 2000: Charting the Course for a New Century*. NTIA Special Publication 88-21. Washington, D.C.: Government Printing Office, October 1988.

Nelson, Sharon. "The Federal and State Role in Promoting Rural Development." Presentation to the Annenburg Telecommunications and Rural Development Forum, Washington, DC, March 1990.

Niles, John. "Advanced Telecommunications for Economic Development in Washington State: A Working Paper from the Telecommunications Task Force-Economic Development Board," Olympia, WA, January 1989.

Noam, Eli. "Questions by Commissioner Eli M. Noam concerning the establishment of economic incentives for quality performance by New York Telephone, as part of the general treatment of its rates." New York Public Service Commission, Case 28961, Fifth Stage, undated (circa 1989).

Northwest Policy Center. *A Northwest Reader: Options for Development*. University of Washington, Seattle, WA, 1989.

Oklahoma Public Utility Commission. Order. Cause No. PUD 000692, January 11, 1991.

OPASTCO. "OTC Technical Paper No. 2: Interactive Television: Technology Linking Rural Areas." OPASTCO: Washington, D.C., December 1989.

Oregon Independent Telephone Association. *Week in Review.* August 2, 1991, p. 1.

Oregon Progress Board. *Oregon Benchmarks: Setting Measurable Standards for Progress.* Report to the 1991 Oregon Legislature, January 1991.

Oregon Task Force on Telecommunications. *Telecommunications: Oregon's Next Trail.* Salem, OR, April 1991.

Pacific Bell. *Intelligent Network Task Force Report.* San Francisco, CA, October 1987.

Parker, Edwin B., Heather E. Hudson, Don A. Dillman, and Andrew D. Roscoe. *Rural America in the Information Age: Telecommunications Policy for Rural Development.* The Aspen Institute and University Press of America, Lanham, MD, 1989.

Pearson, Larry. "A Fresh Look at How Alaskans Communicate." *Center for Information Technology News,* University of Alaska Anchorage, Vol. 1, No. 2, May 1991, p.1.

Public Utility Commission of Texas. "Dockets 8585 and 8218: Stipulation and Agreement." Austin, TX, February 2, 1990.

Pulver, Glen C. "The Changing Economic Scene in Rural America." *Journal of State Government,* Vol. 61, No. 1, January/February 1988, pp. 3–8.

Roberts, Brandon. *States: Catalysts for Development in Rural America.* Washington, DC: Council of State Community Affairs Agencies, 1990.

Rochester Telephone Corporation. *1990 Annual Report.* Rochester, NY, March 1991.

Ross, Doug. "Thinking about Rural Economic Development in the 1990s." Unpublished paper, CSPA Rural Development Academy, The Corporation for Enterprise Development, spring 1990.

Rudd, David. "Regulating the BT Giant: Consultation without Information." *Telecommunications Policy.* Vol. 12, No. 4, December 1988, pp. 318–322.

Rude, Suzanne D. "Developments in State Telecommunications Regulation: Experience in Vermont." Paper presented at the Seventeenth Annual Telecommunications Research Conference, Airlie, VA, October 1989.

Salant, Priscilla. *A Community Researcher's Guide to Rural Data.* Washington, DC: Island Press, 1990.

Saunders, Robert, Jeremy Warford, and Bjorn Wellenius. *Telecommunications and Economic Development.* Baltimore, MD: Johns Hopkins University Press, 1983.

Schmandt, Jurgen, Frederick Williams and Robert H. Wilson. *Telecommunications Policy and Economic Development: The New State Role.* New York: Praeger, 1991.

Schmandt, Jurgen, Frederick Williams, Robert H. Wilson and Sharon Strover. *Telecommunications and Rural Development: A Study of Business and Public Service Applications.* New York: Praeger, 1991.

Schramm, Wilbur. *Big Media, Little Media.* Beverly Hills, CA: Sage, 1977.

Silkman, Richard. Personal communications. State Planning Office, Augusta, ME, 1989, 1991.

SRI International. *Achieving Leadership in Information-Intensive Industries: A Plan to Establish the Nebraska Applied Information Management Institute.* Final Report. Prepared for Greater Omaha Chamber of Commerce, Omaha, NE, June 1991.

Strover, Sharon and Frederick Williams. *Rural Revitalization and Information Technologies in the United States.* Research report prepared for the Aspen Institute and Ford Foundation, 1991.

Tapellini, Donna. "High Tech Home on the Range." *Marketing Computers,* May 1991, pp. 18–19.

Telecom Publishing Group. "Georgia PSD OKs Rural Incentive Tariff." *State Telephone Regulation Report,* Vol. 8, no. 21, Alexandria, VA, November 1, 1990.

Telluride Institute. *Telluride InfoZone.* Telluride, Colorado, 1991.

Teske, Paul E. *After Divestiture: The Political Economy of State Telecommunications Deregulation.* Albany, NY: State University of New York Press, 1990.

U.S. Congress. *Food, Agriculture, Conservation and Freight Act of 1990.* Public Law 101-624, November 29, 1990.

U.S. Congress, House of Representatives. *Bringing the Information Age to Rural America.* Hearings before the Government Information, Justice, and Agriculture Subcommittee of the Committee on Government Operations. Washington, DC: U.S. Government Printing Office, 1991.

U.S. Congress, Office of Technology Assessment. *Critical Connections: Communications for the Future,* OTA-CIT-407. Washington, DC: U.S. Government Printing Office, January 1990.

U.S. Congress, Office of Technology Assessment. *Linking for Learning: A New Course for Education,* OTA-SET-430. Washington, DC: U.S. Government Printing Office, November 1989.

U.S. Congress, Office of Technology Assessment. *Rural America at the Crossroads: Networking for the Future,* OTA-TCT-471. Washington, DC: U.S. Government Printing Office, April 1991.

U.S. Department of Agriculture, Agriculture and Rural Economy Division, Economic Research Service. *Infrastructure Investment and Economic Development: Rural Strategies for the 1990s.* Staff Report No. 9069, Washington, DC, December 1990.

U.S. Department of Agriculture, Economic Research Service. *Rural Conditions and Trends.* Vol. 1, No. 4, winter 1990/91.

U.S. Department of Commerce, Bureau of the Census. "Money Income and Poverty in the United States, 1989." *Current Population Survey,* Series P-60, No. 168, March 1990.

University of Alaska Anchorage. *Chugach Conference Proceedings.* Anchorage, AK, August 1989.

Wall Street Journal. "Analog Switches Get a Chance to go Digital." November 1, 1990, p. B1.

Washington State Economic Development Board. "Washington Works Worldwide: Positioning Ourselves to Compete in the New Global Economy." Olympia, WA, November 1988.

Washington Utilities and Transportation Commission. *Annual Report on the Status of the Washington Telecommunications Industry.* Olympia, WA, January 1987.

Washington Utilities and Transportation Commission. "Comments in the Matter of Comprehensive Study of the Domestic Telecommunications Infrastructure." Olympia, WA, April 1990a.

Washington Utilities and Transportation Commission. "Commission Adopts Extended Area Service Rule." Olympia, WA, December 13, 1990b.

Washington Utilities and Transportation Commission. "The Feasibility of Universal Single-Party Telephone Service in Washington State." Report submitted to the Washington State Legislature. Olympia, WA, December 1989a.

Washington Utilities and Transportation Commission. "Mission and Goals Statement." Olympia, WA, 1985.

Washington Utilities and Transportation Commission. "The Status of the Washington Telecommunications Industry." *Volume I, The 1989 Report on the State of Washington Telecommunications Industry.* Olympia, WA, 1989b.

Washington Utilities and Transportation Commission. "The Status of the Telecommunications Infrastructure in Washington State." *Volume II, The 1989 Report on the Status of the Washington Telecommunications Industry.* Olympia, WA, January 1989c.

Washington Utilities and Transportation Commission. "Telecommunications Regulation in Washington State." Proceedings of a Policy Roundtable held August 11–12, 1988, in Seattle, Washington. *Volume III, The 1989 Report on the Status of the Washington Telecommunications Industry.* Olympia, WA, January 1989d.

Williams, Frederick. "States Step Up to the Challenge." *Telephony,* October 16, 1989, pp. 49–52.

INDEX

References in figures, maps and tables are indicated in **bold type**.

A

access charges   203
    see also *carrier access charge*
agencies
    agricultural extension   6, 31, 83, 134
    commerce   6, 83
    consumer affairs   84
    economic development   6, 16–17
    education   83
    federal   1, 83
    forestry and fisheries   6
    parks and wildlife   6, 83
    social service   6
aggregation of demand   6, 9, 17, 56, 78–79, 133, 135, 137, 197–198
agricultural extension   6, 31, 134
agriculture   2, 31, 52, 83, 120, 134, 141
AgriTechnics International   11, 35, 112, 153, 159, 269
Alabama   8, 59, 63, 113, 114, 115, 118, **118**, 119, 121, 122, **122**, 124–125, 126, 127, 129,
    131, 133, 135, 137, 252, 272
Alaska   55–56, 85, 93, 104, 155, 274
Allen, John   148
Alltel   36
Americans with Disabilities Act   94, 204
American Telephone and Telegraph (AT&T)   18, 36, 38, 88, 89, 119, 120, 121, 125,
    127, 130, 140–141, 142–145, 210, 218, 256, 269
Ameritech   269
amortization   18, 212–214
analog   107–108, 202, 229, 233–237, **236–237**, 267, 268, 269
    switches   41, 202, 229, 233–237, **236–237**, 268
    video   107–108, 271
Appalachian coal fields   26
Appalachian Communication Services (ACS)   87, 269
Arizona   73
Aspen Institute, The   156
audio information services   267
audiotex   201, 269

L

M

ABOUT THE BOOK AND AUTHORS

Many rural communities are experiencing an economic decline for which there is no obvious or easy remedy. Concerned community and state government leaders must seek new ways to forestall structural decline and construct a new economic vision for themselves. And, given the dynamics of today's global economy, any plan for economic development must provide links to national and international economies.

In this groundbreaking study, rural development and communications policy scholars explore the role modern rural telecommunications infrastructures can play in facilitating these goals. The authors illustrate the ways advanced telecommunications can, in combination with strategic community development planning, serve as a catalyst for economic growth. In this regard, they provide prescriptive policy recommendations for governors, state legislatures, economic development departments, state telecommunications regulatory commissions, and the telecommunications industry.

Edwin B. Parker is a telecommunications consultant and former professor of communication at Stanford University. **Heather E. Hudson** is director of the Telecommunication Management and Policy Program in the McLaren School of Business at the University of San Francisco. **Don A. Dillman** is professor of sociology and rural sociology and director of the Social and Economic Sciences Research Center at Washington State University. **Sharon Strover** is associate professor and director of graduate studies in the Radio-TV-Film Department at the University of Texas at Austin. **Frederick Williams** is director of the Center for Research on Communication Technology and Society at the University of Texas–Austin where he occupies the Mary Gibbs Jones Centennial Chair in the College of Communication.